MW01008834

Getting Our Act Together

Together we can often achieve things that are impossible to do on our own. We can prevent something bad from happening, or we can produce something good, even if none of us could do it by ourselves. But when are we morally required to do something of moral importance together with others?

This book develops an original theory of collective moral obligations. These are obligations that individual moral agents hold jointly but not as unified collective agents. The theory does not stipulate a new type of moral obligation but rather suggests that to think of some of our obligations as joint or collective is the best way of making sense of our intuitions regarding collective moral action problems. Where we have reason to believe that our efforts are most efficient as part of a collective endeavour, we may incur collective obligations together with others who are similarly placed as long as we are able to establish compossible individual contributory strategies towards that goal. The book concludes with a discussion of 'massively shared obligations' to major-scale moral problems such as global poverty.

Getting Our Act Together: A Theory of Collective Moral Obligations will appeal to researchers and advanced students working in moral, political and social philosophy, philosophy of action, social epistemology and philosophy of social science.

Anne Schwenkenbecher is Senior Lecturer in Philosophy at Murdoch University, Western Australia. She is the author of *Terrorism: A Philosophical Enquiry* (2012). Her articles on collective action and obligations have appeared in *The Monist, Midwest Studies in Philosophy, Synthese, Ethics & International Affairs* and the *Journal of Applied Philosophy*.

Routledge Studies in Ethics and Moral Theory

Apologies and Moral Repair
Rights, Duties, and Corrective Justice
Andrew I. Cohen

Kantian and Sidgwickian Ethics
The Cosmos of Duty Above and the Moral Law Within
Edited by Tyler Paytas and Tim Henning

Cultivating Our Passionate Attachments
Matthew J. Dennis

Reason and Ethics
The Case Against Objective Value
Joel Marks

Offense and Offensiveness
A Philosophical Account
Andrew Sneddon

Virtue, Narrative, and Self
Explorations of Character in the Philosophy of Mind and Action
Edited by Joseph Ulatowksi and Liezl van Zyl

The Authority of Virtue
Institutions and Character in the Good Society
Tristan J. Rogers

Getting Our Act Together
A Theory of Collective Moral Obligations
Anne Schwenkenbecher

For more information about this series, please visit: www.routledge.com/Routledge-Studies-in-Ethics-and-Moral-Theory/book-series/SE0423

Getting Our Act Together
A Theory of Collective Moral Obligations

Anne Schwenkenbecher

Routledge
Taylor & Francis Group

NEW YORK AND LONDON

First published 2021
by Routledge
52 Vanderbilt Avenue, New York, NY 10017

and by Routledge
2 Park Square, Milton Park, Abingdon, Oxon, OX14 4RN

Routledge is an imprint of the Taylor & Francis Group, an informa business

© 2021 Anne Schwenkenbecher

Library of Congress Cataloging-in-Publication Data
A catalog record for this book has been requested

ISBN: 978-0-367-56112-3 (hbk)
ISBN: 978-1-003-09713-6 (ebk)

Typeset in Sabon
by Apex CoVantage, LLC

Contents

Acknowledgements   x

Introduction   1

1 Collective Obligations in a Nutshell   6

   1.1 The Starting Point 6
   1.2 Jointly Held Obligations 10
   1.3 Collectively Available Options and
   We-Reasoning 11
   1.4 Joint Ability and Ignorance 14
   1.5 When Do We Have Collective Obligations? 17
   1.6 Collective Versus Individual Obligations 20

2 Joint Oughts and the Agency Principle   25

   2.1 Joint Moral 'Oughts' 25
   2.2 Motivating Collective Obligations 28
   2.3 Duty Collectivism and the Agency Principle 31

3 Joint Ability and 'Ought' *Implies* 'Can' for Pluralities
   of Agents   37

   3.1 What Is Meant by 'Joint Ability'? 37
       3.1.1 The Strong View: Ability to Perform
       Joint Actions 38
       3.1.2 The Intermediate View: Joint
       Intentional Activity 43
       3.1.3 The Weak View: Combined Ability 48
   3.2 When Do Agents Have Joint Ability? 51
   3.3 Objections and Challenges 56
   3.4 Types of Pluralities 58

4   Knowing When We Have Collective Moral Obligations   63

   4.1 Considering Options: 'We-Framing' Scenarios 63
   4.2 Weighing Options: Substantive Ethical Theories 68
   *4.3 Weighing Options: Non-substantive Theories of
      Moral Obligation 70*
   *4.4 We-Reasoning and Team-Reasoning About
      Obligations 77*
   4.5 Group Knowledge 90
   *4.6 Simplicity, Complexity: Additional Factors for
      Collective Moral Obligations 91*

5   What Collective Obligations Mean for Individual
   Agents: Contributory Obligations, Non-compliance
   and Joint Blameworthiness   98

   5.1 Individual (Contributory) Obligations 99
   5.2 Failures to Comply With Collective Obligations 106
   5.3 Joint Blameworthiness 108
   5.4 The Knowledge Condition 109

6   A Comparison of Existing Accounts
   of Collective Obligations   114

   *6.1 Meta-Criteria for a Theory of Collective Moral
      Obligations 114*
   6.2 Reductionist Accounts 117
   *6.3 Collective Moral Obligations as Obligations of
      Groups 119*
   6.4 'Shared' and 'Joint' Obligations 127
   *6.5 Collective Moral Obligations From the Perspective
      of the Deliberating Agent 129*
   6.6 In What Sense Is This Still a Collectivist View? 131

7   Massively Shared Obligations and Global Poverty   135

   *7.1 Differences Between Small-Scale and Large-Scale
      Joint-Necessity Problems 135*
   7.2 Global Obligations to Combat Poverty 139
   7.3 Large-Scale Distributive Action 143
   7.4 Massively Shared Collective Obligations 150
   *7.5 Three Objections: Claimability, Enforceability and
      Action-Guidance 152*

Conclusion   161

Glossary   163
References   166
Index   173

Acknowledgements

Philosophical works are often more biographically motivated than scholars may be aware of. It took me a good few years to realise that my interest in collective action and responsibility was closely tied to growing up in a state that cultivated a collective narrative of popular resistance against injustice as its founding myth while also having its own fate sealed through precisely such an act of collective resistance against the injustice it committed against its own citizens. Between 1989 and 1990, through peaceful protests and acts of civil disobedience, the people of East Germany first overthrew their government and finally ended the existence of the very state they were protesting against, the German Democratic Republic (GDR). They took to the streets demanding democratic reforms – with the initial movement being as passionately inspired by a vision of a more humane kind of socialism as it was short-lived. It found an end with German reunification on 3 October 1990 when East Germans became citizens of another country, shortly after Francis Fukuyama (1989) declared the 'End of History' over the (then pending) collapse of the socialist block and the perseverance of capitalist societies.

Suddenly, we – who had grown up with the belief that our state was founded upon the ideals of those who fought Fascisms' injustices and that our socialist society was morally superior to capitalism and imperialism – found ourselves to be the ones in the dock of history. Why had we – or, more precisely, why had our parents and grandparents – not resisted the unjust regime we lived under sooner and more decidedly? Why had they been complicit for so long? Repeatedly, I found myself explaining that the vast majority of people in the GDR had just lived ordinary lives: they complained about problems and performed little acts of micro-resistance among all those acts of social and political conformity, just like people in other societies. Also, it was far from easy to organise resistance, because the stakes were high and surveillance was pervasive. Protests only took off once there was a critical mass of people – just like in any other society. We were probably neither more nor less heroic or complicit than people anywhere else. Or were we?

Over the years, the question I was asked – the question we have been asking ourselves – stayed with me: *when should we 'get our act together' to effect change in the world?* As I am writing these lines, protestors of the Black Lives Matter movement across the world are taking to the streets to denounce racial discrimination and demand justice for those who have been and continue to be victims of systemic racism. Runaway climate change continues to threaten our planet and life as we know it. A global pandemic is bringing the collective nature of any successful effort to ward off public health threats into painful focus.

In trying to answer the question of when we should (get our) act together, in this book, I start with small-scale, one-off cooperation problems and ultimately turn to our obligations to collectively combat large-scale systemic injustice. Unsurprisingly, the clear-cut conclusions that can be drawn for small-scale collective action cases are lacking when it comes to complex, large-scale problems. While I will not explain away this – moral and phenomenal – gap, I aim to show why it exists and which – epistemic and other – factors can play a role in strengthening our collective obligations vis-à-vis large-scale injustice.

We cooperate – often spontaneously – on a small scale. But we are also very good at contributing to large-scale collective ventures that we consider morally important. We vote, we comply with public health recommendations in a global pandemic not just because it protects us but because it protects other people and promotes a public good.

Further, the pursuit of knowledge is a collective endeavour. Writing an academic monograph may seem like a quintessentially individual effort, but it is in a crucial sense collaborative. As such, this book is a perfect illustration of the very thought that guides my argument: we are essentially cooperative creatures who rely on each other all the time. Philosophical ideas and concepts materialise and are shaped through engaging with other people's ideas and views – be they published work or conveyed in conversation. It is through countless discussions with other people that I have been able to develop and continuously improve the ideas in this book. I am extremely grateful to all of those who were willing to engage with me for their intellectual generosity, curiosity and patience. In particular, I would like to thank Valentin Beck, Jelena Belić, Gunnar Björnsson, Olle Blomberg, Sean Bowden, Zlata Bozac, Justin Bruner, David Butler, Simon Caney, Steve Clarke, Stephanie Collins, Garrett Cullity, Niels de Haan, Nenad Dimitrijevic, Ned Dobos, Laura D'Olimpio, Hein Duijf, Daniel Dzah, Lina Eriksson, Toni Erskine, Annika Fiebich, Tim Flanagan, Christina Friedlaender, Alberto Giubilini, Natalie Gold, Henning Hahn, Daniel Halliday, Richard Hamilton, Kendy Hess, Johannes Himmelreich, Violetta Igneski, Tracy Isaacs, Tamara Jugov, Elizabeth Kahn, John Kleinig, Matthew Kopec, Holly Lawford-Smith, Christian Lee, Michael Levine, Alejandra Mancilla, Larry May, Jeff McMahan, Zoltán Miklósi, Seumas Miller, Toby Miller, Andrew Moore, Piero Moraro, Olaf

Müller, Herlinde Pauer-Studer, Philip Pettit, Felix Pinkert, Luke Roelofs, Olivier Roy, Michael Rubin, Julian Savulescu, Stephan Schlothfeldt, Hans-Bernhard Schmid, Vanessa Schouten, Valentin Schröder, David Schweikard, Adam Slavny, Leonie Smith, Nick Southwood, Uwe Steinhoff, Sofia Stemplowska, Arjun Subrahmanyan, Alan Tapper, Emma Thomas, Janna Thompson, Joe Ulatowski, Lachlan Umbers, Suzanne Uniacke, Dave van Mill, Christopher Woodard, Bill Wringe and Veronique Zanetti. I also thank all those who appear in the reference list for their (generally unwitting) contribution to this book. Further, I gratefully acknowledge the hard work of numerous anonymous journal reviewers who have provided me with invaluable feedback over the years. Finally, special thanks go to Routledge editors Allie Simmons and Andrew Weckenmann.

I have been lucky enough to enjoy not only the intellectual input from countless colleagues and friends but also significant financial support from a number of organisations. The original idea for this book was supported by a postdoctoral research fellowship funded by the German Academic Exchange Service (Deutscher Akademischer Austauschdienst) (2010–2011) and hosted at the Centre for Applied Philosophy and Public Ethics at Australian National University. I continued this project while working as a postdoctoral researcher with the European Research Council Advanced Grant Project 'Distortions of Normativity' at the University of Vienna (2011–2012). In 2015, the German Research Foundation (Deutsche Forschungsgemeinschaft, a.k.a. DFG) funded a bilateral Australian-German research workshop on 'Joint Duties' as well as a two-month visiting fellowship at the University of Bayreuth's Department of Philosophy through their 'Grants to Support the Initiation of International Collaboration' scheme. Murdoch University's School of Arts' Study Leave Scheme enabled me to turn several years of research into a full-length manuscript during a sabbatical (2017 and 2018) of which I spent two months at the Australian National University's Research School of Social Science and four months at the Oxford Martin School at Oxford University. I am especially honoured to have been the recipient of a generous Oxford Martin Visiting Fellowship as part of the research programme Collective Responsibility and Infectious Diseases (2017 & 2018). I also want to extend a big thanks to Central European University's Political Science Department and Research Group POLEMO (especially Jelena Belić and Zoltán Miklósi) for running a two-day manuscript workshop on an earlier draft of this book in Budapest (2017). Mark Cooper's and Shayne Martyn's research assistance are much appreciated, as is Murdoch University for providing the funding for it (2017 and 2019). I am deeply grateful for the financial and institutional support I received from the above-mentioned organisations without which this project would not have been realised.

Some of the material in this book has been published before in journal articles or book chapters, and I am grateful for the permission to include extended, revised and updated sections from these previous publications in the book:

- The Introduction contains sections from The Epistemology of Group Duties: What We Know and What We Ought to Do. *Journal of Social Ontology* 2020, published online ahead of print. Published by De Gruyter.
- Chapter 1 was previously published as The Possibility of Collective Moral Obligations. In *Routledge Handbook on Collective Responsibility*, eds. Saba Bazargan-Forward and Deborah Tollefsen. New York: Routledge, 2020, pp. 158–173.
- Chapter 4 contains sections from Collective Moral Obligations: 'We-Reasoning' and the Perspective of the Deliberating Agent. *The Monist* 2019(102): 151–171. Published by Oxford University Press.
- Chapter 6 was previously published as Making Sense of Collective Moral Obligations: A Comparison of Current Approaches. In *Collectivity: Ontology, Ethics and Social Justice*, eds. Tracy Isaacs, Kendy Hess and Violetta Igneski: Rowman and Littlefield, 2018, pp. 109–132.
- Chapter 7 contains sections from Structural Injustice and Massively Shared Obligations. *Journal of Applied Philosophy* (2020), first view. Published by Wiley.

Last but absolutely not least I want to thank my ever-supportive family and my wonderful friends – you are an enormous source of strength to me.

Introduction

Being cooperative is natural to us – we have set up our social world in a way that both presupposes and requires continuous joint efforts. We rely on each other all the time, assuming that others will play their part in these shared endeavours as we are playing ours. From basic coordination when sharing and navigating public spaces, to enjoying social activities with friends and loved ones, to working in a team with others in our professional capacities on complex tasks, "[w]e seem to have a natural capacity to engage in activities with others, which is constitutive of us as social creatures" (Seemann 2007: 217).[1]

Cooperation works really well in many if not most situations we find ourselves in. Still, we regularly encounter collective action problems that challenge us: whether these arise because we have arranged the social world in a suboptimal way or whether something unforeseen and socially unrehearsed occurs – we can get stuck with problems that we have not developed (and may not even be able to develop) behavioural patterns or effective joint responses for.

Philosophers have spent considerable energy on analysing small-scale cases of impromptu collective assistance among random bystanders, for instance (Held 1970; Goodin 2012; Collins 2013; Schwenkenbecher 2014b; Aas 2015; Collins 2019; Schwenkenbecher 2019). Not only practically but also conceptually more challenging are large-scale moral problems, in particular structural injustice. Some of these problems could be substantially improved through *distributive collective action* – attending rallies, changing our day-to-day activities and adopting certain collective behavioural patterns.

But for the great majority of collective moral action problems – especially where groups lack organisational structure and where collaboration is ad hoc – things are more complicated. Collective action is as ubiquitous as it is fraught with risks and failure, especially in its initial phase. Individual efforts are often in vain unless (sufficiently many) others cooperate. They will be costly for those acting unilaterally or pioneering new ideas while often producing no benefit for anyone. Worse, uncoordinated action might even stymie collective efforts to produce such benefits.

In other words, cooperation comes with its very specific set of problems surrounding the uncertainty of others' actions, intentions and motives. This uncertainty may undermine agents' reasons to choose cooperative (multilateral) over non-cooperative (unilateral) options, or their motivation to do so, or even make them fail to perceive of (or frame) a situation as one requiring cooperation at all. Successful communication can be stymied by a variety of factors and even where it works, uncertainties and disagreements concerning the joint goal, its relative (moral) importance, and the individual strategies that will produce that goal will often jeopardise the collective endeavour. In small-scale scenarios with groups of manageable size, continued mutual reassurance is often key to the success of any joint endeavour. In larger, unstructured groups the problem is often in the lack of direct communication between group members and uncertainty regarding group membership.

Philosophy is but one of the academic disciplines trying to illuminate the collective nature of our existence: sociology, psychology, economics and biology – the academic literature on the topic is burgeoning. This book takes a philosophical – and therewith admittedly narrow – perspective on collective aspects of our existence.

More concretely, and more narrowly still, this book is a defence of the idea that people can be *jointly obligated* in the sense of *sharing a collective moral duty*. An intuitive understanding of such requirements regularly surfaces in our actions, yet moral theory has been slow to pick up on them. Take the following case:

> *Commuters:* On a busy weekday morning at Stirling Station in Perth, Western Australia, a man gets trapped between the commuter train and the station's platform. If the train moves he will be crushed. Dozens of people who happen to be on the platform witnessing his predicament join forces in pushing the train to tilt it away from the man and free him.[2]

None of the commuters could have helped the trapped man on their own; in order to assist him they had to collaborate, and so they did. Consider also the following scenario:

> *The global pandemic*: Early in 2020, a coronavirus that originated in the Chinese province of Wuhan in late 2019, starts spreading across the globe. As it is becoming clear just how contagious and aggressive COVID-19 is, countries across the world adopt extreme measures to stop the spread of the virus. Populations are mandated to stay indoors except for essential trips outside, public institutions, bars and restaurants close, and people are asked to practice social distancing to limit the number of people they come into contact with. Places with high levels of compliance report a rapid decline of infections.

This case is very different from the one presented earlier: the circumstances under which the individual collaborators act differ greatly between the two cases. This is important for our moral obligations, as I will show later. Still, I argue that there is a sense in which the people in either scenario had a collective obligation to assist those in need.

It should be obvious by now that I am not interested in the obligations of organisations and corporate agents here. I believe that a lot of very good and very illuminating work has been done with regard to the agency of such groups and their ability to be addressees of moral demands (French 1984; Erskine 2003; List and Pettit 2011; Tollefsen 2015).

Instead, I am interested in groups of agents who are not organised but which – with either some very basic or no level of coordination and organisation – can willingly bring about outcomes. Such pluralities of agents may be groups of passers-by that are able to spontaneously collaborate to assist someone in danger, or they may be groups of people who collect money to help a friend in need, or they may just be people who unite behind a common cause without knowing each other in person. The reason why they are interesting for me is that they can effect change and they can – in some sense – act in the world. The book is trying to answer the question of *when* we can have obligations to perform a certain action or achieve a particular outcome *together*.

It is fair to say that traditional normative ethical theory has almost exclusively focused on what individuals ought to do and how they ought to act *as individuals*.[3] That is, the notion of agency underlying traditional moral theory is individualistic.[4] According to Neil Levy,

> [t]he individual is not merely the primary unit of analysis and bearer of value; for the most part, individualism is taken for granted to such an extent that philosophers are no more aware of their individualism than fish are of the water in which they swim.
>
> (2018: 185)

In this book, I not only try to show how we can expand traditional moral theory to incorporate collectivism but also argue that such an approach better reflects how deeply collectivism is engrained in our everyday thinking and moral practice.

I am interested in finding out when individual moral agents have obligations together with others in cases where they are facing a morally relevant choice and where individual action alone is either insufficient for doing what is morally optimal or even where individual action cannot make a difference to the better at all, leaving aside the substantive question of what makes any particular choice morally optimal.

Collective moral action problems are intriguing because our intuitive or standard responses vary greatly, depending on the specific features of the situation: while we all accept that together with others we have greater capacities than on our own and that bundling those capacities will often lead to better outcomes, we regularly feel torn between participating in the collective effort or choosing what is individually efficacious (but perhaps collectively suboptimal). In those cases, traditional moral theory is often at a loss. As yet, we lack the adequate conceptual tools. This book is meant to provide such tools and further our understanding of our obligations in joint-necessity cases. At the same time, I hope that it makes the reader realise that many of our obligations – or the way we perceive of them – are already in an important sense collective; as such I am not aspiring to posit a new type of moral obligation. I see my task more as providing a conceptual account of something that is already part of our moral practice.

In a bid to overcome the individualist blinkers of canonical ethics, one can occasionally observe a tendency in the recent literature to overstretch the idea of *collective* obligations and responsibility. Some authors have – in my view too easily – declared all kinds of complex problems – including global poverty and climate change – to ground collective obligations, often in a crude top-down fashion, which assumes that our moral obligations are merely imperatives to produce what is collectively morally optimal. My book will take a more cautious approach by focusing specifically on the perspective of the deliberating moral agent. As such, it is partly an argument against an unqualified proliferation of collective obligations, partly advocating a refined understanding of what these obligations are.

My views on the subject of this book have shifted over time. In my earlier articles, in particular my 2013 paper in *Ratio*, I opposed the view that we can have large-scale collective obligations. And even though I am still very sceptical of many of the arguments made in favour of such 'global obligations', in the final chapter of this book, I give a qualified defence of such a view. Most moral agents will hold a variety of different obligations – individual and collective – to contribute to addressing large-scale collective moral action problems. Many of us will not be in a position to initiate collective action but merely to contribute to existing endeavours. This, too, is a way of discharging our collective obligations.

Ultimately, I am hoping that this theory of collective moral obligations can help us better understand some of the conundrums we are facing in an ever more complex, interconnected world. Despite greater-than-ever exposure to information concerning the impacts of our actions and unprecedented levels of opportunity for collaboration across national and cultural boundaries, we might be growing ever more uncertain about what it means to be doing the right thing.

Notes

1. On how humans may have evolved to be cooperative, see Michael Tomasello (Tomasello, M. (2014). *A Natural History of Human Thinking*. Cambridge, MA; London: Harvard University Press; Tomasello, M. (2016). *A Natural History of Human Morality*. Cambridge, MA; London: Harvard University Press).

2. This happened on 7 August 2014 (www.abc.net.au/news/2014-08-06/man-freed-after-leg-trapped-in-gap-on-perth-train-station/5652486). See a similar case from Japan from the same year: www.theguardian.com/world/2013/jul/22/tokyo-train-passengers-rescue-woman-trapped and www.youtube.com/watch?v=39i89NJNCRQ (accessed on 22 February 2017).
3. Systematic development of 'collectivist' ethical theories did not take place until the last quarter of the twentieth century. Early texts include Held, V. (1970). Can a Random Collection of Individuals Be Morally Responsible? *Journal of Philosophy*, 67(14), 471–481; Regan, D. (1980). *Utilitarianism and Co-Operation*. Oxford: Oxford University Press; Parfit, D. (1984). *Reasons and Persons*. Melbourne: Clarendon Press; May, L. (1987). *The Morality of Groups*. Notre Dame, IN: University of Notre Dame Press; May, L. and S. Hoffman (1991). *Collective Responsibility: Five Decades of Debate in Theoretical and Applied Ethics*. Savage, MD: Rowman & Littlefield.
4. Neil Levy argues, "With few exceptions, work on moral responsibility in the Anglophone world is resolutely individualistic" (Levy, N. (2018). Socializing Responsibility. In K. Hutchison, C. MacKenzie and M. Oshana (Eds.), *Social Dimensions of Moral Responsibility* (pp. 185–205). New York: Oxford University Press). Contra Levy, some might think that some ethical theories have been taking collective effects into account in some sense (rule consequentialism, for instance. Here the rule to follow is the one that would produce the best consequences if it were generally adhered to). However, such an approach is still tied to an individualist framework precisely because it does not locate the unit of agency in the collective but in the individual.

1   Collective Obligations in a Nutshell

The philosophical literature on collective agency, collective responsibility, social epistemology and social ontology is burgeoning. Scholarly interest in 'collective' phenomena and theories reflects a persistent desire to tackle an old conundrum – the relationship between individual agents and the collectives they compose. The problem of reconciling these two perspectives is not one for philosophy alone.[1] There is a notable shift away from a strict individualism towards theories that reflect the fundamentally social, cooperative nature of human activities.

This book attempts to shed light on the issue of collective moral obligations – that is, obligations that individuals in loose groups (as opposed to group agents) may have together.[2] I take moral obligations to be a basic feature of our moral repertoire. Put in the simplest possible terms, there are things we ought and things we ought not to do.[3] For instance, we ought not to harm others without good reason and we ought to assist those in need. Further, we might want to distinguish between *pro tanto* and *all-out* obligations. Pro tanto obligations are demands on us that give us some reason to act but which can be overridden by other, more important reasons. All-out obligations are those we ought to meet *all-things-considered*, taking all the different moral considerations into account.

In this first chapter, I will give a brief account of my approach to collective obligations and I will sketch some of my core arguments. Subsequent chapters will provide in-depth discussion of the various contentious issues as well as a comprehensive defence of my view against rival views.

1.1 The Starting Point

I argue that our moral obligations (*pro tanto* and *all-out*) can sometimes be collective in nature. By this I mean that moral obligations can *jointly* attach to two or more agents in that neither agent has that obligation on its own, but they – in some sense – *share* it or have it *in common*. To have a collective obligation is a plural moral predicate much like to play a duet is a plural non-moral predicate. I will explain this in more detail later.

I believe that the notion of collective moral obligations fills a conceptual gap in philosophy. In a sense, one could say that moral philosophy has traditionally been concerned with the question "what ought I to do?",[4] while what we ought to do as communities has been the focus of political philosophy. But some of the things that we *together* can (and potentially ought to) do may be neither the political communities' responsibility nor straightforward individual obligations. Furthermore, even where some desirable goal or action is *primarily* the political community's responsibility, as a matter of fact, political agents (e.g. states and their institutions) often fall short of meeting their obligations. In either case, there may be groups of individual agents who can step up and produce the desired outcomes or perform the required actions. Examples include our joint ability to overcome collective action problems even in the absence of state action, such as closing (or reducing) the so-called global emissions gap (Blok et al. 2012; Wynes and Nicholas 2017). On a national scale, our ability to produce herd immunity against some infectious disease should be seen as collective. I will come back to these examples at the end of the chapter. My starting point will be a simpler, small-scale, real-world example of spontaneous collaboration between complete strangers:

> [*Motorcyclist*] Ten passersby witness a car accident in which a motorcyclist gets trapped underneath a car, which has caught fire on one side. Somebody has to act very quickly to pull him out the other side and in order to do so the car will need to be ever so slightly lifted. None of the passersby can lift the car on their own and pull the man out, but together they can (without taking any undue risks to their own health and safety). As it happened, the people manage to lift the car and save the motorcyclist's life.[5]

For the sake of argument, let us assume that the following is the case: it is obvious to the witnesses of the accident that the man is in imminent danger, and it is fairly clear what needs to be done to get him out of danger.

There are several scholars who argue that under circumstances such as these individual moral agents can be under a *collective obligation* (or have collective responsibility) to assist (Held 1970; May 1992; Wringe 2005; Miller 2010; Wringe 2010; Isaacs 2011; Schwenkenbecher 2013b; Pinkert 2014; Schwenkenbecher 2014b; Wringe 2016; Schwenkenbecher 2019). Collective obligations, on their accounts, are distinct from and not reducible to individual obligations (to contribute to cooperative ventures, for instance).

In the following, I will distinguish different ways of spelling out such collective obligations. But before I do so, let me briefly talk about why anyone might think that we need the notion of collective obligations. One of the starting points of many debates on collective obligations is the observation that in cases like the one earlier, in order to produce the morally best outcome, or in order to perform the action most likely to secure that outcome, individual agents need to cooperate with one another and coordinate their individual actions. It takes more than one person's effort to make a difference to the person in need.

More generally, there is a class of actions (and outcomes) that cannot be performed (or produced) by one person on their own. They require at least two people in order to be realised, and no one individual agent can guarantee the success of the collective endeavour. These cases are characterised by 'joint necessity'.[6] Playing a duet is a joint-necessity type of activity. By definition, it cannot be done by one person. Another example is 'talking past one another'. Joint necessity can be *analytic* (as in the two examples just given), where it is part of what it means to do x that x is done by at least two people. Or joint necessity can be *circumstantial*, where as a matter of fact (rather than as a matter of principle) something cannot be done by one person – for instance, if it takes two or more people to lift a heavy table (or a car, for that matter).

We can further distinguish between *strict* and *wide* joint necessity.[7] For strict joint necessity to apply, the number of available contributors to a collective outcome equals the number of contributors minimally necessary to produce it. What it means to be an available contributor would depend on the outcome in question. For the motorbike accident described earlier, it would mean anyone close enough to see what is happening and able to make some kind of contribution. For strict joint necessity, the success of the joint venture is counterfactually dependent on each available contributor playing their part. It is entirely within my power to stymie any efforts of our duet playing, and the same applies to you.

Wide joint necessity applies where there are more available contributors to a joint outcome than minimally necessary. There are many large-scale examples of wide joint necessity, such as producing herd immunity (against a certain infectious disease), bridging the emissions gap (UNEP 2017) or producing a referendum outcome in favour of marriage equality. In order for herd immunity against a particular communicable disease to be achieved, it is not necessary that everyone who can safely be vaccinated should be in fact vaccinated. Depending on the disease, the figure may be around 90%. What this means is that, in contrast to strict joint-necessity cases, my unilateral defection in a wide joint-necessity case does not *guarantee* collective failure and neither does yours. This might lead someone to the conclusion that therefore individual obligations to contribute to such goods are always less stringent. But I think this would be the wrong conclusion to draw, as I shall show later.

In many joint-necessity scenarios, something morally important is at stake. Especially where lives are in imminent danger, people tend to share the intuition that those who could help ought to do so; for example, those witnessing the motorbike accident ought to assist the trapped person. But this common intuition may create a dilemma, because no individual can guarantee the success of the joint endeavour (or produce the desired collective good).[8] That is, individually, none of these passers-by can assist the trapped motorcyclist. Hence, it cannot be any individual agent's obligation to rescue him. They can only help jointly. So, whose obligation is it? We might want to say that it is the obligation of all of them together. But what does that mean? Is it the 'group' of passers-by that has the obligation to assist? Or is there 'merely' an obligation on each of us to do our best, given others' actions? The answer is not straightforward. In my view, this impasse is regularly felt when we try to make moral decisions: it is the pull between the individualist option (to do something that is under one's individual control only) and the collectivist option (where the success of one's actions often depends on others' contributions).

Scholars have chosen different routes to answer the question about the locus of moral obligation in joint-necessity cases. Roughly, they can be divided into two groups, which I will call 'conservatives' and 'revisionists'. Revisionist scholars will usually introduce new moral vocabulary and concepts to fill what they believe to be a gap in traditional moral theorising where joint necessity is concerned. Many argue that there is some kind of group-level obligation (or responsibility) that applies to loose collections of individuals such as the passers-by in scenarios like our exemplary case (Held 1970; May 1992; Wringe 2010; Isaacs 2011). Other revisionists, including myself, speak of individuals holding joint obligations (Miller 2010; Schwenkenbecher 2013b; Pinkert 2014; Schwenkenbecher 2014b; Schwenkenbecher 2019) or sharing obligations (Björnsson 2014). Conservative scholars, in contrast, do not see the need for new conceptual tools but attempt to resolve collective action puzzles in a way that is maximally continuous with existing theory. They tend to argue that joint-necessity cases give rise to (perhaps slightly more complex than usual) contributory duties only. According to Parfit, for instance, each of the individual passers-by simply has an obligation to contribute if she thinks that enough others contribute to get the joint endeavour off the ground (Parfit 1984). Collins and Lawford-Smith would argue that each ought to take steps towards forming a group that can then act as an agent (Collins 2013; Lawford-Smith 2015), though Collins' view has shifted and in her latest work she appears to endorse a more revisionist approach (2019).

I will discuss the merits of these different types of approaches in more detail in Chapter 6. The obvious downside of the conservative approach is that the obligation to produce the collective good (or to realise the joint endeavour) is not allocated. In our example, then, there is no obligation to free the trapped motorcyclist, even though individual agents have obligations to contribute.[9] Holly Lawford-Smith acknowledges this problem for the conservative approach but bites the bullet because she thinks the advantages of this approach still outweigh its disadvantages (2015). In contrast, the obvious downside of the first type of revisionist approach is this: it seems to be built on the assumption that there is a (novel) entity, a group agent of sorts, that not only can act on the problem at hand but has a sufficient level of unity such that it can hold a moral obligation (or be held morally responsible). Revisionist scholars have tried to avoid this kind of criticism by arguing that being an agent is not a necessary condition for being the bearer of a moral obligation as far as groups (or collections of agents) are concerned (Wringe 2010).

However, my aim here is not to give an overview of the literature but to instead flesh out my own (revisionist) approach to collective obligations and show how it applies in a range of cases.[10] This approach, while revisionist, avoids the objection sketched earlier by refraining from postulating a group agent (even a putative or potential one) and instead conceiving of the obligations to assist in joint-necessity cases as shared or 'joint'.

1.2 Jointly Held Obligations

What does it mean to say that a number of agents *jointly* hold a moral obligation? On my view, collective obligations are not a novel type of obligation but moral obligations held in a collective *mode*: I can individually hold an obligation to do x or we (for instance, you and I) can jointly hold an obligation to do x (for instance, where x is only collectively feasible). To jointly hold an obligation is a plural predicate – it can only meaningfully apply to two or more agents, very much like other (non-moral) plural predicates such as 'playing a duet' or 'walking past one another'. On this approach, the obligation that the passers-by in our example assist the trapped driver is a joint obligation; they hold it together.

Joint obligations give rise to further individual obligations. If you and I jointly have an obligation to lift a heavy table, then each of us has an individual obligation to do our part or make an effort towards the joint endeavour. But joint obligations do not reduce to individual obligations to play our part. In order to see why, let us return to wide joint-necessity cases, where we have more potential contributors than minimally necessary for the success of the collective performance. Suppose that it takes two people to lift a heavy table, but three potential contributors are available. Suppose further that two is also the maximum number of people who can successfully lift the table together, because of the way each needs to position themselves to lift it. So out of the three potential contributors only two should act. It cannot be the case that each of the three has an obligation to act (because a three-way effort will not succeed). Neither should we think that any combination of two people (out of the three) is obligated to contribute. Because if we did, we would either (i) arrive at an impasse where we could not say exactly which two people have these obligations (i.e. we would arrive at the following disjunctive obligation: either a and b are obligated to do their part in lifting the table together, or b and c are so obligated, or a and c). Or, (ii) we would have to make an arbitrary decision on which two people have these obligations.

Instead, I suggest that the joint obligation is on all three and the individual (contributory) obligations will be derived from it. For instance, we may all be under an obligation to see to it that two of us lift the table together and one of us makes sure not to interfere. In order to do this, we will usually have to communicate with each other. This may be non-verbal communication. In everyday life, we often coordinate our actions this way – just think of a scenario where some passers-by rush to help someone who has trouble lifting a pram into a bus while others stay behind ready to step up if necessary.

But we need not always be able to communicate with each other in order to acquire (and discharge) a collective obligation. Sometimes, having the right information concerning the other agents' beliefs will suffice. Suppose that you and I live on opposite shores of a protected lake and in order to preserve the lake's sensitive ecosystem and keep its pristine water clean we are instructed (by the local council) to ensure that no sewage or grey water enters the lake. We also learn that every neighbour is being thus instructed. Now I can do my part of not allowing any polluted water to enter the lake, and so can you. But neither of us can guarantee that the lake's water not be compromised – that outcome we can only produce together. Assuming that the pristine ecosystem is valuable and no overriding concerns exist, we are under an obligation to protect it. This obligation is held by both of us, jointly. It is not an obligation held by either of us, because neither can discharge it alone. Note that this does not require us to act together in the strict sense. Note also that a joint plan is in place (via the local council's communication), which ascribes to each of us a clearly circumscribed role in the collective effort (and which, furthermore, communicates that very fact to each of us).

1.3 Collectively Available Options and We-Reasoning

So, when exactly should we think of our obligations as collective? I shall explain the conditions in the following. To start with, I argue that two (or more) agents have a collective moral obligation to do x if x is an option for action that is only *collectively available* and if each of them has sufficient reason to rank x the highest out of the options available to them.

Let me explain what this means. In a scenario like that of the trapped motorcyclist, each individual could reason in the following way: "I can walk over and attempt to lift the car but on my own I will not be able to lift it. Trying to lift it will only make sense if several other bystanders also contribute."

Naturally, most of us would probably make an attempt to get others to contribute (provided no countervailing circumstances obtain). But why is this so? To me it seems that the reason why one would try to establish collective action in this kind of scenario is that it seems like the (morally) best option.

Before I continue, note two things here: I do not commit to a view on what actually *is* morally best in this scenario; that is, I make my argument independently of any *particular* substantive moral theory. Evidently, different substantive theories vary significantly in what they consider morally best. However, I am hoping that the example used here is one where the major moral theories and common moral intuitions converge. Further, note that calling an option 'morally best' does not imply that I am committed to some kind of consequentialism. The morally best option for a Kantian may be to respect someone's autonomy and for a Virtue Ethicist it may be to act in the way most constitutive of *eudaimonia*.

Returning to our individual decision-maker, let us assume that she perceives the option as best where several passers-by lift the car together. It is important to note that this option is not actually available to *her* (alone), but it is only available to *them*. At the point of making her move to assist the trapped driver, our deliberator does not yet know exactly how many people will be needed and how many of the other passers-by are willing and able to contribute and who they are. Still, she acts on what she perceives to be the optimal option for acting in this case (jointly lifting the car), and she infers her own (and potentially others') individual contributory action(s) from that *collectively available* option.[11]

If that is what our individual deliberator does, then she *we-reasons*. This means that the starting point of her deliberation is not merely the options available to her (individually). Instead, she also includes in her deliberation those options that are only collectively available, such as lifting the car and freeing the trapped motorcyclist. She reasons from the top-down, so to speak. Starting from the best option (which is only collectively available) she derives individual contributory actions.

I am not alleging that someone who acts like our exemplary deliberator *necessarily* engages in we-reasoning, but empirical evidence suggests that people faced with similar scenarios regularly do (Butler et al. 2011; Butler 2012). And my contention here is that they often should.

Let me now explain the idea of 'we-reasoning' in some more detail. The way I am using the term is slightly different from how similar ideas of reasoning from the collective perspective are employed, for example, in philosophy of economics and (non-standard) game theory (Bacharach 2006; Gold and Sugden 2007a, 2007b; Hakli et al. 2010; Butler 2012; Tuomela 2013; Sugden 2015). My notion of 'we-reasoning' is equivalent to what Hakli et al. (2010) called 'we-mode reasoning'. It differs from some notions of 'team-reasoning' in that it is not a joint (or team) effort (Gold and Sugden 2007a, 2007b).

Importantly, I am adopting the term from its original context of decision-theoretic discussions of strategic interaction for the field of moral deliberation and decision-making. As moral agents, we regularly face problems wherein the outcome of our actions depends on how others choose. There are two ways of deliberating about our own choices in such cases. We can either think of our choices as best responses to others' choices (I-mode reasoning) or think of our own choices as contributions to the collectively best option (even when we do not know how others are (likely) to choose) (we-mode reasoning).

Let me illustrate this by returning to the example of the trapped motor-cyclist. The individual passer-by might reason in the following way:

> If sufficiently many others contribute then the morally optimal thing for me to do is to also contribute (provided that this will make a difference to the outcome). If not enough others contribute then the morally optimal thing for me to do is not to try to lift the car on my own, but perhaps to call an ambulance or the police.

This would be an instance of I-mode reasoning (I am adopting this term from Hakli et al. 2010).

Or, the individual passer-by might reason differently:

> The morally best outcome is the one where several people join forces to lift the car and free the trapped driver. In order to secure the mor-ally best outcome, each of us should make an effort towards lifting the car. I should get others to make an effort in lifting the car and signal to others my readiness to contribute to the joint endeavor.

Note that this involves two steps: (i) *we-framing* means to include col-lectively available options in one's option set when deliberating about which option is best and identifying an option that is only collectively available as optimal. In a second step, (ii) the deliberating agent deter-mines her individual course of action as playing her part in the collec-tively optimal course of action. If this is how the individual passer-by reasons about what she should do, then she is employing we-reasoning.[12]

There are many joint-necessity scenarios where by default most of us would reason in this way. Not only would we include collectively avail-able options in our deliberation (we-framing) but we would also take individual steps towards realising those options as well as encourage oth-ers to take the necessary steps. This may (but need not) include commu-nicating our intentions and goals to others, asking them to contribute, or distributing and coordinating tasks and roles. Often we will play our part without having information on what others are doing; we will take a gamble, so to speak (for instance, when we are not diverting grey water into the pristine lake).

Sometimes, individual roles or contributory tasks will be clear from the very start. This may be because there exists a joint plan or a habitual pattern of actions for a particular joint endeavour. Take the example of jointly setting a table, for instance. Or a traditional dance or a tune that people know well enough to perform it together instantly.

At other times, it may be relatively straightforward for individual agents to jointly work out a plan and individual contributions if they can communicate with each other. The other day I asked a friend to help me lift my canoe onto the roof rack of my car. We had to adjust our individual contributory actions on the go, but it was fairly easy to do so. If we did this more often, we might form a habitual pattern and could possibly even do this without important communicative (for instance, visual) cues.

There are other cases where such patterns, while not habitual or engrained, can be easily established by potential contributors without any need for communication between them. It may be obvious what the collectively best choice is and how each person can contribute to realising it as, for instance, in a hi-lo game kind of scenario. This is a payoff-matrix for a hi-lo game. We can easily imagine moral decision-making scenarios that have this structure. Even when each player is ignorant of the other player's choice, it seems obvious that they should pick option A (Table 1.1):

Table 1.1

		Player 2		
		A	B	
Player 1	A	Hi/Hi	0/0	Hi > Lo > 0
	B	0/0	Lo/Lo	

One example would be voting in a referendum on a morally black-and-white matter, such as the right to have an abortion (as in the 2018 Irish referendum to repeal the Eighth Amendment) or the right of same-sex couples to marry (as in the 2017 Australian Marriage Law Postal Survey).

But there are also cases where communication is difficult or even impossible and where individual agents cannot divine their contributions to the joint task without communicating to the other agents. Arguably, in those cases individual agents would be less inclined to we-reason. That is, they may be (and probably should be) less inclined to include options that are only collectively available in their moral deliberation and to take steps towards realising those options.

1.4 Joint Ability and Ignorance

Further, we might say that in such cases the *joint ability* of potential contributors to perform an action or produce an outcome together is severely diminished. That is, there will be circumstances under which the success of joint action is so unlikely that a collection of agents cannot be said to have the level of joint capacity minimally required for ascribing an obligation to them.

Two agents, *a* and *b*, have joint ability[13] to do *x* if there is a least one combination of contributory actions such that

- these are genuine options *a* and *b* have, and, if both are performed in the right way, they produce *x*;
- both contributory actions are compossible;
- *a* and *b* are capable of performing these actions with a view to combining them.

Let me explain the last condition: joint ability is not mere compossibility. Rather, agents must – in principle – be able to willingly combine their actions. That is, they must be in a position to *intentionally perform their contributory action as a contributory action*. This requires at least that agents are able to conceive of a collective pattern of actions, which their own and other agents' individual actions could form part of. It does not require them to believe that others are likely to perform their contributory actions within the pattern but merely that they could conceive of their individual actions as part of such a pattern.[14,15] There must be some reason for agents to form plural intentions in the most minimal sense as intentions the content of which is some collective endeavour (Ludwig 2016).[16] This is important, because otherwise we could ascribe joint ability wherever an outcome could accidentally be jointly produced. But surely, the accidental production of any outcome by some agent (or group thereof) should not be mistaken for a *robust ability* to produce that outcome where this robust ability is the basis for ascribing moral obligations.

Joint ability, then, is highly context-dependent and particularly sensitive to shared (or even common) beliefs.[17] As such, joint ability can be deliberately generated in a given collection of agents by providing information related to collective goals and contributory actions.[18] In fact, public information campaigns concerning specific collective causes do precisely that they communicate collectively desirable patterns of action and outline those individual contributory actions that are most likely to produce the collective pattern. This does not only solve (or prevent) coordination problems, but it also generates joint ability in the sense that people may now reasonably form intentions concerning their contributory actions *as* contributory actions where perhaps such intentions would not normally have been formed. Where small-scale joint-necessity problems are concerned, we commonly (and without thinking much about it) inform others of the problem at hand, the potential patterns of action that will resolve it and encourage others to make their contribution ("Do you mind giving me a hand with this? If you just [do *x*] then I will [do *y*] ").

In other words, knowing of opportunities to address collective action problems will reduce or remove *propositional ignorance* of the issue concerned. A person is propositionally ignorant of a proposition *p* if they do not know *of p* (Le Morvan 2011). For instance, someone may have never heard of anti-microbial resistance and therefore will not form intentions to contribute to the reduction of such resistance by changing her dietary habits, for instance (Giubilini et al. 2017). Further, information campaigns may reduce or eliminate *factive ignorance*, that is, they may correct false beliefs on the matter at hand. For instance, people may believe that there is nothing we can do to stop runaway climate change, but we may learn that there are things we can each do that will have a significant impact on mitigating global warming (Dietz et al. 2009; Blok et al. 2012; Wynes and Nicholas 2017). Factive ignorance, then, can also prevent agents from having reasons to form minimal plural intentions to perform their contributory action *as a contributory action*.

It is easy to see that in our main example, the case of the trapped motorcyclist, we will hardly need to worry about propositional ignorance. To each of the passers-by it is immediately obvious that the person is in need of help and that he must be pulled out from underneath the burning car. Where the respective (collective action) problem is less immediate (as is the case for problems concerning 'distant strangers', for instance), propositional ignorance will become a major factor in collective apathy and inaction.

In our exemplary case, there may be some factive ignorance as to whether the random group of strangers is in fact capable of lifting the car and extracting the driver, but in the real-world case, the passers-by were confident enough to try. The more immediate a problem, the less likely it is that agents are propositionally ignorant concerning that issue. Factive ignorance, in contrast, can have all kinds of causes, including emotional and psychological factors, and as such is often difficult to combat.

If we think that forming intentions to act depends on having certain beliefs (as I have been alleging), then interesting questions arise where we think that an agent or a group of agents can be held responsible for their suboptimal epistemic position. Take the example where a group of agents is factively ignorant of some harm they are collectively causing and they therefore continue to perform the actions that in aggregation cause harm. For instance, this was the case before the climate greenhouse effect was widely known. On my account, people who lived during the Industrial Revolution were not in fact jointly able to prevent global warming because their epistemic position was not such that they could have formed the intention to reduce (or abstain from) their fossil-fuel burning activities as part of an effort to prevent global warming.[19] This is not because there were no (feasible or economical) alternatives to burning fossil fuels, and neither is it because they were not (accidentally or incidentally) capable of preventing the release of massive amounts of greenhouse gases (GHGs) in the atmosphere, but rather because they could not have formed the relevant intentions to contribute to a joint effort to prevent aggregate harm, because they were ignorant of that harm. In other words, their ignorance undermined their joint ability. But were they responsible for that ignorance? And if so, can we say that they were culpable for their lack of joint ability? I cannot discuss here which criteria should make us consider an agent blameworthy of her ignorance, and there exists ample literature on this topic (Rosen 2003; Peels 2010; Le Morvan 2011; Peels 2016; Zimmerman 2016). Joint ability and the epistemic background conditions will be discussed in more detail in Chapter 3 and revisited in Chapter 7.

1.5 When Do We Have Collective Obligations?

To sum up what has been said so far: in order for two or more agents to jointly hold an obligation to address some joint-necessity problem they must have the joint ability to address that problem. We also discussed that in deliberating about the right (individual) course of action vis-à-vis collective action problems, agents regularly we-frame the case at hand – that is, they include options in their deliberation that are only collectively available – and they we-reason with regard to their individual contributory actions.

It is a necessary condition for collective obligations that potential collaborators facing a joint-necessity case have grounds to privilege we-reasoning over reasoning in I-mode. But under which circumstances do agents have such grounds? It is easier to give negative conditions for when agents lack such grounds. For instance, they will have no grounds for engaging in we-reasoning if they do not recognise the problem as a joint-necessity case. Further, they may not recognise a joint-necessity case as a morally pressing problem in need of resolution. Or else they may not be aware of other agents' potential to contribute. Finally, they may have reason to believe that they are on their own with regard to the problem, because agents appear unwilling to contribute. However, if the problem is pressing enough, the conscientious agent must not give up at this point but ought to attempt to secure the cooperation of others.

The picture of joint obligations drawn here aligns best with a non-objective view of moral obligations. On an objective view of moral obligations, we ought to do what is objectively best (or right) regardless of whether we *know* what that is. So even if we act conscientiously, on the basis of the best available information, and are rigorous in our decision-making, we may still fail to meet our actual moral obligations. Likewise, we may meet them accidentally. I do not have the space here to argue against the objective view of moral obligations and will instead refer the reader to Michael Zimmerman's work on this issue (1996, 2014).

The notion of collective obligations defended here aligns best with what Zimmerman (1996) calls the "prospective view of moral obligations".[20] To put it in a nutshell: on the prospective view, we ought to do what is prospectively best, that is, what our best bet is given the obtainable evidence and provided we have conscientiously availed ourselves of the evidence. This means that our moral obligations depend on our reasonable, justified (but not necessarily true) beliefs concerning the problem at hand.

The prospective view of moral obligations makes better sense of the intuition that agents have no collective obligation to address a joint-necessity problem where they reasonably believe an individually available option to be superior to an only collectively available option; or where they reasonably disagree on which collectively available option is best and they therefore cannot agree on a course of action; or where they are unlikely to figure out the collectively optimal solution in the time available to them. These kinds of complications, where they cannot easily be resolved between willing agents, can cancel collective obligations.

To illustrate the prospective view of collective obligations, let us once more return to the case of the trapped motorcyclist: the passers-by are likely to include the option of (collectively) lifting the car and extracting the driver in their set of options for moral deliberation unless they have reason to believe, for example, that there is no one available to help them. Of course, because the stakes are so high that they may still try on their own to pull out the driver, essentially testing if the option of rescuing him is individually available. However, this action is simply a way of availing themselves of evidence in a conscientious manner. Passers-by will usually attempt to investigate others' willingness to contribute – this serves to determine which options are available to *them*[21] and, potentially, it can be the moment where individual roles or contributions are distributed. Further, it generates common knowledge among potential contributors and therewith increases (or even establishes) joint ability. The same action can also deliver important information for each individual deliberator with regard to how others rank the available options and the extent to which they are willing to make their contribution. What they are obligated to do will depend on what they have good reason to believe is the best option, given that they have availed themselves of the evidence. That evidence will often include information about other agents' willingness and ability to contribute.

Such information will often be crucial for whether or not the pro tanto joint obligation becomes an all-out obligation. To reiterate, an all-out obligation is an obligation *all-things-considered*. Whether or not anyone (or any group) has an obligation, all-things-considered depends on how highly a particular option for action ranks for the respective individual(s) among competing options. Or, in other words, it depends on whether the reasons that speak in favour of that option outweigh the reasons speaking in favour of any of the alternative options. Awareness of others' likelihood to contribute will strengthen those reasons in favour of the collectively available option, other things being equal.[22]

On my view of collective moral obligations, two or more moral agents jointly hold an all-out obligation to perform an action or produce an outcome corresponding to a collectively available option if each of these agents, provided that she is conscientious,

i. has reason to believe that the collectively available option (joint rescue) is morally best;

ii. has reason to include that option in her deliberation about her obligations (we-framing the problem);

iii. has reason to infer her individual course of action based on (i) and (ii) (we-reasoning about the problem) and the ability to do so; And if the agent

iv. is jointly capable with the other(s) of discharging the task at hand.[23,24,25]

The first three conditions may be met either consecutively or simultaneously. Further, we-framing (ii) and determining individual courses of action (iii) will usually (but not necessarily) mean that agents communicate among each other, even though this need not be verbal communication. If one of the passers-by in our example observes another placing their hands on the car in an attempt to lift it, then they usually have a reason as per (ii) and (iii).

It is obvious now that our main examples came with a few implicit assumptions, which are responsible for the initial plausibility of the claim that the agents involved have some all-out duty to assist. This was necessary to get the argument off the ground. For instance, the scenarios were characterised by a certain moral simplicity. The features of the situations described were such that rescuing the person (or protecting the lake) would presumably be the morally best response. That is, most major moral theories would converge in their action recommendation. Further, in taking these scenarios out of context and discussing them at a certain level of abstraction, we simply ignored other factors that would play a role for moral deliberation. For instance, we did not discuss any competing obligations that our passers-by (or the lakeside neighbours) may have but simply assumed that there were none that would override the obligation to assist. Further, in the cases presented the objectively best option corresponded to the option that was perceived to be best by potential contributors (i.e. the objective and the prospective view on obligations would align in these cases as to their action recommendation). Further, the joint rescue case is a one-off problem that requires no recurring sacrifice. Apart from moral simplicity, we also assumed epistemic simplicity: the problems were fairly obvious to an ordinary agent and so were the solutions. The number of potential contributors was manageable, and they could communicate directly with one another. Naturally, more often than not these favourable conditions will not obtain. What impact does moral and epistemic uncertainty have on our collective obligations? The short answer is: the same impact as they have on our individual obligations. We frequently make decisions about what we ought to do under conditions of uncertainty and risk. As such, assumptions concerning which of our many pro tanto obligation become all-out obligations will always be somewhat approximate.

However, it may seem that *more* needs to be known or possibly investigated by individual agents if they are to jointly hold an obligation, compared to individually held obligations. This is true insofar as some knowledge concerning the others' willingness and ability to contribute to a joint endeavour are concerned. On the other hand, joint agency often calls for the sharing of (epistemic and other) expertise and burdens. Often, we do not *each* need to know how exactly to address some problem in order to jointly address it, as long as between us we have enough expertise to do so. In this regard, the threshold to acquiring collective obligations may in fact be lower than it is for individual obligations, or, put differently, the former may at times be more easily defeated than the latter. I will discuss this in more detail in Chapter 5.

1.6 Collective Versus Individual Obligations

Let me conclude the first chapter by pointing to the advantages the collective obligations view holds over individualist competitors. A more detailed discussion of alternative approaches can be found in Chapter 6. Earlier, I already pointed to some of the disadvantages of the individualist approach. Here is what I believe the collectivist approach that I am proposing has to offer:

(a) Harmony with our moral intuitions concerning blame

Earlier, I pointed out that for individualist (conservative) approaches there is no obligation to free the trapped motorcyclist. Consequently, if people stand by idly and fail to assist the trapped man, we could blame them only for not playing their part in the operation, but we could not apportion blame for letting the motorcyclist die. But our intuitions in that and other cases seem to suggest otherwise: ascriptions of wrongdoing and blame should concern not merely people's failure to contribute to the joint action but their failure to actually assist to do the action required. One could argue that the collectivist reading of duties follows our intuitions more closely than the individualistic reading. We think that the idle bystanders should be held responsible and blameworthy for the man's death because they walked away when they could and should have helped. On the collective obligations view, the individuals are culpable of *jointly* failing to assist the victim of the attack and they potentially jointly blameworthy (see Section 5.3).

(b) Generating a unified picture of our moral obligations

This takes us to the second argument in favour of a non-individualist, revisionist reading of the obligations involved in the above-discussed scenario. According to Wringe, the notion of collective duties gives us "a more unified picture of the moral scene, since it postulates one underlying obligation which explains a range of individual obligations, rather than a large number of unconnected primitive obligations" (2016: 12). He admits that the individualist (conservative) approach, which he calls the "primitive obligation to co-operate account", seemingly has a similar advantage: it appears simpler than the account proposed here, because it operates with only one kind of moral duty instead of two kinds (ibid.). However, Wringe argues, whether or not the resulting theory is really simpler than one that accepts collective duties cannot be shown without seeing them both worked out in detail.[26] Furthermore, "we should notice that it is not clear that collective obligations are a distinct kind of obligation rather than a familiar kind of obligation falling on a new kind of thing" (ibid.).

(c) Providing an explanation for our duties to contribute to collective endeavours

The third reason to prefer the collectivist approach is that it better accounts for the existence of an obligation to assist in joint-necessity cases in the first place than the "primitive account". If we do not have the capacity to assist someone, we are under no obligation to do so. In the above-described cases, capacity to assist results from the fact that the individuals have a joint ability but no individual ability to assist. Only together with others can the individual passers-by help those in need. Their individual action would not have any effect if others did not perform corresponding actions towards a joint goal. Hence, the individual passers-by cannot be required to lift the car by virtue of their individual duty to assist. They can only be required to do so because of the possibility of joint action. Furthermore, they cannot hold individual duties *to collaborate* with others, because whether or not others collaborate is outside their control and power. Hence, the duty to collaborate in order to assist cannot be an individual duty. It makes sense, then, to consider the individual obligations to contribute as *arising or resulting from* the collective or joint obligation. According to Wringe, that the latter are more basic than the former is shown by the fact that the collective obligation remains the same even if the individuals who hold respective contributory duties change (Wringe 2016: 11). Apart from being more basic, the existence of the joint obligation *explains* the existence of the individual obligation, as Wringe (2016: 9) has argued. Relatedly, Allard Tamminga and Frank Hindriks argue that a member obligation – an obligation to contribute to a collective endeavour

> is of necessity a member obligation specified by a plan consisting of one or more optimal group actions. This means that a member obligation essentially includes a reference to a group. Group obligations are conceptually prior to member obligations, since the group members determine their member obligations by reasoning from the group obligations.
>
> (2020: 1103)

(d)   Resolve individual decision dilemmas (action-guidance)

As moral agents we are often faced with the problem of having to decide between performing individually efficacious but overall non-optimal actions and performing contributory actions, which are individually non-efficacious, but collectively optimal. The concept of collective obligations can help us guide our actions when these decision dilemmas arise and help us choose the right action. If we do not have a concept of collective obligations, we may standardly feel pressured to choose the non-optimal action, while feeling that we are not justified in choosing the collective action. I take it that Christopher Woodard has made an argument of this kind (Woodard 2003).

(e)   Overcoming the individual impotence objection

It is often argued that one has no obligation to do something where one's action makes no difference to the outcome. For example, Walter Sinnott-Armstrong has argued along these lines, rejecting an obligation to reduce one's individual carbon footprint, because no individuals' emissions make a difference to the warming climate (Sinnott-Armstrong 2005). I am calling this the *individual impotence objection*. This objection is undesirable, because it condones collective inaction where a joint effort can make a difference. Endorsing the view that our individual obligations can have their source in collectively optimal patterns of action (and in collective obligations for that matter) will help us defeat the impotence objection.

Notes

1. To give just three examples from outside philosophy: Behavioural economists like Michael Bacharach emphasize the importance of 'team reasoning' in strategic interaction, and evolutionary biologist Michael Tomasello posits the adaptive advantage from 'collective intentionality' in our ancestors' thinking.

(Bacharach, M. (2006). *Beyond Individual Choice: Teams and Frames in Game Theory*. Princeton, NJ: Princeton University Press; Tomasello, M. (2014). *A Natural History of Human Thinking*. Cambridge, MA; London: Harvard University Press.) Olson, M. (1971). *The Logic of Collective Action: Public Goods and the Theory of Groups*. Cambridge, MA: Harvard University Press.

2. I am referring to group agents as described by List and Pettit (2011) or Tollefsen (2015).

3. I cannot say much more about this without abandoning the required level of generality. How moral obligations as such are grounded is a question that cannot be addressed here. In particular, I will refrain from committing to any 'substantive' moral theory.

4. Exceptions include Donald Regan's and Derek Parfit's works (Regan, D. (1980). *Utilitarianism and Co-Operation*. Oxford: Oxford University Press; Parfit, D. (1984). Five Mistakes in Moral Mathematics. In *Reasons and Persons* (Vol. 1, pp. 55–83). Oxford: Clarendon Press)

5. See www.telegraph.co.uk/news/worldnews/northamerica/usa/8761446/ Trapped-motorcyclist-saved-by-bystanders-who-lifted-burning-car.html. There are countless other examples of strangers collaborating spontaneously to save the life of perfect strangers or to protect them from harm. See, for instance, www.abc.net.au/news/2014-08-06/man-freed-after-leg-trapped-in-gap-on-perth-train-station/5652486 (both accessed 7 July 2018).

6. I am adopting this term from Lawford-Smith (2012).

7. I first introduced this distinction in Schwenkenbecher (2017).

8. Another problem may arise if this turns out to be a wide joint-necessity case, because it would then seem that in addition to being individually unable to guarantee the success of the collective endeavour, each passer-by is also not, strictly speaking, necessary for its success. I leave this problem aside here and will return to it later.

9. Consequently, in a case of collective omission, no one would be blameworthy for the failure to free him. Further, if individual contributory obligations are understood as conditional, we run into the problem of mutual release. Simultaneous non-action by all potential contributors voids obligations of the kind "I ought to help if the others do" (see Goodin 2012).

10. For a more detailed defence of this account, see Schwenkenbecher (2019).

11. An option for acting is 'collectively available' if it is an option for two or more agents acting (or producing an outcome) together, but not something an individual can do (or bring about). For instance, the option of getting married is not available to me as an individual. It is only available to me and another person together.

12. A more detailed account of the difference between I-mode reasoning and we-mode reasoning can be found in Schwenkenbecher (2019).

13. Joint ability is temporal and comes in degrees.

14. It is the failure of the last condition that undermines joint ability in Zofia Stemplowska's example: "[A]n action of each of three billion people touching his or her nose next Tuesday is correctly classified as unfeasible because there are not three billion people who could know next Tuesday how to do it or that their individual contributions are needed. (Of course it remains open that this may become possible in future, in which case the action will become feasible then.)" Stemplowska, Z. (2016). Feasibility: Individual and Collective. *Social Philosophy and Policy*, 33(1–2), 273–291.

15. In a wide joint-necessity case, the same clause applies. It must be possible for each to intentionally perform their contributory action, which may mean to refrain from contributing where their contribution is either superfluous or detrimental to the success of the joint endeavour.

16. Minimally, plural intentions are individual intentions with a plural content. Maximally, they are interdependent, interlocking intentions (Bratman 2014).
17. A belief that x obtains is *shared* between two agents if each agent believes that x obtains. It is a *common belief* if it is shared *and* if each agent knows that it is shared (first-order common belief). See also Roy, O. and A. Schwenkenbecher (2019). Shared Intentions, Loose Groups, and Pooled Knowledge. *Synthese*, online first.
18. This is what Scott Shapiro refers to as a 'shared plan'. Shapiro, S. (2014). Massively Shared Agency. In M. Vargas and G. Yaffe (Eds.), *Rational and Social Agency: Essays on the philosophy of Michael Bratman* (pp. 257–293). Oxford: Oxford University Press.
19. One might extend this period of blameless ignorance to the second half of the twentieth century. I am assuming that Svante Arrhenius' discovery of the greenhouse effect towards the end of the nineteenth century was not public knowledge for a long time. However, at the very least with the adoption of the UNFCCC in Rio de Janeiro in 1992, climate change and the greenhouse effects should have been widely known.
20. It should be noted, though, that Zimmerman is an individualist about moral obligations and would probably not subscribe to the idea of collective obligations defended here.
21. Bacharach (2006) and others (e.g. Butler et al. 2011) insist that we-reasoning involves what they call 'agency transformation'. This means that individuals consider the group the locus of agency, rather than themselves (see also Woodard 2011).
22. Another way to put this is to say that it depends on which moral reason(s) for action outweighs all others (see, e.g., Woodard 2011).
23. It should be noted that these conditions are jointly sufficient for pro tanto collective obligations but are not all necessary. This is because such obligations can also arise in the absence of joint necessity where one person alone can produce a morally optimal outcome or perform the corresponding action, but it is a matter of fairness that another agent (or other agents) would help her in doing so. Cases of joint obligations arising from distributive justice rather than joint necessity are not discussed here.
24. Finally, whether or not a pro tanto collective obligation becomes an all-out collective obligation depends on whether or not for the contributing agents there are competing overriding (collective or individual) duties. Or, to put it differently, it depends on whether or not the group-based reasons for contributing to the collective endeavour weigh heavier than other reasons (on group-based reasons for action, see Woodard 2003, 2017).
25. I would like to thank Niels de Haan for comments that helped me refine these conditions.
26. If we look at two such approaches – Bob Goodin's (2012) complex conditional obligations or Stephanie Collins' (2013) proposal – they hardly appear simpler than what I propose here. I will return to both of them later (Goodin, R. E. (2012). Excused by the Unwillingness of Others? *Analysis*, 72(1), 18–24; Collins, S. (2013). Collectives' Duties and Collectivisation Duties. *Australasian Journal of Philosophy*, 91(2), 231–248.)

2 Joint Oughts and the Agency Principle

2.1 Joint Moral 'Oughts'

In the first chapter, I suggested that collective obligations are jointly held by agents. But what exactly does that mean? On my (non-distributive) view, if there is an obligation that jointly attaches to two or more individuals, then it is distinct from (but gives rise to) their individual contributory obligations. Collective obligations do not reduce to an aggregation of individual obligations to contribute to collective actions. Agents hold them *together* rather than individually. In Chapter 5, I will say more about what it means for two or more agents to hold an obligation together. Collective obligations are characterised by a *normative primacy of the collective level*: the collective level is considered primary and the question of individual obligations as secondary (Isaacs 2011; Schwenkenbecher 2014b; Wringe 2016). Further, the more strongly collective our obligations are, the greater are what I call *normative links between group members*. Here are a few examples for how a set of agents who collectively have an obligation can be normatively linked: they may be required to take some responsibility for the success of the collective action, such as coordinating the joint activity and generating the kind of group knowledge required for the group members to be able to fulfil their contributory actions. Further, it may mean that group members have to pick up the slack left by others. All this, however, presupposes that certain epistemic conditions hold within the group, for example, that information is shared in the right way. Finally, group members may also be linked by considerations of fairness in the distribution of contributory roles. More on all this is in Chapters 5 and 7.

But let me return to the basics of the collective obligations view. In contrast to my view, on a distributive view of collective obligations, every member of a set of agents has a certain (share of that) obligation, but that there is no plural obligation above and beyond that. The collective obligation is the sum of the individual obligations. The collective obligation is usually discharged if every person of that set plays his or her 'part'. Note that for some types of actions it will be hard, if not impossible, to individuate parts. That is, actions that are highly interdependent may not easily be analysable in terms of discreet individual contributions. Likewise, it might be difficult to individuate contributory duties when the collaborative actions are interdependent and highly integrated.

There are also significant differences between my view and the views of other collectivist revisionists. Importantly, my view does not claim that pluralities or sets of agents can hold duties in terms of their being 'potential' or 'putative' agents, as Wringe and Isaacs do (and possibly Held, too). My own view is that when acting or producing an outcome jointly, individual agents are not necessarily forming a novel collective agent. In fact, they may not even be performing a joint action, or act together, in the strict sense. To say that they are a plurality of individuals capable of acting jointly and under an obligation to act jointly seems to perhaps shift the focus more to the relationship between these individuals, rather than the nature of the group as a (somewhat) distinct agent.

But are these just disagreements about words? Perhaps it does not matter how exactly we describe the entity holding the duty to assist? It matters for a number of reasons, in my view. Mainly, non-collectivists are at odds with our basic and derivative intuition, as I will explain in more detail later. Further, collectivist accounts aspire to unify our theoretical account of moral obligations in an explanatory and ontological sense. They think that the concept of collective obligation can explain and ground individual contributory duties. Non-collectivists usually have no such aspirations and where they do they are arguably less successful in fulfilling them. I will provide evidence for this claim throughout the book and more explicitly take it up again in Chapter 6. Further, the view I propose can better explain why we may have obligations to take up the slack left by others in the group or why we may bear some responsibility for the overall outcome. However, collectivism about moral obligations can violate the agency principle – a problem that I will discuss further down in this very chapter. Ultimately, both approaches have some downsides. But, in my view, for the kind of collectivist approach I propose the advantages are greater than the disadvantages.

So far, I have only very roughly sketched a number of key concepts. Before I continue explaining my view, let me refine some of the central concepts in this book. What are moral obligations? I understand moral obligations in this book as moral requirements on agents to perform actions or patterns of actions, usually with a view to producing certain outcomes, rather than requirements to adopt certain attitudes.

Some people understand moral obligations to be fundamentally about actions and see actions as requiring corresponding intentions. In other words, one might think that to have a moral duty means to have a duty to perform an action (or sets thereof or else an inaction), which in turn implies that one at least is capable of forming the corresponding kind of intention. Philosophers of action think that actions are tied to and defined by specific intentions and as such they differ from mere activity or behaviour.

If that were the picture endorsed at the individual level, one might be tempted to transfer it to the collective level. One might think that in order for a plurality of agents to have a collective or joint obligation it must be capable of performing a collective action proper. In the philosophy of collective action, the notion of collective (or plural, or shared or joint) intention is central. Much of this literature is dedicated to figuring out just exactly how these intentions can arise and how they differ from individual intentions.

One might then think that a necessary condition for collective obligations of a plurality of agents is their ability to jointly perform an action, including their ability to form the kind of plural intention required for an action to properly count as a joint action. And, in fact, philosophers have in the past turned to existing accounts of joint agency when exploring the idea of joint obligations, including myself (Schwenkenbecher 2013b). However, I will not follow this interpretation of 'joint ability' here, because I now think it is too restrictive. I will later explore the notion of joint ability in more detail (Chapter 3). For now I will merely point out that our account of collective obligations will depend on our account of collective ability.

Further, and as indicated in Chapter 1, my focus is on pro tanto obligations. Pro tanto obligations are potential obligations to do something. They are the morally important considerations in favour of acting in a particular way that have to be weighed against other considerations in order to arrive at an *all-out* obligation. We arrive at an *all-out* obligation once we have considered all morally relevant aspects of an action (or inaction). All-out obligations are action-guiding and final.

Some philosophers think that obligations *are moral reasons* for action (Parfit 1984). I cannot discuss this issue here, but will instead adopt a position that permits this kind of view, while not affirming it. For the purpose of my argument, I suggest that to have an obligation to do x means to have a moral reason to do x. This can but need not be an overriding reason. Some see moral reasons as pro tanto obligations and overriding moral reasons as all-out obligations.

Let me turn to another crucial distinction: that between moral obligations, duties and responsibility. I am using the first two – obligations and duties – synonymously throughout the book, even though some scholars have argued that they differ. According to Hart (1955), obligations arise from relationships between specific people, such as an obligation to keep a promise. Duties, in contrast, can be held with regard to strangers. I will not follow Hart's distinction here. Another way to draw the difference between duties and obligations is this: while someone's duty always corresponds to another one's right, the same is not true for obligations. Furthermore, according to some scholars, this tracks the difference between perfect and imperfect duties. In any case, I will use obligations and duties interchangeably and will not concern myself with the issue of imperfect versus perfect duties.

What about responsibility? I deliberately refrain from framing the debate in this book in terms of moral responsibility. The concept of moral responsibility, as I understand it and as it is commonly used, is much broader than that of obligation. Sometimes, they are used synonymously; however, responsibility refers to more than requirements on agents. It may refer to an agent's capacity for moral reasoning and agency, for instance. It may refer to moral complicity, shared blame or moral taint with regard to collective practices or states of affairs. Maike Albertzart (2015) argued explicitly against the use of 'responsibility' in collective contexts and in favour of the focus on 'obligation' or 'duty'. The former term, in her view, has too strong a ring of causal contribution that it is unhelpful for understanding aggregate harm, for instance.

Further, the scholarly debate on collective moral responsibility is to a large extent focused on *retrospective* responsibility for harm brought about by groups of people: societies, constituencies, or firms and their employees (May 1987, 1992; Thompson 2006; Pettit 2007; Isaacs 2011). Some of the authors discussed here, such as Virginia Held, have formulated their approaches to collective obligation in terms of responsibility. I will not be talking about retrospective responsibility here, mainly because I believe that a lot of good work has already been done in the area, while there is very little work on the topic of collective duties. Further, I believe that we can address both questions – that of retrospective responsibility and that of prospective duties – separately. True, if we have retrospective responsibility for a moral wrong, we tend to have some kind of prospective duty to fix the problem or else to otherwise remedy our wrongdoing. But this may not always be the case. For instance, we may not be able to fix a problem that we are responsible for having brought about. The potential sources of forward-looking duties or obligations extend beyond cases where we have infringed a negative duty or are retrospectively responsible for a wrong. In other words, we can have forward-looking duties (to assist, to further justice etc.) without having previously violated a duty.

Finally, my discussion of collective obligation does not presuppose or rely on any specific first-order normative theory. All major ethical theories would suggest that we ought to help those in need. I will come back to these questions in Section 3.2.

So much for the very basics: I am sure that the reader will still have some questions concerning these issues, but I hope that these questions will be answered in the course of the next chapters, where I develop my view in more detail.

2.2 Motivating Collective Obligations

At this point, let us return to our simple starting example of the trapped motorcyclist. At the time of arriving, the passers-by have no preconceived plan as to how to free the trapped man. They are, however, well capable of working out such a plan and of enacting it together.

I call the 'basic intuition' the intuitive view that the passers-by ought to lift the car and free the trapped man together. The 'derivative intuition' is the view that if people fail to assist the man, then they are possibly blameworthy for letting him die (provided no mitigating circumstances apply). I assume that most people would share these intuitions given certain conditions, for example, that helping is not overly demanding or risky and that the task at hand is fairly obvious and doable.

One of the reasons why we need to move beyond conservative (individualist) accounts of moral obligations in joint-necessity cases is that they fail to satisfy these two intuitions. In order to see that, let me show what it would mean to spell out the duties involved as duties *of* individuals.

According to an individualist reading, the individual passers-by hold no duty to free the trapped man. Such a duty simply does not exist because there is no agent that could hold that duty given that there is no agent that could discharge the duty. Each individual, however, has a moral duty to perform individual actions towards a joint goal such as communicating with the other person, suggesting possible individual group patterns and individual contributory actions, and, if necessary, performing a contributory action towards the joint goal such as contributing to lifting the tree. A view of this kind has been defended by Stephanie Collins, for instance (Collins 2013), and – to some extent[1] – by Holly Lawford-Smith (2012).

Now, to be fair on individualists, they think all sorts of duties arise as part of the individual duty – for instance, the duty to be responsive, to show willingness to contribute, to take steps towards forming a group agent and so forth. But still, an individualist would have to accept that, strictly speaking, there is no obligation to free the trapped motorcyclist.

As a result, it seems that if we were to ascribe blameworthiness in case the passers-by failed to assist and the trapped man died, no one would be blameworthy for his death. We could only blame the individual agents for failing to play their part, for instance, for not having taken steps towards acting jointly.[2]

One might doubt that this is a strong argument against individual approaches to collective assistance cases for two reasons. First, one might question the importance of intuitions in moral theorising, perhaps because they can be unreliable or inconsistent. Second, some readers may not share these intuitions. I will address these worries in turn.

First, let me address the methodological point. For some of those critical of using intuitions, perhaps the problem is resolved by simply referring to the aforementioned as 'considered judgements' rather than as 'intuitions'. To the extent that we think moral reasoning may use the method of reflective equilibrium we must allow for considered judgements to be part of moral reasoning. In other words, if we think that considered judgements may be used to challenge abstract principles and modify them, we should accept their use in this argument.

Second, it may be the case that some readers do not share these intuitions. Perhaps they have no strong intuitions either way or else they have strong individualist convictions. These readers may well not be convinced by the point made earlier, but I hope they will see the merit of a collectivist approach as the discussion continues. Further down, in Chapter 6, I will showcase the advantages of a collectivist approach in more detail as well as the reasons against duty-individualism.

Furthermore, some versions of duty-individualism are problematic in yet a different way. If the obligations concerned are not only individual obligations but also conditional, the *problem of mutual excuse* may arise. If, for instance, each has an obligation to make an effort towards establishing the joint endeavour (or towards contributing to it) only if the others also make an effort (or else the others' behaviour shows signs of making such an effort).

Problem of mutual excuse: If the passers-by refuse to do anything at all or even walk away simultaneously, then on some versions of conditional individual duties each of them gives the other an excuse for not contributing (because the other one does not and individually one's efforts are futile) while simultaneously being excused by the other's equivalent refusal. In short, if both do nothing, they nullify each other's obligations by conveniently (simultaneously) denying the other's conditional obligation's antecedent.

This means that if both do nothing in such cases no wrongdoing has occurred. Again, one might think that this seems only intuitively wrong and intuitions are unreliable. However, this time even those with individualist intuitions should be dissatisfied.

Bob Goodin has offered a way out of the mutual excuse dilemma (Goodin 2012). Let me illustrate it using a simplified version of a joint rescue case involving only two contributors:

> [Hikers] Two hikers encounter a man trapped under fallen tree, whose only chance of survival consists in them lifting the tree off him (Image 2.1).

Goodin showed that simple conditional commitments are not enough even if both agents are committed to the maximally ethical action. "I will lift the tree if you will" does not commit them to acting unilaterally and satisfying the condition (ibid.). Goodin's solution is to argue that individuals

Image 2.1 Hikers

must commit to the following complex condition: *I will if you will* and *I will if (you will if I will)*. In other words, if the others' commitment to the joint action depends on your own commitment to it, and vice versa, then you should commit to contributing to the joint action not only if the other contributes but also if the other's commitment is thus dependent on yours.

It appears that Goodin defends the following set of duties for the two people facing the trapped man in *hikers*. For each of you, it is the case:

> You have a duty to contribute to lifting the tree (or to establish joint action) if your friend contributes.
> AND
> You have a duty to contribute (or to establish joint action) if it is the case that your friend will contribute if you do.

Does this solve the problem? Perhaps yes, but in doing so it creates a new problem. Let us assume that it is not entirely obvious to you whether or not your friend will contribute if you do. In establishing whether that is in fact the case, you need to first communicate with her and find out whether she is willing to do her part if you do. Imagine that you fail to enquire as to your friend's conditional willingness to contribute. You now have another excuse not to assist: you had no idea that your friend did subscribe to the condition. In this case, we would probably want to say to you that you should have found out from her. But why should you do this? If the answer to this question is that you ought to communicate with the other passers-by because you have an obligation to somehow help the trapped man then our argument has become circular. My point, as elaborated in detail later, is that you have this obligation to enquire because you already have a collective obligation to assist together with the others. This collective obligation can explain why you have the individual obligation to enquire with your friend. But nothing explains it in the individualist case. Further, this solution does not escape the problem of failing to confirm our intuitions. If you and your friend fail to lift the tree and free the trapped man, on this account, you have each failed in a complex conditional duty to contribute but not in a duty to save the man. The reader may at this point still not be convinced of the collectivist approach, but perhaps she can appreciate that duty-individualism comes at a certain price.

2.3 Duty Collectivism and the Agency Principle

The advantage of the individualist approach is clear. It satisfies both the agency and capacity principles, usually deemed to be core tenets of moral theory, in a straightforward way.

> *Agency principle:* Only agents can hold moral duties.
> *Capacity principle:* An agent can only hold a moral duty if the agent is capable of discharging that duty.

I will discuss the capacity principle, or the principle that 'ought' *implies* 'can', in more detail in Chapter 3, but let me briefly sketch the argument to come.[3] On any standard reading of the capacity principle no passer-by 'can' lift the car on their own, and hence no one has a duty to do so. The individualistic reading satisfies the capacity principle by suggesting that in the previous examples each individual holds a moral duty to perform an action towards solving the problem. The capacity principle is met, because no individual member of the group has duties beyond her capacity.

Duty-collectivism can still satisfy the capacity principle if we are prepared to extend it to include joint actions and jointly acting agents:

> *Singular-agent capacity principle*: For singular – individual or group – agents *'ought' implies 'can'* means that if a singular agent ought to do x, this implies that she can do x, and if she cannot do x then she need not do x.[4]
>
> *Plurality-of-agents capacity principle:* For a plurality of – individual or group – agents *'ought' implies 'can'* means that if agents jointly ought to do x, this implies that they jointly can do x, and if they cannot jointly do x then they need not jointly do x. (Schwenkenbecher 2014b)

More needs to be said about the capacity principle and about what joint ability exactly is. I will set this issue aside and discuss it further down (Chapter 3). At this point, we will simply assume that there is some plausible version of the capacity principle and that it can be thus extended to cover pluralities of agents. The capacity principle is satisfied if agents *jointly can* discharge the duty.

But what about the agency principle – is not the collectivist reading in violation of the agency principle according to which only agents can hold moral duties? There are two possible ways to answer this question: we can claim that it *is* met because only individual moral agents hold duties on my view, albeit jointly (the 'ought' itself is *joint*), or else we can bite the bullet grant that the agency principle is not met. Let me address each proposal in turn.

The first possible answer is that the agency principle *is* satisfied because it is the individual group members who hold the moral duty to assist (in joint mode).[5] That is, the duty to do x – to lift the tree and free the trapped man – is not held by novel entity consisting of you and your friend. Rather, two individual agents hold the duty together. This answer presupposes that there are (at least) two different *modes* in which agents can hold duties: the individual mode and the joint mode. An agent can hold a duty individually – where this implies that she is the one in control of and responsible for performing the action the duty requires. Or two or more agents can hold one duty jointly – where this implies that only jointly are they in control of and responsible for performing the action the duty requires.

This answer might be unorthodox for some and, or, worse, they might think it wholly implausible. How can two agents hold a duty *jointly*? And how is this not the same as saying that the plurality or group of agents holds the duty? Plural predicates in non-moral contexts are those predicates that apply to two or more agents. If two people, for example, walk past one another, then it is not the group of them that has walked past itself. Rather, 'walking past one another' is a plural predicate – it is something only two agents can do. Other examples include 'to play a duet', or else 'to drift apart' or 'to go separate ways', for that matter. It does not seem so far-fetched that moral imperatives could apply across agents, too.

Collective obligations, then, are different from individual obligations in that they apply jointly to agents. The plural moral predicate 'to be jointly obligated' or 'jointly ought' could behave very much in the same way as the standard individual 'ought', except that it may not be applied to individual agents.[6]

The second possible answer to the previous question – whether or not my account of joint duties violates the capacity principle – is to grant that the capacity principle *is* violated. That is, one could grant that on the account I propose non-agents can hold moral obligations. Why is it problematic if the agency principle is not met? Should we agree that collectives that are not agents are incapable of performing actions? Or should we discard of the agency principle?

In this section, I will briefly discuss the importance of the agency principle and why or why not its violation matters. While conservative scholars insist that only individual agents and constituted group agents are properly agentive, capable of performing actions and capable of being addressees of moral demands (Lawford-Smith 2012; Collins 2013), revisionists are more comfortable with the idea that the agency principle may be implausible and superfluous. Bill Wringe (2010) argues that the agency principle is often endorsed because it seems that an obligation need to be addressable to some agent and that only agents can act in the sense relevant for meeting the capacity principle.

Wringe, however, tries to show that the addressee and the subject of an obligation can come apart: while we should accept the principle of addressability of obligations, we should deny that the addressee of an obligation needs to be the subject of that obligation. (2010: 217). He writes that

the correct conception of agency is derivative from a prior grip on the range of moral obligations that exits. On this account, it is not that certain entities are morally obligated in virtue of the fact that they are agents; *rather, we should take them to be agents in virtue of the fact that they are the subjects of moral obligation.*

(p. 221, my emphasis)

According to Wringe, there are two motivations for the agency principle, and he rejects them both. The first motivation is that if 'ought' *implies* 'can' it seems that in order for there to be an 'ought' or an obligation there must be an agent who can do whatever the obligation requires (ibid. 221). The second motivation, Wringe alleges, is that "statements about obligations are only intelligible if they have some kind of 'addressee'". This addressability requirement might be motivated by "the idea that it is part of the point of statements of obligation that they can be capable of affecting deliberation" (2010: 225).

Let us assume that these are the two main motivations for endorsing the agency principle. According to the first one, only agents 'can' do the things that are required by the capacity principle. But we need not accept such a view. The first motivation is easily dismissed if what it means is that there must be an agent in the strong sense, that is, an individual with full agentive capacity or a group agent in order to do whatever the obligation requires – in order to lift a tree, for instance. We can see clearly that this does not require an agent proper, but only two agents who are capable of acting together. Let us use an everyday-type scenario. Let us assume that for some reason you and your colleague have to move a desk in your office. You cannot do it on your own and neither does your colleague – it is a very heavy and large desk. Let us say that the reason you need to move it is that removalists accidentally trapped the office cat between the wall and a recess in the rear panel of the desk. They went home before you noticed and now you and your colleague are the only two people left at the office. The poor animal will not be able to get out unless you move the desk away from the wall. You and your colleague are not an agent, but you can still move the desk together – you can do whatever the obligation requires. And without doubt that is exactly what you would do in a situation like that. Some might say that in this situation you and your colleague are in fact forming one agent. But to do so would beg the question. When is it the case that two agents form a novel and distinct group agent? Scholars such as List and Pettit have done a lot of work in this area, arguing that constituted groups such as corporations can be moral agents. It would take a detailed argument to show that the two people lifting a desk are in fact a group agent. None of the scholars claiming this (Lawford-Smith, Collins, Killoren and Williams) have provided such an argument. And I believe that it would be unlikely to get off the ground because drawing the line between group agents and non-group agents that way would brush over important nuances: two people lifting a desk together constitute a very different phenomenon from the action of a group agent – for example, the university – purchasing the desk.

Wringe objects to this first motivation for the agency principle in a similar way by saying that the 'can' involved in the capacity principle does not require an agent, strictly speaking, but merely a 'potential agent', "which can now become an agent can do any of the things which it could do if it were an agent" (2010: 22, FN 11). He goes on to say that groups which – despite not being agents – can be transformed into agents already meet the conditions for agency:

> In fact, the idea that constituting oneself as a collective agent requires that one is already a collective agent is one that seems to lead pretty quickly to a *reductio ad absurdum* of the claim that there are collective agents (unless one holds, implausibly, that such agents, when they exist, have existed from eternity). The way to avoid the *reductio* is to insist that if collective agents can exist, they can also come into existence, and that a body's constituting itself as a collective agent is not itself an exercise of collective agency, but is something achieved by the acts of individuals who act in such a way as to bring the collective into existence.
>
> (2010: 224)

My disagreement with Wringe reflects my previous point. He appears to be saying that in order to be able to act together an unstructured group of agents must transform itself into an agent or that in acting together individuals transform into an agent. This kind of language somewhat blurs the lines between agents acting jointly on the one hand and agents acting as (or transforming into) a group agent on the other hand (Pettit and Schweikard 2006; List and Pettit 2011). However, being capable of joint action or of jointly producing an outcome is not the same (and is in fact weaker) than being a collective agent.

Let me point out, however, that it is still an open question what exactly the conditions are under which members of an unstructured group have joint ability. In order to reject the first motivation for the agency principle, we merely need to assume that there is *some* way in which agents *can* jointly do things without forming a group agent proper. I will discuss the exact parameters of joint ability further down (Chapter 2). Suffice it to say here – again – that joint ability is not the same as being a group agent.

The second motivation for the agency principle is that only agents can hold duties because only agents can be proper addressees of moral requirements. This, in turn, is because only agents, according to Wringe's take on this view, can deliberate about such requirements (2010: 225).

In fending off this second motivation, Wringe proposes that addressee and subject of the obligation can sometimes come apart (2010: 225). In a case like hikers, he would say that the subject of the obligation is the group (you and your friend). In other words, the collective consisting of you and your friend has the obligation to lift the tree. However, the addressees are you and your friend, as individuals. It is the addressees' task to see to it that the obligation gets discharged, for instance, to organise themselves if that is necessary (2010: 227f). Another, and perhaps more straightforward, way to question the second motivation for the agency principle is to say that it is two or more agents who can jointly deliberate over their moral requirements without being an agent. As long as the hikers in our case can communicate with each other nothing stands in the way of them deliberating on the best course of action. Further, where there is a salient optimal pattern of actions individual deliberation may well suffice for joint ability (see Chapter 4).

It seems then that the fact that the collective obligations view violates the agency principle is no decisive argument against it. Further, we might accept the possibility of joint oughts discussed earlier. In that case, the joint duties view is definitely in the clear as far as the agency principle is concerned.

Notes

1. I am saying 'to some extent' because Lawford-Smith focuses on agents who are already structured and in that sense are in fact group agents. Her main example is that of a removalist company (2012). Further, it should be noted that Collins' view in her 2013 paper differs significantly from that in her 2019 book *Group Duties*.
2. Sean Aas seems to agree. In response to Stephanie Collins' example of the beachgoers who must coordinate their actions to save someone from drowning, he writes that "[i]t seems hard . . . to resist the claim that the swimmers are obligated, collectively, to save the [drowning, A.S.] swimmer, even if they do not take any steps to 'collectivize'" Aas, S. (2015). Distributing Collective Obligation. *Journal of Ethics and Social Philosophy*, 9(3), 14.
3. Importantly, even where individual agents are concerned it is not settled what exactly this principle says. This problem is exacerbated for collective agents, obviously, with Pinkert Pinkert, F. (2014). What We Together Can (Be Required to) Do. *Midwest Studies in Philosophy*, 38(1), 187–202, and Lawford-Smith, H. (2015). What 'We'? *Journal of Social Ontology*, 1(2), 225–249 – the only ones I know to have attempted to tackle it so far.
4. Alex King has argued that the sense of 'implies' in 'ought' *implies* 'can' must be strong enough to support the contrapositive – 'can' *implies* – 'ought', even though he does not defend the principle as such. In King, A. (2017). 'Ought Implies Can': Not So Pragmatic After All. *Philosophy and Phenomenological Research*, 95(3), 637–661.
5. This argument was made before by Björnsson, G. (2014). Essentially Shared Obligations. *Midwest Studies in Philosophy*, 38(1), 103–120, and in Schwenkenbecher, A. Ibid. Joint Moral Duties, 58–74.
6. I first expressed this idea in Schwenkenbecher (2013b). A similar idea appears in Pinkert (2014).

3 Joint Ability and 'Ought' *Implies* 'Can' for Pluralities of Agents

The next important issue is the capacity principle and its plural form, or the sense in which a plurality of agents' jointly can act or bring about an outcome. This is a necessary criterion for ascribing collective obligations. What does it mean for a plurality of agents to have joint ability? The first section contains a somewhat detailed discussion of existing accounts of joint action, so readers mainly interested in my notion of joint ability may want to skip this and move straight to Section 3.2.

3.1 What Is Meant by 'Joint Ability'?

What is the sense of joint ability required by the capacity principle? In other words, which sense of 'can' satisfies 'ought' *implies* 'can' for unstructured groups?[1] One might think that accounts of individual ability are a good starting point for an enquiry into joint ability. One way of thinking about ability is in terms of dispositions:

> An agent has the ability to A in circumstances C if and only if she has the disposition to A when, in circumstances C, she tries to A. So, according to the dispositional analysis, I am able to smash all the windows in my house if and only if I am disposed to succeed in smashing all the windows in my house when I try. . . . The schematic letter 'A' in the dispositional analysis is to be replaced by verb phrases that express actions that are voluntary, in the sense that they are actions that one can in principle try to perform.
>
> (Fara 2008: 848–849)[2]

Along similar lines, Alex King (2017) writes that in the capacity principle what is meant by 'can' is that "you're able to do things that (a) you would do (or tend to do) if you tried and (b) you have the opportunity to do" (p. 2). Zimmerman points to the requirement of control: "[t]o be obligated to do *A*, then, *S* must be in control of whether or not he does *A*; it must be personally optional for *S*" (1996: 40). According to Zimmerman, *S* must be able to do *A* or refrain from doing *A*. Peter Vranas (2007) claims that saying that an agent *can* do something means that "the agent has both the ability and the opportunity to do the thing" (p. 169).

The key elements of these accounts of individual ability are the 'likelihood to do x if one tried to do x', 'having the opportunity to do x' and 'being in control of whether or not one does x'.

But how useful are these approaches for our enquiry? After all, what it means for a plurality of individuals to have the ability to act jointly is different from what it means for an individual to act. Naturally, a set of agents' collective ability depends on their individual abilities. But there must be something else, something more than the sum of individuals' abilities to do their share that makes a plurality of agents capable of doing something.

As mentioned earlier, some might argue that a collective (or joint) obligation is an obligation to act collectively or jointly in the sense of performing a joint action, narrowly construed (Pettit and Schweikard 2006; Bratman 2014). In fact, I have so argued in the past (2013b, 2014b), and I believe that Bill Wringe (2010, 2016) and Sean Aas (2015) are committed to such a view.

But is this too narrow? After all, pluralities of agents can bring about outcomes intentionally even if they are not performing joint or collective action proper, and this may suffice in order for them to be able to hold a duty collectively.

In the following, let me distinguish three ways in which we may understand joint ability:

* In the strongest sense as the ability of a plurality of agents *to perform a joint action*, narrowly construed;
* In the intermediate sense as the ability of a plurality of agents *to engage in joint intentional activity*, where agents form intentions to participate in some collective endeavour;
* In the weakest sense as the ability of a plurality of agents *to jointly produce an outcome* regardless of the participants' intentions.

Ultimately, the notion of joint ability defended here will sit somewhere between the intermediate and the weak interpretations.

3.1.1 The Strong View: Ability to Perform Joint Actions

What is meant by such a joint action? Let me distinguish, for the point of clarity between group action as an action of an incorporated or structured group agent such as a corporation or a state one the one hand, and joint action by a loose, un-structured group of people (what I have been calling a 'plurality of agents') on the other. I am assuming that those who have tried to give accounts of joint action as distinct from group action (as the action of structured group agents) are getting it more or less right.[3]

What is usually considered crucial in the discussion of corporate agency – and what is missing in the case of joint agency – is the fact that incorporated agents have a certain decision-making and decision-implementing structure, sometimes referred to as a 'constitution' (List and Pettit 2011). It is the constitution that allows the group to adopt views, form intentions, and decide on ways to implement their intentions by way of actions. A group's constitution is "a set of rules, formal or informal for determining how the inputs of individuals are to be put together to generate group judgments as outputs" (ibid. p. 89). Groups must abide by standards of rationality such as consistency and deductive closure in order to be agents. Consequently, if a group has no such constitution, it cannot form group judgements and therefore cannot act *as a group*, that is, as an agent over and above the individuals constituting it. According to this view, group judgements are caused by individual judgements, but are not reducible to them: the former supervene on the latter.[4]

In any case, the groups I am concerned with in this book have no constitution and their respective actions differ from the actions that group agents can perform. There is no doubt that people do things together in ways that do not fall under 'group agency' as described earlier. You and I might sing a duet, three musicians might lift a piano or two lifesavers might jointly pull a drowning man out of the surf. These kinds of action are often referred to as 'joint action', and that is how I will use the term here to distinguish it from group action as the action of structured or incorporated groups.

Some scholars seem to believe that any time agents act together they are forming a group or collective agent (Lawford-Smith 2012; Collins 2013; Killoren and Williams 2013) while others seem to be interpreting group agency as a type of joint agency (Miller 1992). However, the differences between the phenomena these different approaches attempt to capture – two people singing a duet or a university divesting from fossil fuels, for example – are significant and should not be brushed aside. While all attempts to provide a theoretical account of collective agency that covers its different forms necessarily simplify, some of those simplifications will bury important nuances. Most scholars therefore distinguish between group agency proper and joint agency.

Let me now turn to exploring some of the existing accounts of *joint agency*. First, I will introduce the idea and, then, I will show that some of the accounts put forward need some amendment.

Most scholars agree that some minimal conditions need to be in place in order for something that is done by more than one agent to count as a joint action. This will usually include a shared or joint goal and some level of belief or knowledge regarding other people's intentions to contribute to the shared goal and special 'plural' intentions. In the following, let me explain the account of joint action proposed by Pettit and Schweikard's (2006), which also resembles Michael Bratman's (2014).

According to Pettit and Schweikard, individual agents "combine to perform" a joint action (2006: 19). Apart from their individual contributory actions there is also an action they perform together. Take the example of singing a duet. Each singer follows their own score, but with a view to producing a harmony together with the other. Or take an orchestra at the concert hall playing Vivaldi's *Spring* from the *Four Seasons*: each musician plays her individual part, together they play Vivaldi's *Spring*.

Arguably, that action is different from an alternative scenario: imagine that each musician practises their part at home, and without their knowledge, their solo recital is being transmitted to a studio and mixed with all the other musician's performances. The outcome – the complete score – might sound very similar to what we heard in the concert hall, but surely the musicians are not playing this piece together in the same sense.

Basic account of joint action

These are the basic elements of joint action:

Two (or more) agents act jointly if it is the case that

  (i) each performs their part in the joint action
  (ii) together they perform the joint action
  (iii) each intends

- to do her part as in (i); and
- that[5] they act together as in (ii)

Many accounts of joint agency do require that each participant in a joint action have certain beliefs about the other participants' intentions. Bratman (2014) argues that shared or plural intentions are held 'by way of' others' shared intentions – that is because of and in alignment with those.

Pettit and Schweikard argue that in order for people to "perform a joint action in enacting a certain performance" they need to "each believe in common" that others intend to do their bit, that others intend that they (together) perform the joint action and that "they each intend to do their bit because of believing this" (2006: 23–24). Accordingly, people only act jointly if each believes that the others also intend to act jointly and that they intend to contribute their share towards the joint performance. People do not act jointly if they accidentally or ignorantly contribute to the same outcome. Also, people do not act jointly in the proper sense if they believe that others do not intend to do so.

Further, Pettit and Schweikard consider it necessary that agents have common beliefs concerning others' intentions and beliefs regarding others' intentions. Bratman (2014) put forward similar (sufficient and not necessary) conditions, which he argues need to be out in the open. Olle Blomberg – correctly in my view – argued that such a condition would be too strong as a necessary condition (Blomberg 2016). I will return to the question of group knowledge later.

Joint or shared actions as described by Pettit and Schweikard (2006) and Bratman (2014) where participants' beliefs concerning the joint action and their intentions are out in the open, and each is certain to be able to rely on the others' contributions will usually require participants to communicate directly with one another. It is much harder to achieve this level of interlocking beliefs where participants can only communicate indirectly, for instance through the help of a coordinator (Roy and Schwenkenbecher 2019), or where they cannot communicate at all.

There will be actions where – in the absence of a constitution or a set of rules concerning the contribution of each – interlocking beliefs and intentions are necessary in order for the joint action to succeed. Say that several musicians meet at a public jam session. They do not know each other and they will not play standards but improvise on the basis of their spontaneous ideas. Perhaps one of them starts with a beat, another plays a cord progression and the rest of them join in. In order to perform together, each must be aware of and reacting to what the others are doing. Each might take the lead at times. In contrast to the performers of Vivaldi's *Spring*, there is no score or script – they cannot merely perform a pre-set sequence. These kinds of actions seem to require strongly interlocking intentions, mutual responsiveness and an ongoing – explicit or implicit – re-assurance between participants of the shared intentions and goals.

However, surely not all types of actions that people perform together in some sense are like this. There may well be other types of actions that individuals perform together and which do not require the same levels of interlocking and regular mutual assurance. To be fair, though, Bratman purports to put forward *sufficient* criteria for shared agency. Pettit and Schweikard, though, argue that their conditions are *jointly necessary*.

Let me illustrate what has been discussed by returning to the aforementioned real-world case: on 6 August 2014, commuters at Perth Stirling station (Western Australia) pushed aside a 30t train to rescue a passenger who had been trapped between the train and the platform. The *Independent* reported online:

> A commuter whose leg became trapped between a train and the platform edge was freed by his fellow passengers, who collectively managed to push the entire train up and away from him. . . . In dramatic CCTV footage, commuters can be seen rushing to the man's assistance and tipping the whole carriage away from him until he managed to free his leg.[6]

Each person could see that around her were others who were also pushing against the train. Each had grounds to believe that those around her were also intent on jointly assisting the trapped person. But none of them would have these beliefs concerning every single commuter. Commuter trains are long. Each person would have been able to see the people closest to her, but she would have had no idea of how many others there are and whether or not they were jointly capable of pushing the train away from the trapped person. Their plural intentions and respective beliefs would have been at most de dicto and not de re. Further, it would not have been *known* to the individuals which beliefs the others would have been holding concerning the collective endeavour. They could infer the beliefs and intentions of those in their proximity, based on their actions and perhaps utterances, but they would not have formed beliefs concerning those whom they were not directly aware of.

It seems to me that the conditions put forward by Pettit and Schweikard (2006) do not obviously cater for this scenario. Concretely, it seems to be the case in our commuter scenario that all commuters' beliefs can only be de dicto: they possibly believe in common

- that others – whoever these others are apart from the ones they can directly observe – intend to do their bit,
- that others intend that they (whoever exactly is meant by that apart from those they can directly observe) perform the joint action, and
- that each intends to do their bit because of believing this.

Pettit and Schweikard's and most of the popular accounts of shared agency use examples where there is a clearly identifiable and usually fairly small group of people who can easily coordinate and communicate, and where group membership is obvious.[7] But they do not examine larger and looser groups such as the commuters at the train station. There, the boundaries of the group are blurred and the information concerning who is part of the group is not available to any of the individual agents.

In a situation like commuters the individual participants may well make implicit assumptions about others' willingness and intentions to contribute even if they do not know exactly who these others are and how large the group is. However, they have little reason to assume that everybody in the group has formed beliefs concerning everybody else's beliefs and intentions with regard to the collective effort. So, the level of interdependent group knowledge would be weak and common knowledge would not obtain.

Nonetheless, it seems strange to deny that the commuters are engaged in a type of joint action. Let us once more return to basic account of collective action and add to it the factors we just discussed:

Extended basic account of joint action

Two (or more) agents act jointly if it is the case that

(i) each performs her part in the joint action
(ii) together they perform the joint action

(iii) each intends

- to do her part as in (i); and
- that they act together as in (ii)

(iv) each believes (iii) de dicto
(v) each believes that (iv)

Still, even on this improved account of joint action, our real-world case will most likely not meet conditions (iv) and (v). We have several options now. We can either conclude that the commuters are not performing a collective action; they are 'merely' producing some outcome collectively. This seems to be what Pettit and Schweikard are committed to. Or, we could say that they are performing a collective action and that the above-mentioned authors' accounts need to be further amended accordingly. Again, Bratman (2014) might be happy to say that the commuters do perform a collective action, because his account merely puts forward sufficient conditions.

Finally, we could take an altogether different route: we could simply put the question of collective action or joint action aside and say that in order to have a joint obligation a plurality of agents need not be able to perform a collective or joint action in the strict sense.

What speaks in favour of this view is that agents may not need to perform an *action* to discharge a duty. Zimmerman argues that, strictly speaking, obligations are not restricted to actions (1996: 40f), and Björnsson makes a similar point (2014). Not everything we have control over neatly fits into the concept of action (such as decisions, mental phenomena, motives, intentions, attitudes) (Zimmerman 1996: 41–42). Assuming that pluralities of agents need not perform an action, strictly speaking, in order to discharge a collective obligation, let me now explore a different concept – that of *shared intentional activity*. Perhaps that is all that is needed for a group of agents to have joint ability in the sense required for moral duties.

3.1.2 *The Intermediate View: Joint Intentional Activity*

This section focuses on a weaker notion of collective action – that of shared intentional activity. Scott Shapiro (2014) has defended the concept of *shared intentional activity* in his critique of Michael Bratman's approach to shared agency, where he argues that collective agency is more easily had than Bratman and other philosophers of action think.[8] It is important to note that Shapiro sees shared intentional activity not as an additional type of collective agency, distinct from the stronger accounts just discussed, but instead he believes that these accounts are too demanding and that his weaker and more general account should instead be endorsed. He does not deny that there can be 'strong' collective agency as described earlier, but thinks that it is a special subtype of the more general phenomenon of *shared intentional activity*, which he aims to give an account of.

Shapiro (2014) points out that plural intentions that are reflexive and mutually interlocking (as, e.g., proposed by Bratman 2014) are only required when cooperating agents are the sole authors of their shared and individual plans to act, but not when there already exist plans for such action (provided, perhaps, by a public authority). Shapiro criticises the way in which not just Bratman, but most philosophers of action, approach collective agency: "philosophers of action have largely concentrated on analyzing shared activities among highly committed participants. . . . This restriction, however, has rendered these theories inapplicable to instances of massively shared agency" (2014: 258).

The idea that shared agency required shared interlocking intentions instead suggesting that "shared intentionally activity is activity guided by a shared *plan*" (p. 277). What does it mean for a plan to be shared?

> A plan is shared by a group to J when (1) the plan was designed, at least in part, for the members of the group so that they may engage in the joint activity J and (2) each member accepts the plan.
>
> (2014: 278)

Accepting a plan does not imply that each member know the full content of the plan but that the content is publicly accessible for those who wish to find out. According to Scott Shapiro,

> A group G engages in shared intentional activity to J . . . when . . .
>
> (1) There is a shared plan for G to J;
> (2) Each member of G intentionally follows her part of the shared plan;
> (3) Members of G resolve their conflicts about J-ing in a peaceful and open manner;
> (4) It is common knowledge that (1), (2), and (3); and
> (5) J takes place in virtue of (1) and (2)
>
> (2014: 277)

The second condition is somewhat ambiguous. It could mean that each member is required to intend her contributory action and to actually perform it. Or else, it could mean that each member must do her part of the shared plan (or perform the contributory action) where doing it is part of or the result of an intentional action. In any case, I assume that Shapiro means the first and stronger interpretation of the second condition.

We can see that this is a less demanding account of shared agency, or of acting together than Bratman's or Pettit and Schweikard's. Concretely, agents need not have formed their intentions by way of others' intentions.

However, it still has fairly strict epistemic requirements: in order to be engaged in shared intentional activity there has to be common knowledge between the group members of the fact that each intentionally performs her contributory action.

Common knowledge has been understood in different ways. Bratman (2014) suggests it is equivalent to knowledge being 'out in the open' in a group of people and refrains from describing it in more detail or providing a formal definition. However, generally speaking, in order for common knowledge of x to obtain in a group, the individual members of the group need to have knowledge about what the others know with regard to x. Or else, common knowledge is often formulated in terms of beliefs such that common knowledge of x requires that each group member (i) believe x, (ii) believe that each member believe x, (iii) believe that that each group member believe that each other group member believe x, and so on.

A simple example will show that our beliefs are often iterative and reflexive in this way even if we are not explicitly aware of that. Take the following case: you and I are talking about a common friend – Michael. I say to you that Michael was just granted Australian citizenship and I am sincere. Let us call that belief b_m. Now I believe b_m and you – having no reason to mistrust me – believe that, too. We share that belief. But what I also believe – in addition to *my* believing b_m – is that *you* believe b_m. After all, I just told you and you nodded and said "Oh, that's great news". And, clearly, you believe that I believe b_m. So each of us in that situation has second-order beliefs. Now, if pressured, each of us would probably also infer third-order beliefs: I believe that you believe that I believe b_m. After all, it makes sense for you to believe that I believe the very thing I just told you. And so on.

Ordinarily, we tend not to be explicitly aware of iterations beyond a certain level, and we are certainly not capable of having an awareness of infinite belief iterations. This suggests a qualification of the iterative account of common knowledge: beyond two or three iterations, our higher-order beliefs would be implicit, rather than something we actually infer, let alone are explicitly aware of. Further, there may be cases where common knowledge obtains up to some level of iteration but not infinitely. We can account for this by saying that something – for instance, b_m – is common knowledge up to a certain level n.

Certainly, in everyday communication we regularly make inferences about what other people believe, including what they believe concerning our beliefs. Here is another example: if I stand on the footpath holding my parasol on a sunny day and a person walks past me and remarks on the fact that it is not raining, I infer that she wrongly believes that my parasol is an umbrella and also that she believes that I wrongly believe that it is raining or soon will be. I may then venture to correct her first-order belief and say that what I am holding is a parasol. This should tell her two things: (i) that I believe that she believes that I am holding an umbrella and (ii) that I believe that she is mistaken in that belief.

Let us assume that she replies with "Oh, I see". This suggests that she is adjusting her first-order belief (i.e. her belief concerning my holding an umbrella). Now we both share a first-order belief (that I am in fact holding a parasol) and several higher-order beliefs: I believe that she believes I am holding a parasol, she believes that I believe that, and so forth.

In any case, this short excursion into common knowledge is simply meant to show that such knowledge is easily had where individuals can directly communicate with each other. But it is more difficult to achieve where individuals cannot directly communicate, and there may be cases where it is impossible to achieve (Roy and Schwenkenbecher 2019).

Most importantly, common knowledge may not be obtainable in those cases Shapiro has tried to give an account of: massive-scale collective action. After all, his goal was to describe the kind of transient, dispersed, and often alienated agency of the contemporary world that spans across the globe. But we will not usually have common knowledge concerning other people's intentions to follow their part of a shared plan in large-scale collective endeavours. This would require that we each have beliefs about (each of) the other group members following their part of the plan, plus beliefs about their beliefs concerning our beliefs and so forth. This seems too strong. We could increase the plausibility of such a claim by requiring merely that such beliefs be de dicto (as we did in the previous section). This would allow us to have beliefs about others beliefs even if we did not know who they are (or even how many of them). But even so common knowledge will not be achieved by people in large, dispersed and often only very loosely connected groups were communication would often be one-way and we may have no reason to form beliefs about others' beliefs or if we did we may often believe that (most) others are not similarly engaged in some collective endeavour.

In fact, neither common knowledge nor interlocking plural intentions may be required for massively shared agency.[9] Shapiro himself says about the merits of his own approach:

> It turns out, therefore, that not only is shared agency possible in the absence of *shared* plural intentions, it can obtain even without *any* plural intention. What is necessary is that someone formulates a plan for the group to follow and communicate that plan to the group. *If that plan is efficacious in coordinating planning, action, and resolving conflict that is, if it satisfies the functional role that shared intentions normally serve, it will issue in shared agency.*
>
> (2014: 282, my emphasis)

In short, Shapiro argues that as long as there is a plan that is known to the members of the group and that serves the coordinating function of shared (or plural) intentions we can have shared agency without such intentions.

But we must not lose sight of our actual question: what is the sense of 'jointly can' or 'joint ability' that we need in order to be able to ascribe joint obligations to a plurality of agents including large and dispersed groups of the kind Shapiro tried to account for?

Our discussion of Shapiro brought about the following suggestion: that in order to be successful in doing something together (and I am deliberately using this vague term here) we sometimes only need to share a plan that works. A plan that works is one which identifies a group strategy for achieving whatever goal is adopted and individual strategies (or parts of the shared plan or (sets of) contributory actions – I am using all these terms interchangeably) that will realise the group strategy and ensure – under normal circumstances – that the goal is achieved. Further, the individual members of the group must be capable of performing their part(s) of the shared plan.

But is this correct? Take the following example:

> [*Housemates*] Suppose you and I are housemates and our landlord has told us to keep our house clean at all times. What does it take for us to do so? Imagine for the sake of argument that I work during the day and you work during the night. We are not usually at home at the same time. What it takes for you and me to keep the house clean is that I keep the house clean when I am around and you keep it clean when you are around. According to Shapiro, if we follow this plan in the way described then we are engaged in shared intentional activity.

Note that, strictly speaking, we need not have a shared plan in order to keep the house clean. Just imagine that the landlord sent us a note demanding that the house be kept clean at all times, but none of us has read it. It slipped in between some advertising in the mail and we threw it out unread. So we have no plan. We are perfectly able to keep the house clean without either of us intending to keep the house clean at all times or without sharing a plan to that extent. I might just feel that I want to keep it clean when I am at home and you might feel the same way. We might be concerned with our individual plans only. Or else, we might have been brought up to always clean after ourselves so it has become second nature to us to do so. Nevertheless, we both succeed in keeping the house clean at all times. Also, note that *only jointly* are we able to keep the house clean *at all times*. This is because it is not under my control whether the house is clean when I am not around and the same applies to you.

Are we engaged in *shared intentional activity*? Not on Shapiro's account. But are we *jointly able* to keep the house clean at all times even in the absence of a shared (and publicly known) plan? Are the two of us who know nothing of the landlord's demand and care little about what the other person does jointly able to do something like keeping the house clean at all times?

It seems that the answer to this question must be affirmative, because in an sense, we are perfectly jointly able to keep the house clean at all times in the absence of a shared plan. This is because we each have the ability to do our part and both parts are compossible and we can produce the desired outcome without a shared plan. But is this too weak a notion of joint ability? I will argue further down that joint ability goes beyond individual ability plus compossibility when it comes to ascribing collective obligations.

3.1.3   The Weak View: Combined Ability

Have we thrown out the baby with the bathwater? Is joint ability nothing more than the sum of individual abilities? Was this not what we started out denying? Let me further scrutinise the minimalist view sketched earlier.

On that account, joint ability is fundamentally only the sum of two (or more) agents' abilities where *their successful combination* (i.e. the combination which produces the joint outcome or which manifests as the joint action) *is not only possible, but if the agents tried* (to combine them) *they would be disposed to succeed.* That is, on the weak view, you and I are jointly able to keep the house clean if there is a *combination of individual contributory actions* towards keeping the house clean that is not only possible but we are disposed to produce the desired outcome (or action) given that we try.

Now let us stop here a moment. What does it mean that *we try*? What is involved in our trying? Would it involve each of us being aware that this is *us* trying to do something *together*? Because we are not concerned with each of us trying to do something individually, it seems that the answer must be 'yes'. What does 'trying' to combine one's individual actions and abilities entail? If I try to combine my action with yours – with the aim of (us) doing something that we can only do together – I will do so with a view a view to establishing some joint activity or generating a joint outcome. That is, I will have an intention that is directed at that joint activity and joint goal.

(Preliminary definition): *Joint ability* is then understood as

> the sum of two (or more) agents' abilities where *their successful combination* produces a joint action or manifests as a joint outcome and *if the agents tried* (to combine them) *they would be disposed to succeed.*

Let me contrast this with the view on joint ability that was formulated by Felix Pinkert (2014). According to Felix Pinkert's account of (immediate) joint ability:[10]

> Agents *aa* are immediately jointly able to *Φ* if and only if there is exactly one salient possible collective pattern of actions of the

relevant *aa*'s that constitutes *aa* Φ-ing, and which is such that every relevant agent believes of the action which is her part in that pattern that she needs to perform this action if *aa* is to Φ.

(2014: 194)

He adds in a footnote that

each relevant agent believes of her part that she needs to perform it, rather than that she believes that she needs to perform her part in the pattern. . . . [T]he agents do not need to have beliefs about the salient collective pattern of actions as a whole, but only need to have beliefs about those actions that are their individual part of that pattern.

(ibid.)

That is, on Pinkert's view, in order for two agents *a* and *b* to have joint ability to perform action *x* two conditions must be met:

- There must be *exactly one* salient pattern of actions of *a* and *b* that would produce *x* (or result in *x*); and
- Both *a* and *b* have *true beliefs* that they *need to perform* their respective contributory actions x_a and x_b irrespective of that pattern.

What does it mean to say that *a* and *b* believe that they *need* to perform their individual part? Pinkert does not require them to know that these are part of a pattern of actions, or, therefore, to desire the joint action or to aim at producing that action. Let us return once more to the example of the *Housemates* whose house is to be kept clean at all times. Perhaps I have a belief that I need to keep the house clean when I am around and you have a belief that you need to keep it clean when you are around. But in what sense do we each believe that we 'need' to do that? It is not that I know I need to keep the house clean when I am around *because (or if)* I want it to be clean at all times. Pinkert does not require me to aspire to the joint pattern of action or even have it in mind. It is perfectly fine, on his view, if each of the two group members simply – for one reason or another – believe that they need to perform these actions.

So in what sense can I believe that I 'need' to keep the house clean when I am at home? 'Need' in this context could mean 'ought'. But in that case, Pinkert's view would commit him to the following: you and I only have a joint duty to keep the house clean if we have joint ability to keep the house clean, which in turn requires that we each believe that we ought to keep the house clean when we can. In other words, we ought to keep the house clean if each of us believes that we ought to do our part. But this is not very informative, as it merely explicates our joint duty rather than telling us anything about the conditions under which we have it. In other words, it is implausible to think that two agents only have the joint ability to do something together if they are under some (independent) moral (or perhaps prudential or other) imperative to perform the respective contributory actions. This seems to conflate joint ability with joint duties, or else, necessary criteria for the latter with sufficient criteria.

Another way of spelling out Pinkert's conditions is as requiring that in order for a plurality of agents to have joint ability, each member must have reasons to perform their part regardless of whether these reasons reference the joint action or outcome. If you and I believe that we each need to keep the house clean we have some kind of – more or less compelling – reason to do it. But this is too demanding, because it suggests that two or more agents can only have joint ability if they have some reason to do their part in performing the joint action. Surely, we are jointly able to do things (at a point in time) even if we have no reason to do them (at that point in time).

Let me turn to another crucial component of Pinkert's account. In order for there to be immediate joint ability – that is a plurality of agents' ability to jointly perform an action or produce an outcome through their actions without prior coordination or communication – there has to be *exactly one salient possible collective pattern of actions*, according to Pinkert. In order for there to be mediate joint ability, it must be possible for the agents to establish a salient pattern of actions.

But this, also, is too restrictive. All we really have to do in order to produce joint outcomes is to perform the correct combination of contributory actions – that is, one successful combination. This successful combination might be the only one that is possible or it might be one of many. It may be obvious or not. And in order to be *able* to perform the successful combination, we need not have true beliefs concerning the likely success of a *particular* combination ex ante. In fact, we may simply be trying out different combinations, hoping that one will work.

On Pinkert's account, the collective pattern needs to be salient because without prior coordination it must be the option that agents would choose because it is 'obvious', because it sticks out. Or, in other words, if *x* is something that agents wanted to produce then the salient collective pattern of actions producing *x* (out of several that would produce *x*) is the one, which is obvious to reasonable agents.

Accordingly, what is not obvious is not obligatory. But again, this is too strong, *unless* the participants have only *exactly one shot* at getting this right. If I have only one opportunity to pick the right contributory action and so do you then we may indeed be quite likely to get it wrong unless it is really obvious. It is only in those scenarios that Pinkert's proposal holds, I believe.

Further, note that if both agents hold true beliefs concerning their individual contributory actions (which are 'needed') then it is not necessary to also require exactly one collective pattern to be salient. In fact, it does not matter whether some possible collective pattern is salient to them as long as they have true beliefs in what is required ('needed') of them. In short, the condition that there should be exactly one successful salient combination should be dropped. Even where there is no salient option, agents may be able to succeed in acting jointly.[11]

Is it necessary for the two (or more) agents to *know* that they have that joint ability in order to have it? Zimmerman argues that (individual) agents need not know about their (individual) ability in order to have that ability in the sense required for a moral obligation (1996):

> Many, indeed most, of the things that I can (in the present sense) do are things I know nothing about. Those worlds that are presently accessible to me are such that, at best, I only know a tiny fraction of their features.
>
> (p. 50)

I cannot see why this should be different for joint ability.[12]

However, certain factors make it harder to actually perform joint actions even where joint ability as such exists. Increasing the number of possible contributory actions and combinations thereof while keeping the number of successful combinations constant will make it harder to pick the successful combination if that combination is not salient. I think what this suggests is that joint ability might be scalar, depending on how hard it is for a plurality of agents to successfully combine their individual contributory actions to produce a joint action or outcome. In other words, we must not think of joint ability as a binary property. And if joint ability comes in degrees there would be a context-dependent threshold below which a plurality of agents have insufficient joint ability to hold collective obligations. The level of joint ability implied by joint obligations will, among other factors, depend on the content of that obligation.

One might further object by saying that in the cases where there is no salient strategy or no communication to establish such a group strategy it is merely *possible* for us to jointly do something, but we are not – strictly speaking – *jointly able* to do so. For instance, in the example used earlier it might be merely *possible* for the housemates to keep the house clean at all times but not robustly possible in the way required for moral obligations. We may then grant that for two agents to have joint ability to do *x* they must be able to *intentionally combine* their contributory actions.

3.2 When Do Agents Have Joint Ability?

To recapitulate, when we look at joint ability, there are two fundamental issues to distinguish: the first is the ability of each individual to do their part or to play their role in the collective action. The second is the sum of these individual agents' abilities where *their successful combination* (i.e.

the combination which produces the joint action or manifests as the joint outcome) *is not only possible but, if they tried* (to combine them), *they would be disposed to succeed.*

Further, as I said earlier, to the extent that joint ability is at least in part about individual ability the same issues arise for collective action as for individual action. So there is no need to give the issue of individual ability specific attention here. Others have done so exhaustively (Zimmerman 1996; Vranas 2007; Maier 2014).

But the current discussion is about the question of two or more agents' ability to do something *together* or jointly. What makes it the case that two people are able to perform an action together or produce an outcome together? That is, what is the most general account of what is required for joint ability? In the following I will develop the account of joint ability sketched in the previous section in more detail.

In order to be able to jointly do x, a plurality of agents a and b must be able to perform the right combination of contributory acts to x that will produce (or result in) x. The joint action or outcome x must be doable for a and b if they try. This means that a and b must each be able to do at least one instantiation of the participatory or contributory actions x_a and x_b and they must be able to combine those such that x_a and x_b result in or produce x.

Let us return to the aforementioned two-person rescue case (and add some more detail to it):

> *[Hikers]* You and a friend are hiking in a remote part of the country and you encounter a man trapped under a large, fallen tree in the middle of nowhere, who cannot free himself and is stuck. There is no way to get external assistance – your mobile phones have no reception, the closest public phone is a 2-day walk away, your satellite phone is out of battery and you forgot your emergency radio beacon. In short – you are on your own. If you leave him there he would most likely die, because there are no other people in the area to help (or at least this is very unlikely – the area is so remote). But there is no real problem, because it is easy for you two to help the trapped man. You and your friend can just lift the tree under which he is trapped off him. Doing so is the only option available to help the trapped man.

Each of the two people assisting the trapped hiker must have the ability to do some lifting, to recognise how the tree must be lifted in order to actually free the trapped man and so forth. For instance, there could be three different ways of lifting the tree together:

a.   has the following options at her disposal: x_{a1}, x_{a2}, x_{a3} *(and so on)*
b.   has the following options at her disposal: x_{b1}, x_{b2}, x_{b3} *(and so on)*

Some combinations of x_a and x_b will produce x, some will not.
Several different cases are possible:

1.   The overdetermined case: any combination of x_a and x_b will produce
     x. Here a and b must each be able to do at least one instantiation of
     x_a and x_b.
     For instance, when we are collecting money towards a farewell pres-
     ent then, any action involving putting money into the collection box
     in the staff kitchen (within a certain time-frame) will make it the case
     that jointly the people who contributed collect the respective amount.
2.   There is exactly one such combination x_a and x_b. For instance, x_{a1}
     and x_{b3} could be the only successful combination.
3.   Other cases: there are several successful combinations of x_a and x_b.

Sometimes, the members of the group may have exactly one attempt at
getting it right, that is, they need to get it right the first time. If it is difficult for a and b to figure out the right combination (or else if they only
have one attempt), then they may well be excused if they fail to do x
(should there have been a duty to do so).

Often, a and b's joint ability will depend on a's ability to match her
choice to b's. Take the example of ballroom dancing: one dancer has the
leading part and the other follows. A couple's ability to dance together then
would depend on one of them being able to lead in the right way (such that
the other one is capable of following) and the other being able to follow.

The more generic the cooperative activity, the more likely are the
participants going to be able to successfully jointly perform it without
organisation or set structures. And vice versa, the more singular, intricate,
specialised or sophisticated the cooperative activity, the greater are our
chances of failing at them. For instance, lifting a table is a generic activity
that is easy to jointly perform, as long as at least one participant picks
a contributory action that is part of a potentially successful pairing of
contributory actions and the other one is able to pick the matching contributory action to make the joint action happen. One of the two people
attempting to lift the table may just position herself at one end of the
table and push her hands underneath the table top, waiting for the other
to position herself in the correct way at the opposite end so as to make
it possible to actually lift the table. This would involve the other not
positioning herself right next to the first, because that would not result in
lifting the table. Often in these situations at least one of the participant
will announce what they think is the best strategy: "I will take hold of
this end of the table; how about you take hold of the other?" This is a
way of singling out a specific combination and encouraging the other to
perform their part. If done publicly (or openly), this makes a particular
combination of contributory actions salient (and therewith increases the
likelihood of the successful performance of the joint activity).

It is important to note that – depending on the kind of action in place and on whether or not the plurality can have several shots at getting it right – the agents may well make a particular combination salient, or obvious, by trial and error.

Joint ability, then, is highly context-dependent. We could, for instance, assume that there are 100 different potential contributory actions x_a and x_b for each hiker for lifting the tree off the trapped person and only one such combination will lead to success. Whether or not the two hikers are jointly able to lift the tree will depend on whether or not it is possible for them to find the right combination of contributory actions within reasonable times limits.

Hence, there are four aspects that determine the degree of a plurality of agents' joint ability:

1. the number of possible combinations of individual contributory actions in relation to the number of successful combinations
2. the salience of the successful combinations: how obvious is it which combination(s) work(s)?
3. how easy is it for the group members to agree on a particular combination of contributory actions (assuming that is more than one and there is no single salient one)
4. how many attempts to they have; are there time constraints?

This leaves us with the following:

Definition of joint ability

> Two agents a and b have joint ability to do x if a has individual ability to do x_a and b has individual ability to do x_b where x_a and x_b produce x, both actions are compossible, and a and b are in principle capable of intentionally combining them.

Or, put differently:

> Two agents a and b have joint ability to do x if there is a least one combination of contributory actions x_a and x_b such that
>
> - these are genuine options a and b have, and, if both are performed in the right way, they produce x
> - both contributory actions are compossible
> - a and b are capable of performing these actions with a view to combining them.[13]
>
> X_a and x_b can be act-types or act-tokens.

As I said earlier, it makes sense to think of pluralities of agents who have joint ability as a having such ability to different degrees. It can be more or less difficult to establish joint action for a plurality of agents and this means that their endeavour can be more or less likely to fail. Whether or not a combination is salient or whether individual agents hold true beliefs in that regard will make it more or less likely that they produce x or else harder to excuse their failure to produce x if there was an obligation to so. If they fail in producing x, this may be for a lack of the appropriate degree of joint ability.

For the cases described earlier, it was assumed that the group's joint ability was high. Hence, its members acquired joint obligations to save the lives of the persons in danger. At the other end of the spectrum, groups with no joint ability cannot hold joint moral duties. Then there would be groups that have some level of joint ability but not the maximum level. A plurality's joint ability can be diminished by a number of factors, including limitations to the group members' individual abilities to perform the contributory action. If the obstacles are too great, then the group has no joint ability and its members cannot jointly hold duties.

It also makes sense to think of a group's capacity to perform a joint action – its joint ability – as temporal. A group can have joint ability at one moment in time and lose that ability in the next moment, for instance, if there are no longer enough group members to perform the task.

Further, it is possible for an agent to increase a group's joint ability or to make it the case that they have joint ability at all. Making one combination of actions salient, taking leadership, ascribing contributory actions to others, researching successful combinations and so forth – all these actions will increase joint ability. Further, where there is no joint ability at all it can be produced: I can teach you how to dance and therewith create our joint ability to dance. Or else I can show you how to clean the house and thus enable us to jointly keep it clean. Because joint ability is a necessary condition for joint obligation these 'enabling' actions can make it the case that a plurality of agents acquires joint obligations where previously they did not have them. Again, *I can sometimes unilaterally make it the case that a plurality of agents has joint ability where they previously did not have it. I can therefore unilaterally make it the case that a plurality of agents is a candidate for joint obligations when previously they were not.*

In contrast, individual agents can sometimes unilaterally undermine joint ability. If in the *hikers* scenario, one of the potential helpers instead of lifting the tree walks away, she therewith undermines their joint ability to act. It would seem that she also undermines any collective obligation she and the other passer-by may have, or does she? At this point, Michael Zimmerman's thoughts on remote obligations may be useful. Zimmerman thinks that I can now be able to do something later (1996). For instance, I may now be able to make a salad later. Hence, I may have an obligation now to make a salad later. This is a *remote* obligation, whereas an obligation to do something at the time the obligation arises is an *immediate* obligation. Here is what Zimmerman says: if someone (at a particular point in time under particular circumstances) ought to do something at a later point in time, then it is the case that at this (first) point in time he or she is able to do that thing at a later point in time – "if S ought, at *T* in *W*, to do *A* at *T'*, then S can, at *T* in *W*, do *A* at *T'*" (1996: 97). According to Zimmerman, this solves the problem of self-imposed impossibility and necessity (1996: 97). I cannot simply nullify an obligation by preventing myself from fulfilling it. Likewise, we may say, an agent cannot escape a joint obligation with another by way of undermining their joint ability to act.

3.3 Objections and Challenges

Let me now turn to the challenges of the (minimal) approach to joint ability developed earlier. Zofia Stemplowska (2016) has argued that outside group agents collective action can only be *possible* but not feasible, and that it is feasibility and not possibility that reflects the sense of 'can' or ability in 'ought implies can'.

She grants that some collective action to φ is possible even if the individuals don't even know how to φ as long as they know how to do their part $φ_n$. They need not even know that they are part of a collective action. However, when there is no intentional (collective) agent, collective action φ towards S is never *feasible*.

If Stemplowska were correct then my proposed account of joint ability would indeed be too weak. We would only have established what is possible for pluralities of agents but not what they 'can' do in the sense required by 'ought implies can'. But what exactly does Stemplowska mean when she writes that such actions are not feasible? She writes that "[t]he feasibility of actions depends on there being an intentional agent, single, or collective, who can perform the action in question" (p. 19). Stemplowska at various points seems to suggest that only fully fledged collective agents or group agents can perform (collective) actions proper, but this view, as I have previously argued, is misguided.

Her main point is nonetheless of interest: if it is a mere possibility that a plurality of agents produce an outcome *x* (or *φ*s) *then* the 'can'-condition in 'ought implies can' is not met. That is, in her view, more is needed for a group to have the ability to do *x* in the required sense. One of these additional conditions is knowledge of the outcome *x* or knowledge of the fact that their x_n is needed.

However, this is too restrictive. Surely, there are many things that we can do together where it is not the case that each participant knows how the final action *x* is done or achieved. This is especially true of organised group agents. Stemplowska grants that I need only know that my x_n is needed. But then again, in many collective action cases, a particular individual agent's contribution may actually *not* be needed. It may be that several agents have a collective obligation but I do not need to do anything. It may be that my group has the ability to do x without me having to do part of x. I will discuss this and the relevant distinction between strict and wide joint necessity in detail in Section 5.1 on membership obligations. In short, there may be cases where it is not entirely clear how an action x is achieved and not everybody's contribution is necessary.

Holly Lawford-Smith in "What 'we'?" shows herself to be sceptical of the idea of joint obligations of unstructured groups (2015) for – roughly – similar reasons. She, too, doubts that unstructured groups, what she calls 'non-collectives' can reliably perform actions in the sense required by 'ought implies can'.

She gives the example of a meat farm going out of business because of a chain of unplanned events leading to costumers ordering less than they usually would: "some fall sick, some have to travel, some are gifted produce from alternative sources" (p. 234).

She argues that even though the farm's going out of business is a good thing from an environmental point of view, there could not have been an obligation on those who brought about its demise to do just that. This is because the events that led to it are just too much a matter of luck. "The action [of reducing the orders to the extent that the farm goes out of business] 'can' eventuate, but only flukily" (p. 235), Lawford-Smith writes.

This argument is meant to show that the customers could not have been obligated to bring about the farm's going out of business, because the different events, which in sum caused this outcome, could easily have been different. However, that the customers did not intentionally make the farm go out of business in this scenario is no argument against *their ability* to do so in principle.

To illustrate that, let us turn to the following scenario: suppose that the staff kitchen at work is rarely ever clean. However, one day, just before the Christmas break, several staff members clear away their rubbish and each tidies up a little bit. As a result the kitchen is finally clean. But, as it happens, each action that contributed to the kitchen being clean could have happened differently on that day. Say that Prof X had a bit of time to waste before her husband was coming to pick her up. So she wiped the kitchen bench and threw away all the stuff that was sitting on the kitchen bench. Let us say that Dr Y was hungry and walked into the kitchen in search for food (somebody else's, in fact. Dr Y never buys anything – she steals other people's food!). She grabbed something from the fridge, found that it was past the use-by date and then chucked it into the bin. She grabbed the second item from the fridge – same thing. And so on. As a result, the fridge was cleaned out. Finally, Mr Z, the administrator came into the kitchen to warm up his lunch in the microwave. The lid of the food container came off and soiled the microwave so badly that he felt compelled to clean it even though it was not clean before he used it. As a result the microwave was clean, too.

On Lawford-Smith's account, the staff members are not able to keep the kitchen clean and they could not have been obligated to keep it clean, because their actions could have all been different. Had Prof X's husband not been late, had Dr Y not been hungry and had Mr Z's food not exploded, the kitchen would still be dirty. But, obviously, none of this shows that they were not able to keep the kitchen clean or that they could not be under an obligation to keep it clean. The fact that they did not perform a joint action to keep the kitchen clean nor intentionally participated in a collective endeavour to do so does absolutely not show anything about their ability to do so. They are perfectly able to keep it clean despite the fact that most staff kitchens are not clean. One might insist that there is a difference between contingent joint success as in this scenario and reliable ability to jointly succeed. But it is not clear to me that this difference depends on the existence of an organised structure or shared plan of sorts.

But Lawford-Smith has another argument against obligations of unstructured groups. Such collective obligations – as I call them – only work, according to Lawford-Smith, "where everyone can be presumed to share an end, and where what each person needs to do is roughly the same (or where the differentiated roles are a matter of common awareness"[14] (p. 237).

These two conditions are not met where humanity as a whole is concerned, she argues, though for subsets thereof, made up of mutually responsive agents, they might be met. She acknowledges that she could concede that in such cases pluralities of agents can hold joint obligations, but opts against it for two reasons. First, she thinks that groups of mutually responsive agents should count as group agents [my terminology]. I have argued throughout that it is important to distinguish group action proper from collective action carried out by agents in unstructured groups. The work colleagues mentioned earlier are perfectly able to keep the kitchen clean together. If they do so they are not forming a group agent, even if they do so by way of being responsive to the others. Or put differently, I think it would not be helpful to declare such collectives 'group agents'. I showed in Section 3.1 that the most common accounts of joint agency assume that groups that are not agents in their own right can perform collective actions. Further, in order to discharge an obligation, agents may not be required to perform an action in the strict sense. Second, Lawford-Smith argues on pragmatic grounds that her position will yield better results – it is more likely to make the world a better place (p. 238). However, whether or not the ascription of collective obligations to large pluralities or unstructured groups really does render these obligations ineffectual is very much an open question. I will briefly return to this issue in Chapter 7.

3.4 Types of Pluralities

Little has been said so far about what kinds of groups are candidates for joint ability. There are many kinds of groups or pluralities of agents with the capacity to produce outcomes or perform actions upon which collective obligations might fall. In the literature on social ontology, different types of groups have been discussed as potential candidates for obligations: *group agents* in the narrow sense (List and Pettit 2011), *goal-oriented collectives* (Erskine 2014), *putative* groups (May 1992; Isaacs 2011), and *mobs* (May 1987, 1989) to name a few. Can we make general claims about the ontological status of a group and how it relates to the group's suitability as a candidate for collective obligations?

Generally speaking, the above-mentioned types of groups have been distinguished according to the degree with which they are 'structured' in the sense of having an organisational structure or a 'constitution' (List and Pettit 2011) and respective decision-making mechanisms. My focus, however, has been on groups which lack such structures and mechanisms at least in the formal sense. It should be noted, however, that groups should be considered as structured or unstructured with regard to specific purposes. In other words, just because people are part of or members of a group agent does not mean that they are a 'structured' collective in the right sense. Assume, for instance, that the two hikers in our example own an accounting firm together – they are members of a structured group. In fact, they constitute the group in its entirety because they are the only two associates. When the two accountants come across the person trapped by the fallen tree, however, their firm's organisational and decision-making structure (or constitution) is irrelevant as far as the emergency is concerned. Or, in other words, their structure is not of the right kind given the required action (lifting the tree). It is in this sense that they are an unstructured group with regard to the circumstances. Here is another example: my university department is an organised or structured group for the purpose of teaching students, administration and research. But it is not organised for the purpose of getting a farewell present for a colleague, for example. If the members of my department want to do something like that, they need to organise it themselves. With regard to that specific task, they are closer to an unstructured group.

In other words, members of a structured group can be unstructured in a particular respect. That is, they can be unstructured with a view to a particular goal or task that lies outside of the task they have been organised for. Whether or not they are able to organise themselves with ease to perform such tasks will depend on the group's social, normative and epistemic cohesion. A group's level of collective self-awareness and capacity for joint attention will be a major factor for their degree of joint ability (Schmid 2016; Seemann 2016). Unsurprisingly, a sense of group identity will increase the likelihood of collective action (McGarty 2009; Thomas 2009b; Faulmueller et al. 2010; Slovic 2010; Thomas 2010, 2013; Bicchieri 2017). On my account, this is normatively relevant: other things being equal, a sense of group identity[15] will strengthen agents' moral reasons to we-frame collective action problems and to pursue collectively available options (more on that in Chapter 4).

As we have seen, there are different candidates for joint ability – what it means for an unstructured collective that they 'can' do something in the sense required by the capacity principle. Moving from the strongest to the weakest conception of joint ability, these are

- ability to perform a joint action (in the strong sense, with plural intentions);
- ability to engage in joint intentional activity;
- ability to produce an outcome that is the successful combination of individual actions.

I have defended a weak conception of joint ability as the basis for joint obligations. But keep in mind that agents need to be able to *deliberately combine* their actions. What exactly this means will be spelled out in the next chapter. Further, we need to keep in mind that joint ability is scalar and that below a certain 'threshold' a plurality's joint ability to do something is insufficient for grounding a collective obligation, that is, where the likelihood that the agents jointly produce x is very low. The ease with which joint action can be established or a joint action can be performed by a number of individuals in a random group may differ greatly depending on their circumstances. This may sound vague to some. This vagueness, however, is no problem unique to the concept of joint ability. Rather, it concerns all accounts of *ability to act* and *feasibility* that operate with probabilities. If we generally accept this aspect of such accounts, then there is no reason not to also accept it here.

We need to keep in mind that this has been a discussion of joint ability only. Joint ability is not a sufficient but merely a necessary condition for joint duties. Because I have control over my own actions, but not over other people's actions, the obstacles to acting jointly seem to generally be greater than the obstacles to acting individually. However, this impression is only partly correct: we are infinitely more capable of performing actions and producing outcomes jointly with others than we would be if left to our own devices and abilities.

Notes

1. The 'ought' in question is a moral 'ought'. Different scholars have understood the implicature differently. Prominently, Walter Sinnott-Armstrong argued that 'ought' merely conversationally implies 'can': "Roughly, saying that p conversationally implies q when saying p for a certain purpose cannot be explained except by supposing that the speaker thinks that q and thinks that the hearer can figure out that the speaker thinks that q, etc." (p. 256). According to Sinnott-Armstrong, then, the principle expresses an aspect of interpersonal communication. However, Alex King has much more recently (and convincingly, in my view) shown that this and all other pragmatic views of 'ought' *implies* 'can' fail because they are too weak to deliver the contrapositive 'cannot' therefore 'not ought'. (Sinnott-Armstrong, W.

(1984). 'Ought' Conversationally Implies 'Can'. *Philosophical Review*, 93(2), 249–261; King, A. (2017). 'Ought Implies Can': Not So Pragmatic After All. *Philosophy and Phenomenological Research*, 95(3), 637–661.) Michael Zimmerman's account, in fact, implies that "'ought' implies 'can'" is true and analytic. See Zimmerman, M. J. (1996). *The Concept of Moral Obligation*. Cambridge: Cambridge University Press, p. 79.

2. Michael Fara argues against the conditional analysis of abilities. I cannot rehearse his argument here but will merely point to his article on this issue: Fara, M. (2008). Masked Abilities and Compatibilism. *Mind*, 117(468), 843–865.

3. Christian List and Philip Pettit's *Group Agency* focuses mainly on corporate agency, while I take Pettit and Schweikard (2006), Raimo Tuomela's *Social Ontology* and Michael Bratman's *Shared Agency* to give an account of joint agency outside structured group agents. Kirk Ludwig argues in *From Individual to Plural Agency: Collective Action* that his account of collective agency covers both phenomena and that we do not need separate accounts for them. I believe that my argument is perfectly compatible with his proposal. (Pettit, P. and D. Schweikard (2006). Joint Actions and Group Agents. *Philosophy of the Social Sciences*, 36(1), 18–39; List, C. and P. Pettit (2011). *Group Agency: The Possibility, Design, and Status of Corporate Agents*. Oxford; New York: Oxford University Press; Tuomela, R. (2013). *Social Ontology: Collective Intentionality and Group Agents*. New York: Oxford University Press; Bratman, M. E. (2014). *Shared Agency: A Planning Theory of Acting Together*. New York: Oxford University Press; Ludwig, K. (2016). *From Individual to Plural Agency: Collective Action I*. Oxford: Oxford University Press.)

4. The most obvious objection to such a view, that entities such as groups cannot have the intentional states required for being an agent, is usually countered with a functionalist understanding of intentions: on such functionalist accounts of intentionality, a group – or a system with a certain structure – can form 'representational and goal-seeking states' – beliefs, desires, judgements or plans. These can function in the same way as intentions of individual agents do. List and Pettit write: "We make no assumptions about the precise physical nature of intentional states. They may be of a wide variety of kinds. . . . We only require that they be configurations of the agent . . . that play the appropriate functional role" (2011: 21). Many of those who defend the idea of group (moral) agency adopt a functionalist view of intention. (Pettit, P. and D. Schweikard (2006). Joint Actions and Group Agents. *Philosophy of the Social Sciences*, 36(1), 18–39; List, C. and P. Pettit (2011). *Group Agency: The Possibility, Design, and Status of Corporate Agents*. Oxford; New York: Oxford University Press; Bratman, M. E. (2014). *Shared Agency: A Planning Theory of Acting Together*. New York: Oxford University Press, but not all French, P. A. (1984). *Collective and Corporate Responsibility*. New York: Columbia University Press; Ludwig, K. (2016). *From Individual to Plural Agency: Collective Action I*. Oxford: Oxford University Press.)

5. I am following Michael Bratman (2014) in that an individual agent can intend *that* she and another agent act together. In contrast to 'intending *to*', this does not require that it be within the individual's control to perform the joint action.

6. See www.independent.co.uk/news/world/australasia/commuters-band-together-to-push-train-off-man-who-trapped-leg-in-gap-between-carriage-and-platform-9650779.html (accessed on 16 June 2020).
   See also www.youtube.com/watch?v=YORxs9E2Ex0. A similar collective rescue took place in Tokyo earlier the same year: www.independent.co.uk/news/world/asia/mind-the-gap-commuters-in-japan-push-30000kg-train-carriage-off-trapped-woman-8727952.html (both accessed on 15 February

2017). Passers-by rescue a motorcyclist from underneath a burning car on 13 Sep 2011: www.youtube.com/watch?v=aIGTyANMFb4 (accessed on 16 February 2017).

7. For instance, Bratman's two painters, who together paint a house (2014), or Lawford-Smith's four removalists, who together life a piano (2012).

8. For an even weaker and more general account, see Kirk Ludwig (2016).

9. Moreover, interlocking plural intentions do not require common knowledge but merely so-called pooled knowledge, which is an asymmetric type of group knowledge where a coordinator ensures that members' beliefs are interlocking even if there is no common knowledge. Roy, O. and A. Schwenkenbecher (2019). Shared Intentions, Loose Groups, and Pooled Knowledge. *Synthese*, online first. See also Blomberg, O. (2016). Common Knowledge and Reductionism about Shared Agency. *Australasian Journal of Philosophy*, 94(2), 315–326.

10. I should note – again – that Pinkert has a second category – mediate joint ability – where in the absence of a salient collective pattern the participants in the potential collective action must first be able to make such a pattern salient. But we need not discuss that second category separately here. My critique would apply equally to both.

11. Pinkert's own notion of mediate joint ability, which is the agents' ability to jointly find a salient pattern or make one salient for that matter, may prove too strong, too. This is because it may not require all agents in a plurality to jointly make a pattern salient; it may only require one of them to make it salient by public announcement or the like. In the real world, this is often how we solve collective action problems: one person takes the lead and proposes a course of action and others adopt whatever they deem to be corresponding individual strategies.

12. Gunnar Björnsson (2014) defends a similar view.

13. This last requirement goes beyond compossibility – it is the requirement that both could in principle willingly combine their actions, that is, perform them with a view to contributing to the joint outcome or action.

14. It is in this context that her following comments should be understood: "the adoption of different moral norms by groups of persons . . . will affect the extent to which we judge that a non-collective can *reliably perform an action*" (2015: 236, my emphasis). That is, if everyone thinks that we should always stand up for people threatened on the subway, then it will make it the case that a non-collective will more reliably perform such an action. I actually agree this is an important point, but I think it fits differently into the bigger picture: On my account, such shared moral background assumptions will not increase the agents' joint ability, that is the ability to jointly produce the outcome if they try, but it will increase the likelihood that they try and that they share an obligation.

15. Other than identity, motivations for collective action include efficacy, emotion and morality. See van Zomeren, M. (2013). Four Core Social-Psychological Motivations to Undertake Collective Action. *Social and Personality Psychology Compass*, 7(6), 378–388.

4 Knowing When We Have Collective Moral Obligations

The reader of the previous discussion may have started to feel uneasy. Surely, this very minimal concept of joint ability is not strong enough to ground joint moral obligations, right? Of course, joint ability is merely a necessary criterion for joint obligations. Would the members of a group, the agents who could potentially act together, not have to have some minimal knowledge of the fact that there are other people they could act together with, and, more fundamentally even, that the problem calls for a collective solution?

In addressing these questions, I will return to the example of the two hikers and the trapped man discussed before. We agreed that the hikers have an obligation to save the trapped man by jointly lifting the tree off him. Under what circumstances do they have a moral obligation to do that? Or, in other words, what has to be the case for two (or more) agents to have an obligation together? I will answer this question by way of discussing *the process of moral reasoning* involved. I will argue that we have collective obligations precisely when we have reason to 'we-frame' a collective action problem. Further, I will show that the collective obligations view is not tied to any particular substantive, first-order ethical theory but, however, that it is most plausibly coupled with a prospective view of moral obligations.

4.1 Considering Options: 'We-Framing' Scenarios

Before I continue, let us pause for a moment and consider the following: in establishing what we ought to do were we facing a scenario like *Hikers*, which steps do we need to take in our moral deliberation? If we are reasonable and morally conscientious observers, we will instantly recognise this scenario as one requiring us to act. In our deliberation, we need to establish first what the available options are and second which one of them is best. (For now, I am leaving open the substantive question of what the morally best option is.)

According to Zimmerman (2014), a morally relevant option – that is, one that must be considered by the deliberating agent – is something that is available to the agent, something that she has the capacity and opportunity to do. Being an individualist about moral obligations, Zimmerman phrased this in terms of individual agency, capacity and opportunity. But note that in *Hikers* the two potential helpers have options for acting individually and options for acting together.

In establishing what their options are, the two hikers *could* confine themselves to only considering what they can do *individually*: each of them could try to lift the tree on their own (probably in vain), each of them could walk to the end of the trail and try to call help from there (which is going to take a long time with potentially severe consequences for the trapped man).

Or each can try to get the other person to help them lifting the tree. But let us pause here: why is this even an option worth thinking about? Why is this something that the individual would or should consider?

It is not too far-fetched to presume that most (or even all) of us would consider this option in the scenario described. But why would we do that? If your answer is "because together we can help the trapped man" or "because together we can lift the tree" then you have performed the kind of deliberative manoeuvre that some game theorists and philosophers of action call 'agency transformation' (Hakli et al. 2010; Butler 2012) or 'reasoning transformation' (Bacharach 2006).

Rather than merely considering options that are available to each of us *individually* – we regularly considers options that are only *collectively* available. That is, in considering what needs to be done in order for us to lift the tree together you are considering an option that is ultimately not available to you – the respective action's success lies outside your control. According to the above-mentioned authors, this is nothing unusual at all. We regularly do this and in doing so switch between seeing ourselves as individual agents who have certain options available to them on the one hand, and regarding ourselves as part of potential teams or groups of people with collectively available options on the other hand.

It is important to note that this 'switch' constitutes a transformation in *agency* and is not the same as *payoff* or *preference transformation*. The latter two ideas capture changes in an agent's decisions based on changes in their individual payoffs or their individual preferences.[1] For instance, agents might favour the collectively available option the payoff attached to that option is greater than the payoff attached to the individual option. Undoubtedly, these kinds of transformation regularly take place, but they are not equivalent to the transformation of agency which the above-mentioned authors are trying to capture. Similarly, preference transformation, too, falls short of explaining why we sometimes choose to go for the exclusively collectively achievable outcome over other (individually preferable) outcomes (Bacharach 2006; Butler 2012). We might be tempted to explain (away) someone's consideration of collective options in a joint-necessity case as tied to the greater payoff attached to the collectively possible outcome or a change in their preferences, but according to the above-mentioned authors an altogether different type of transformation could be taking place.

Agency transformation is best understood as shifting from considering *my* options to considering *our* options, thus shifting from the individual to the collective as the unit of agency in our reasoning process. Tuomela, Hakli and Miller call this *we-mode reasoning*, as opposed to *I-mode reasoning* (Hakli et al. 2010; Tuomela 2013). Such a transformation in reasoning occurs where an agent "abandons the usual way of reasoning to a best act, best-reply reasoning" (Bacharach 2006: 60). Instead of merely picking one's individually best option while holding all other aspects of the situation fixed, the agent reasons from the outcomes that are available to the group to the strategy that she must choose. When that happens the agent is engaged in so-called 'we-reasoning', or sometimes referred to as 'we-mode-reasoning' (Hakli et al. 2010).

In the following, let me explain this idea in more detail. But before I do so, let me make an important point concerning the terminology involved. There are many discussions of the concept of 'we-reasoning' and related ideas, but some of these do not clearly delineate what really are distinct ideas. The most common concepts in this debate are: *we-framing*, *we-reasoning* and *team-reasoning*. Here is how I understand each of these and how I will use them in the following.

We-framing I call the cognitive act of perceiving a joint-necessity scenario as a problem for (or of) the (or a) group. It is something an individual does. I 'we-frame' a problematic situation if I consider it to be a problem *for us*. It need not be a conscious decision for an agent to we-frame some scenario; it may be an unconscious, non-deliberate framing. I assume that propensities to we-frame differ between individuals and also depend on the background conditions. That is, you may – in general – be more likely to we-frame joint-necessity scenarios than I am, and we each may be more likely to we-frame joint necessity scenarios under some circumstances rather than other circumstances. Agents should be able to switch between frames or perhaps even to simultaneously I-frame and we-frame the same scenario, though nothing in my argument depends on this assumption.

We-reasoning is a *type of deliberation* whereby an individual agent independently establishes the course of action *she should take* with a view to an outcome that is only collectively available. We-reasoning explains why agents choose 'hi' in the Hilo game or else when they choose to cooperate in a prisoners' dilemma (Hakli et al. 2010; Butler et al. 2011; Butler 2012). I will explore the idea of we-reasoning in more detail in Section 4.4.

Finally, *team-reasoning* is a type of deliberation that agents do *together*. It is a way of jointly establishing team (or collective) preferences as well as collective and individual strategies for satisfying those preferences. That is, it involves identifying what individual members of the team need to do in order to satisfy the team's preferences or achieve the team's goal. Note that my use of the term 'team-reasoning' differs from that of other authors, for some of whom it covers both individual-based and group-based reasoning (Gold and Sugden 2007a, 2007b; Hakli et al. 2010; Tamminga and Duijf 2017).[2] Team-reasoning seems to require at least a basic commitment of the agents involved to the group and the group goal. Naturally, the epistemic requirements for team-reasoning are much more demanding than those for we-reasoning, because it requires agents to communicate with each other.

In sum, *we-framing* and *we-reasoning* are something that individuals do on their own, while *team-reasoning* is something that agents do together. Complex collective moral action problems will usually require team-reasoning in order to be solved. Simple coordination problems may be successfully solved through independent we-reasoning.

Earlier, I mentioned that I consider we-framing to be the starting point of we-reasoning. I think it is helpful to return to this distinction in order to refine our account of moral deliberation vis-à-vis collective obligations. We-framing is the (epistemic) act of identifying a particular problem (or otherwise a scenario requiring some action or reaction on one's part) as a problem for a group that one is part of. *We-framing a situation is, then, the act of including the collectively available option in one's option set when deliberating.* In other words, in considering the collective option we are in fact we-framing a scenario (or problem). We may do so to the exclusion of the individual perspective, give greater weight to the collective over the individual perspective, or consider both simultaneously.

In moral deliberation we will – in a second step – rank the options available to us, both the options that are individually available and the ones that are only jointly available. So under which circumstances – generally speaking – are we required[3] to include jointly available options among our options for moral deliberation?

My main concern in this section is with *we-framing* and when we should we-frame a joint-necessity case. I believe that this will be the first step towards establishing when our obligations are collective in character, rather than individual. Is it something about the features of a particular situation that makes we-framing and we-reasoning appropriate in determining one's obligations? There is no easy answer to this and perhaps no general answer is possible at all. But let me try to give one, even if it is tentative.

A first possible answer is that we should we-frame problematic situations when it is *obvious* that the best outcome we could potentially achieve can only be brought about collectively. In the previous chapter, I suggested that in order for a group to have joint ability there need not be a salient or 'obvious' collective solution. I think that this analysis was accurate and that, contrary to Pinkert's view, the correct place for the idea of salience or obviousness is here: it is relevant to the process of *moral deliberation*, not to the question of joint ability.

So, when is it the case that a solution is salient or obvious in the sense required? One possibility is that there is a clear Pareto-optimal outcome. Fully rational agents would be able to recognise a Pareto-optimal outcome.

Yet I believe that we will not be able to give a general, abstract account of what it means for an option to be salient, because such salience is a matter of circumstances and individual conditioning. This may be a very dissatisfying answer for the reader, as it seems to introduce an aspect of relativism into our notion of collective obligations. But what is 'obvious' or 'salient' is neither inter-culturally nor inter-personally stable. The salience of a collective option would depend on multiple contextual and background factors. For instance, it would depend on the extent to which relevant facts about the collective option(s) are common or public knowledge[4] and on whether actions of the required type form part of our regular behavioural repertoire. Take the example of moving a table: lifting and moving large items such as furniture together with others is a fairly standard joint action for most people. Being a standard joint action will make an option a salient candidate in our option set. In contrast, jointly assisting an injured person or the victim of a car accident is not so much part of most people's regular collective action repertoire. Therefore, for an agent not to consider this option but to only consider her individually available options may not constitute a failure of deliberation.

But a requirement to we-frame joint-necessity scenarios goes beyond having adequate responses in standard joint action scenarios. We can (and arguably sometimes ought to) make collective options salient through our own actions, for instance by generating group-based beliefs and expectations when we inform others how *we* rank available options and which one *we* are expecting them to choose. In other words, taking the lead, organising a plurality of agents to jointly do something, or instructing people on how to cooperate is something that invites others to also we-frame a shared experience and it can make cooperative options salient. Depending on an agent's knowledge and experience, a specific collective option may well be salient to one person even when it is not (yet) obvious to the other agents in the group. Here is an example: on a camping trip with a group of friends many years ago we pitched our tents in the dark after arriving late at our campsite. The next morning, we realised that we had set up camp in a horse paddock and found ourselves in the midst of ten or so horses that, though not aggressive, were still large, free-roaming animals that cared very little for our delicate camping gear and had started inspecting our tents with their teeth. Unnerved at the ill-behaved visitors, my friends were ready to break up the camp in a hurry and flee the scene. I managed to convince everyone that jointly driving the horses into the adjacent paddock for the time being was not only a preferable option but also one that was jointly available to us (while it was not available to me, individually).

In other words, sometimes it may only require one agent – with the right kind of knowledge – to we-frame a scenario and to communicate to others what they perceive to be the best option. Naturally, the credibility of that person will play a role in whether or not the others choose to include that option in their deliberation. One of the many things that can go wrong in doing things together is that people disagree on what to do about a given situation. Depending on the circumstances, people may be excused for failing to establish the joint endeavour (or for giving the collective option due consideration) or be found guilty of committing a wrong where they should have listened to the person taking the lead.

To sum up, no clear-cut criterion can be given for the circumstances under which a collective option should be included in the set of options an agent considers in the process of her moral deliberation. The best we can do is to invoke some 'reasonable person standard', much like Virginia Held and Tracy Isaacs have done (Held 1970; Isaacs 2011).

If there is a publicly known collective effort to produce a certain joint outcome or if there is a known public good to be maintained, then a reasonable person should include that collective strategy in her set of options for moral deliberation. For instance, in the face of a pandemic we have reason to expect people to follow advice by public health experts who will lay out the optimal pattern of collective behaviour such as wearing face masks and keeping at a safe distance from other people. We think that each agent should include the collective endeavour to stop the spread of the pandemic in her set of options. In other words, even large-scale (including global) collective endeavours and the collective patterns of action that produce them can thus be known to the reasonable person and so can form part of the set of options reasonable moral agents should consider in their moral deliberation.

Let me now turn to the next issue. Assume that an agent is considering one or several collectively available options in her moral deliberation. The next step for her is to decide which option is best and which one she – therefore – ought to do or pursue. That is – how should she determine the morally right choice? This question can be broken down into three different problems

(1) What is the correct moral substantive moral theory?
(2) What is the correct view on moral obligations?
(3) How should the agent reason about her options?

These questions will be addressed in the following three sections.

4.2 Weighing Options: Substantive Ethical Theories

Once an agent has established which options they should take into account, including options that are only collectively available, she needs to assess the value of these options. To be fair, what I have been describing on the last pages may happen within a split second. Many responses to morally dire situations are deeply engrained in our psyche and we intuitively grasp the availability of (collective and individual) options and their moral ranking. Especially, where a danger is imminent, do we not run through any elaborate process of weighing up options? But this does not mean that the more fine-grained discussion of ideal moral decision-making is futile. After all, when we make split-second decisions we sometimes get it wrong. In fact, putting us under pressure to react quickly can be a way of provoking knee-jerk reactions that produce suboptimal outcomes. Further, there are plenty of collective moral action problems that are removed from us in time and space, in a way that both requires and allows for our decisions to be more discerning.

In any case, how an agent would weigh and rank the different (individually and collectively) available options would seem to depend on the specific substantive moral view they hold. I think it is realistic to say that most people do not consistently adhere to any one of the major substantive ethical theories such as Deontology, Consequentialism, Virtue Ethics or Care Ethics, or any of the subsidiaries thereof such as Kantian Ethics, or Act-Utilitarianism. But does it matter for the question I am investigating which moral view people actually subscribe to? Or should we ask instead which substantive moral theory is correct?

In order to be able to say whether or not a plurality of agents failed in their collective obligation, we need to be able to explain why they had that obligation in the first place. Obviously, a failure to act on a collective obligation can arise in different ways. Agents could, for instance, fail to take a collectively available option into account and only consider individual options instead. This could be an epistemic failure (to we-frame), as explained in the previous section or a deliberative (procedural) failure in moral reasoning, as detailed in Section 4.4. However, the failure may also be substantive: they may be getting the ranking of their options wrong.

The important thing to note is that for the account presented here it does not matter which substantive moral theory is correct. As it happens, in scenarios like *Hikers, Motorcyclist* or *Commuters* all major substantive theories and common-sense morality appear to converge on what the morally required action or option is. Cases where all moral theories and common-sense morality intersect in their assessment are those where we can unequivocally ascribe collective obligations. Naturally, cases where substantive views diverge are much more difficult to assess. I will say more about this problem later. It need not concern us just yet, because in principle our theory of collective obligations can be used with any substantive theory.

Having said that, it seems that standard act-consequentialism cannot easily accommodate collective obligations being focused as it is on individual acts and their direct impacts rather than on sets of acts. Individual acts that form part of a collective endeavour are conceived merely in regard to the difference they make to the collective outcome, but not in terms of being parts of an overall desirable whole. In contrast, rule consequentialism would not appear to have this problem.

If agents adhere to different substantive moral views then they may rank the available options differently and therefore possibly fail to collaborate where it would be morally best to do so (Lawford-Smith 2015). So, the fact that agents have either false or conflicting views about what morality requires can lead to a failure of producing the morally optimal result. But even though collective action can be more fragile than individual action, in that there are more ways in which it can fail, this problem is not unique to the issue of *collective* obligations. Every time an agent misjudges what morality requires they will fail to do what they ought to do (unless they produce the right result accidentally or incidentally).

Further, if agents disagree on the ranking of options, they may not disagree on every single option. Perhaps there is a common denominator and they settle on what they think is second or third best, therewith avoiding what they each consider worst. There may be cases, however, where no common denominator can be found.

Note that this last option, settling on a common denominator, may or may not be available, depending on which non-substantive view of moral obligation one adheres to. If you think that what you ought to do is determined by the evidence you have then you are more likely to arrive at a shared perspective with another person than if you believe that moral obligations are fundamentally separate from (evidence-based, justified) beliefs. In short, I believe that adhering to a prospective view of moral obligation, rather than to an objective view, will make it more likely that potential collaborators find common denominators. In the following section, I explain what I mean by that and I discuss these different non-substantive views of moral obligation, building on work by Michael Zimmerman.

4.3 Weighing Options: Non-substantive Theories of Moral Obligation

People have raised the following worry in relation to my account of collective obligations: if we are required to take collectively but not individually available options into account when deliberating about our moral obligations, then it seems that we have to take a sheer endless number of possibilities into account. That is because there are endless opportunities for bringing about morally desirable outcomes together with others. It seems that if we accept that our moral obligations may sometimes be jointly held with others that the moral demands on us multiply to a worrying degree.

I believe that this worry and also the one just raised concerning the very real possibility of agents adhering to different substantive views can be countered by committing to a particular account of moral obligation. I argue in the following that if we endorse a notion of collective obligations we should also endorse what Michael Zimmerman has called the *prospective view* of moral obligations and that we should reject the *objective* and *subjective views* of moral obligations.

In the following, I briefly explain Zimmerman's discussion of the objective, the subjective and the prospective of moral obligation and then debate the different implications of these three views for the concept of collective obligations. I will not challenge Zimmerman's view as such.

Here is how Zimmerman characterises the objective view of moral obligation:

> One ought to perform an act if and only if it is in fact the best option one has.
>
> (2014: 2)

By 'best option' he means what is best "*in terms of what matters morally*, insofar as our moral obligations are concerned". This formulation leaves open which substantive moral theory we subscribe to. It is based on the – in my view, reasonable – claim that what all substantive moral theories have in common is that they have a view on what is best in terms of morality (even though they do not necessarily formulate their view using the superlative).

An option, Zimmerman explains,

> is something that one *can* choose, in some suitably robust sense of 'can' that signifies a kind of personal possibility that goes beyond mere logical or physical possibility and is roughly equivalent to one's having both the capacity to do something and the opportunity to exercise that capacity.
>
> (2014: 3)

Further, an obligation does not only concern actions we perform but can also concern not acting (p. 5). Importantly, according to the objective view of moral obligation what one ought to do is "what is *actually* best" (p. 7). If we think about our *hikers* scenario, we most likely agree that what is actually best is for both hikers to lift the tree together and free the trapped man.

Imagine a scenario where there are two fork lifts at the scene and it would be safer for both the hikers and the trapped man to use one of those rather than lifting the tree manually. In that case, lifting the tree manually is only the second-best option, but lifting it with a machine is best. Let us assume, though, that you have been warned that one of the fork lifts is faulty and will catch fire when turned on, rendering the other unusable, too, plus most likely injuring you to an extent that will prevent you from lifting the tree manually. The other fork lift works just fine. The problem is: you do not know which one is which and you have no way of finding out.[5]

It is clear how the options should rank: lifting the tree manually is second best. Not doing anything is third best (because while you do not rescue the trapped man at least you do not harm yourself). The worst option is the one where you pick the faulty machine, you get injured and you still fail to save the trapped man. The best is the one where you pick the functioning machine. Most people would agree that it is too risky to make a random guess and that the two hikers should instead lift the tree manually. On the objective view, you seem to be committing some kind of wrong by picking what you know is not the best option: manually lifting the tree is not morally optimal.

But we might find this view unsatisfying (and many philosophers do). Zimmerman, in fact, rejects the objective view (1996, 2014) not only because it makes it extremely hard to fulfil our moral obligations. Zimmerman's main objection to that view is that it yields some counterintuitive results in scenarios with incomplete knowledge (2014: 30ff) such as the one just discussed. In that scenario, the agents concerned have four options and they can pick the second and third best options, but they have no way of finding out how to choose the best (or the worst) option. The objective view suggests that it is wrong to choose the second-best option, because only choosing the best option is morally right. Zimmerman thinks that choosing the second-best option is morally right in such cases, contrary to the objective view. After all, if we go for one of the unknown options there is a 50% chance that we pick the morally worst option (in the example Zimmerman uses, which goes back to Frank Jackson (1991), this option would involve causing a person's death).

I will not rehearse the arguments against the objective view in any detail here, but instead hope that the reader will find it similarly unconvincing. In light of the problems the objective view has, many find the *subjective view* of moral obligations more plausible. According to the subjective view, "[o]ne ought to perform an act if and only if one believes that it is the best option one has" (Zimmerman 2014: 7), that is, "one ought to do what is *apparently* best" (ibid.). Zimmerman rejects the subjective view, arguing that it is possible for a conscientious person to know what she believes to be best and yet not know what she ought to do, given that as a conscientious person they would tend to be aware of their own fallibility (2014: 27). That is, I may both believe that trying to find a way to lift the tree together with you is my best option and be aware that I may be wrong in that belief. According to Zimmerman, the subjective view does not allow for this intuitively plausible idea and would render conscientious inquiries pointless (ibid.).

As an alternative to both the subjective and the objective views Zimmerman puts forward the *prospective view* of moral obligation:

> One ought to perform an act if and only if it is one's prospectively best option.
>
> (2014: 32)

What is meant by "prospectively best option"? According to Zimmerman, this is "the *best bet* regarding the actual values at stake" (2014: 34), or whatever maximises *projected* value, where we

> understand the prospectively best option to be that which maximizes projected value, that is, that option which constitutes one's best bet in light of the probabilities of the various possible outcomes of one's options and of the various possible values of these outcomes.
>
> (ibid.: 59–60)

In contrast to the subjective view that one's beliefs determine one's moral obligations, on the prospective view what matters is what evidence there is and whether this evidence supports the belief regarding one's obligation (2014: 64).

We can see how the prospective view has an advantage over the subjective view. On the latter, my actual beliefs matter for what I ought to do, regardless of the quality of these beliefs, for instance their plausibility. On the former view, there must be evidence for my belief and that evidence must in fact support *that* belief rather than a different belief. Or, in other words, my belief must be justified by my evidence. Zimmerman explains that this concerns "the evidence of what that person in fact *avails* himself", rather than all available evidence (2014: 72). Further,

> [i]t is precisely his recognition of the fact that he is subject to this twofold fallibility – fallibility with respect to gauging what it is most reasonable to do in light of his beliefs, and fallibility with respect to gauging the reasonableness of the beliefs themselves – that prompts the conscientious person to undertake his conscientious inquiries.
>
> (ibid.: 75–76)

In other words, Zimmerman believes that the conscientious person, who is morally motivated, will try to find evidence in order to form a reasonable view on what their best bet is. However, they can fulfil their moral obligations even if they are aware that they do not have all the information or evidence they could have. If they have to make a call – and most of us cannot examine evidence forever – then whatever their evidence supports at that point plus their value judgements will determine what they ought to do. This may not be what is actually – that is, objectively – best, but it will be the best they can do in that situation and this, according to Zimmerman, determines the content of their obligation. We can see how the prospective view does not produce the counterintuitive implications of the objective view from comparing their recommendations for the variation of the *hikers* case involving the two forklifts. The prospective view tells us to choose the second-best (safe) option.

But what difference would the adoption of either of these views – objective, subjective or the prospective – make for our account of collective obligations? Let me first point out an obvious incongruity: Zimmerman has formulated his position in individualist terms. He is an individualist about moral obligations and does not subscribe to the here-defended idea of joint or collective obligations. However, I think his analysis can be adjusted to work with the collective view. Here is my collective version of the prospective view:

> Two (or more) agents jointly ought to perform an act[6] if and only if it is their prospectively best option.

Here is how I understand this version: between them, two agents (for simplicity's sake let us focus on cases with two agents for now) have several individually and collectively available options. They ought to pick the one, which is prospectively best, that is the one that produces the greatest value with the highest probability. Here is an example of the collectively and individually available options for the hikers who encounter the man trapped by the tree:[7]

- Collectively available:
  - Lifting the tree together
  - Continuing the walk together, etc.

- Individually available:
  - Continuing the walk on their own
  - Trying to lift the tree on their own, etc.

In other words, the hikers have to determine two things on the basis of their evidence: which (either collectively or individually available)[8] option has the greatest value and the probability with which that value gets produced if the option is picked. These two together determine the 'projected value'.

Note that two different kinds of probability relating to a collective option must be distinguished. First, there is the probability that collectively the agents produce a particular outcome (and realise the value attached to it) given that they try. Second, there is the probability that the agents collectively *try* to produce an outcome, that is, the probability with which an option is *available*. Zimmerman's individualist account of moral obligation only refers to the first kind of probability.[9] Information concerning the first type of probability may not always be readily available. Zimmerman offers the following solution for cases where my evidence is insufficient for assigning probabilities to options: "we could invoke a principle of indifference according to which each option should . . . be assigned an equal probability" (2014: 68).

For the individual deliberating agent there is no need to speculate about the second type of probability at this point. We already identified in the last section that the second probability consideration has already taken place in the first step described previously: it feeds into the agent's decision about which options to consider, that is, whether or not to we-frame the situation. Further, assessing the second type of probability can form part of collective deliberation. Note that the mere fact that a group of two or more agents is engaged in collective rather than individual-based reasoning (see Section 4.4) will make it more likely that they succeed in producing their collective option(s). In other words, the form of the deliberative process itself will influence its result: our probability assessment of the availability of collective options will differ depending on whether or not we can communicate with the other. Further, one's own actions (taking the lead, for instance, or signalling willingness) can make certain options more likely. There will be many joint-necessity scenarios where no such communication or exchange of evidence is possible. I believe (and argue further down) that in such scenarios collective moral obligations can still obtain.

In sum, if the prospective view is correct then agents who face a joint-necessity problem and who have both individually and collectively available options are collectively obligated to do x if and only if x is the prospectively best option (out of all available options) for both agents. That is, they are collectively obligated to do x if on the basis of their evidence x is 'their best bet' in the sense of being the option that most likely secures the greatest value.

Having briefly explored a collectivist interpretation of the prospective, view let me now turn to explaining how it is preferable to the objective view when it comes to collective obligations.

The objective view of moral obligations in combination with the notion of collective obligations would lead to an implausible and possibly disheartening proliferation of moral obligations: not only are our moral obligations independent of our beliefs (and therefore we can never be sure if what we believe is morally required is what is in fact required). Also, our set of options would include far more options than we have hitherto been aware of. The possibilities for joining forces together with others to generate morally desirable outcomes are countless and most of these possibilities we would not be aware of, or have beliefs about. Because the options we have of doing things together with others are far more numerous than the options we have for individual action, an objective view of collective obligations would lead to a dizzying (and implausible) proliferation of those obligations.

Both the subjective and the prospective view make some allowance for the limitations of our individual perspectives. Out of these two it seems to be above all the prospective view that can ground a secondary (epistemic) obligation not only to find evidence but also to find out what options there are. The prospective view links our obligations to evidence that is available to us: we are obligated to do what is prospectively best (reasonable-person standards apply). We may not be in a position to find out what is objectively the best collective option, but we are under an obligation to avail ourselves of accessible evidence in the process of moral deliberation.

Doing so will also make it more likely that we will find a common perspective with our potential collaborators. Where we are in a position to share information in the deliberative process, we can make sure that our potential collaborators have the same evidence as we do. If agents consciously endorse the prospective view they are more likely to be pragmatic about their collective options: because what is morally required depends on their evidence, according to this view, agents may be motivated to share evidence and as such may be more willing to align their assessment of what is morally best with that of their potential collaborator. That is, the likelihood of arriving at a shared ranking of options is greater.

Remember that there are two different parts to the calculation of prospective oughts: the probability of each option and the value of each option. For both of these calculations each potential collaborator must be sensitive to the evidence presented by the respective other. This concerns not only one's own evidence in relation to the value of the options. In addition, sharing this evidence is itself evidence as to the collective option's likelihood of success and provides collaborators with an indication of how one is likely to act. In other words, in sharing, distributing and availing oneself of evidence we generate new evidence that others can then act on.

On the prospective view, not only must our beliefs be supported by the immediately available evidence, but we may have to search for and avail ourselves of further evidence, according to Zimmerman. That way, we may well approximate the option that is objectively best. Interestingly, Zimmerman thinks that virtue ethics, Kantian ethics and act-utilitarianism are all versions of the objective view of moral obligation. If he is correct, then our rejection of the objective view implies a rejection of these substantive moral theories. In any case, the discussion in this book focuses mainly on scenarios where all moral theories (plus common-sense morality) converge in their assessment.

One last comment is due on the issue of consequences of individual decisions. It seems that the view I defend is more plausible if combined with possibilism about obligations. The difference between possibilists and actualists is usually understood as the difference between which consequences of an action – actual or possible – matter for our obligations (Jackson and Pargetter 1986; Zimmerman 1996). I am not able to go into any detail on this debate here. Let me point to Christopher Woodard, who suggests that possibilism is better understood as a claim about the 'unit of action' extending beyond the individual action. In the case of Professor Procrastinate discussed by Jackson and Pargetter (1986), an academic who is prone to procrastination must decide whether or not to accept an invitation to review a book. He knows he should accept the invite and write the review, but he is aware of his tendency to procrastinate, and so he believes that if he accepts, he will not actually end up writing the review. Jackson and Pargetter wonder "whether, in addition to what is possible for the agent, we sometimes need to take into account what the agent would actually do in certain circumstances" (1986: 233). According to Woodard, possibilists think of the decision to accept and the writing of the review as one 'unit of action'. This is the 'unit of action' the consequence of which is best out of all 'units of action' available (the other options being [accept and fail]; [decline]) (2011). Similarly, in thinking about collective obligations we may have to think about what options would overall be best where the unit of action is not just our individual contributory action but includes also the other agent(s)' collaborative efforts.[10]

4.4 We-Reasoning and Team-Reasoning About Obligations

Let us assume that an agent engages in the kind of deliberative process described earlier. So far, I have described this process as something she does by herself. But even if – as a result of that process – she concludes that a particular option is best – for instance, the one where she lifts the tree together with the other hiker – she still needs to think about what exactly it is that she should do.

In the hi-lo game this is obvious: she should choose 'hi' over 'lo'. In the case of the hikers, each agent needs to do her part of the lifting. But perhaps there are different ways in which the tree can be lifted. Agents will need to synchronise their individual contributory actions.

At this point it is important to distinguish two types[11] of cases:

(i) Cases where *individual we-reasoning* suffices for determining individual strategies. This is a kind of independent (i.e. individual) moral reasoning, which Hakli et al. have called we-mode we-reasoning (or the first stage of collective reasoning) – more on that in a moment.

(ii) Cases where agents need to deliberate together. This is a type of inter-dependent, group-based reasoning. This is what I call *team-reasoning*.[12]

On my account, how individuals should reason (and whether they should progress to team-reasoning) depends on the kind of problem they are facing. In scenarios like Hilo there is no real need to do anything other than individual we-mode reasoning. In the following, let me explain both kinds of reasoning and how they allow agents to conclude what their contributory actions and obligations are.

First, I will discuss independent we-reasoning.[13] The concept of 'we-reasoning' is being discussed both in non-standard game theory (Bacharach 1999; Butler et al. 2011; Butler 2012) and philosophy of economics (Gold and Sugden 2007a; Hakli et al. 2010; Tuomela 2013).[14] 'We-reasoning' is thought to both explain cooperative behaviour in situations that resemble prisoners' dilemmas (PD) and optimal choices in coordination games like stag hunt and the 'hi-lo' game (Bacharach 1999; Butler et al. 2011). Some even think that 'we-reasoning' can prevent the emergence of collective action dilemmas (Hakli et al. 2010).

I am using the term 'we-reasoning' here in the same sense as Raul Hakli et al. (2010) used the term 'we-mode reasoning', which is 'we-reasoning in the we-mode' rather than we-reasoning in the 'pro-group I-mode'.[15] That is, I will use the terms 'we-reasoning' and 'we-mode reasoning' synonymously and contrast them with 'I-mode reasoning' (plain or pro-group). I will explain the difference between these terms in the following paragraphs. I consider 'we-framing' (Butler et al. 2011) to be the starting point for 'we-reasoning'.

As I explained earlier, we-framing is the act of identifying collectively available options and including them in one's option set for deliberation. We-reasoning is the continuation of that process, in a sense, to determine individual strategies or action choices. When an agent we-reasons, she decides what she needs to do in order bring about the collective outcome she has identified as optimal.

According to Butler et al. (2011) and Bacharach (2006), the idea of 'we-reasoning' can explain what standard game theory cannot explain: why players co-operate in a one-shot PD and why most players choose the Pareto-optimal solution in a hi-lo game (and also in a stag hunt game). Hi-lo is a coordination game with two equilibria, whereas one is Pareto-optimal and one is not. Here is the payoff-matrix for a two-player hi-lo game (Table 4.1):

Table 4.1

	A	B
A	Hi/Hi	0/0
B	0/0	Lo/Lo

Hi > Lo > 0

What seems intuitively plausible to most people cannot easily be explained by game theory: that most players choose hi/hi in the hi-lo game, rather than choosing the second equilibrium lo/lo. Nash equilibrium, the standard solution concept of classic game theory, delivers two solutions – (A,A) and (B,B): "*If* I think you will choose B then the act it's best for me to choose is B, and *if* you think I will choose B then it's best for you to choose B" (Bacharach 2006: 44). What it does not deliver is any clear indication that it is rational for both to select A over B and it cannot predict that they will.

According to Bacharach, the hi-lo game constitutes a paradox for standard game theory, because the theory cannot predict or explain that people will choose hi/hi. Furthermore, it is at odds with common intuitions about the rational choice being hi/hi:

> A paradox is a mismatch between such high-quality intuitions and the deliverances of an accepted theory. The clash between the obvious rationality of the choice A and the inability of game theory to single out A is a paradox. It is a weak paradox, because game theory does not predict that A will not be chosen. It is a paradox nonetheless, a failure of theory to agree with intuition [A = hi; B = lo].
>
> (Bacharach 2006: 44–45)

Bacharach argues that players in fact we-reason about their choices: they choose hi/hi over lo/lo, because their starting point is the question "what should *we* do?" rather than "what should *I* do?".[16] According to Natalie Gold and Robert Sugden (2007a), in team reasoning "agency is attributed to the group", which in turn gives rise to collective intentions (p. 137).[17]

Hakli, Miller, and Tuomela distinguish "we-mode reasoning" from "I-mode reasoning".[18] In the I-mode a rational agent tries to satisfy her preferences by selecting strategies that are best replies to others' expected strategies. This is the mode rational players adopt according to standard game theory. In contrast, in the we-mode the individual agents view the situation from the point of view of a group agent and its preferences and utilities (2010: 298).

Christopher Woodard makes the same point in a different way (2003, 2017). He argues that people will regularly have group-based reasons for action, as opposed to act-based reasons:

> The core issue is that act-based reasons are based on 'horizontal' or 'vertical' comparisons between outcomes: comparisons of the difference Row can make (vertical comparisons) or of the difference Column can make (horizontal comparisons). But our intuition that there is more reason for each player to choose Hi than Lo concerns a *diagonal* comparison: between the outcome of Lo-Lo and the outcome of Hi-Hi. The concept of group-based reasons enables us to point to a reason that is based on this comparison. We can say that the pattern of action (Hi-Hi) is best, and that this gives each player a reason to play her part (Hi) in that pattern.
>
> (2017: 110)

Hakli et al. furthermore distinguish *plain I-mode reasoning* from so-called *pro-group I-mode reasoning*. In plain I-mode, agents select actions that, given their expectations of the other agents' actions, best satisfy their preferences (which may be other-regarding). In pro-group I-mode, agents "select actions that, given their expectations of other agents' actions, best satisfy their preferences, which are group-regarding" (Hakli et al. 2010: 299ff).

In both pro-group I-mode reasoning and we-mode reasoning agents aim at the benefit of (or highest payoff for) the group, but the reasoning process differs and possibly the results, too, because they do not in all cases entail the same equilibrium behaviours. Confusingly, Hakli et al. (2010) use the term 'we-reasoning' for both pro-group I-mode reasoning and we-mode reasoning. As I said previously, I am using the term 'we-reasoning' only for 'we-mode reasoning', that is, the kind of reasoning where an agency transformation has taken place and players approach the problem from the point of view of the group. Another way to explain the difference is to distinguish between acting for the sake of a group versus acting as part of the group, as Christopher Woodard put it. In pro-group I-mode an agent acts for the sake of the group, while in we-mode she acts as part of the group (Woodard 2003: 216).

Pro-group I-mode reasoning and we-mode reasoning can produce different equilibria. Pro-group I-mode thinking cannot eliminate the Pareto-inefficient equilibrium in the hi-lo game: "the we-mode tends to create more collective order than the pro-group mode: It can decrease the amount of equilibria but it cannot increase them" (Hakli et al. 2010: 306). Only the we-mode guarantees that the Pareto-optimal equilibrium be chosen in games like the hi-lo game (ibid.).

According to Hakli et al., in the I-mode the individual agents can only select strategies, but in the we-mode agents adopt the point of the view of the group and can therefore select outcomes (2010: 298).[19] The important difference is that 'we-reasoning' is not a type of preference transformation (individual preferences are no longer self-regarding, but group-regarding), but it constitutes a kind of agency transformation.[20] This idea of agency transformation is central also to Bacharach's work (2006) and echoed in Butler et al. (2011).[21]

Hakli et al. make an empirical (psychological) claim as well as a claim about rationality: "[a]ssuming that rational agents aim at maximizing utility, in some cases agents should reason in the we-mode rather than in the I-mode" and "in many cases our account of we-mode reasoning gives a more correct description of how people actually reason than the I-mode description given by traditional game theory" (2010: 306–307). In other words, not only do agents in cases of certain strategic interaction we-reason, they *should* we-reason in those scenarios.

For the purpose of this chapter, I will assume that the aforementioned authors are roughly correct in claiming that a distinct type of reasoning (regularly) takes place when individual agents (wish to and do) cooperate. In other words, I accept that the we-reasoning-analysis explains why players choose the Pareto-optimal outcome. Further, I assume that Hakli et al. (2010) have good reason to claim that players should we-reason.

Clearly, there are many situations where – as in our previous examples – in order to achieve the morally optimal outcome we need to coordinate our actions and choices with others. Note that I am now talking about morally optimal outcomes, which is something that might be thought to be at odds with what game theoretic analysis considers optimal. However, it is perfectly compatible with game theoretic analysis that the players' preferences are of a moral nature: that the greatest reward for them is to achieve the morally best outcome. Therefore, I see no problem in running the standard hi-lo game and the morally optimising hi-lo game parallel.

Let me return to the example of the people who could collectively keep their house clean at all times. What both of them together can do is different from what each can do. None of them can ensure – on their own – that the collective goal is achieved (they *can* on their own merely ensure that it is not achieved). If the second person is not pulling their weight, then whatever the first person does will not suffice for achieving the goal of keeping the house clean at all times.

If adopting I-mode reasoning, the situation would seem to present itself to the individual agents as one where their obligations to participate in the collective action depend on what the other person is doing. Here is another way to put this: morally speaking, person *A*'s best (i.e. value-maximising) response to person *B*'s doing her part in the collective action is to also do her part. Also, if *B* does not do her part, then it is the best response for *A* not to do her part.

For the sake of argument, let us assume that there is some other – second best – good that they could secure jointly. Say that the two *Housemates* are hobby musicians who would like to play together at a friend's wedding in a month's time. They will not have time to practise together, but they can practise their individual parts on their own, and in fact they need to do that in order to do a decent performance at the wedding. If only one of them knows their part then the performance will still go wrong. They both need to know their parts. Let us assume that if they do not spend time cleaning the house, then they will use the additional time practising their parts. In other words, assuming that a clean house is the best collective outcome, their respective abilities to play their parts well would be second best.[22] They can only practise if they do not clean.

It may be better to keep the house clean, but there is still significant moral gain in practising music. But in order for the second option to eventuate both need to pick it. The pay-off for this option (or its moral value) is significantly lower than keeping the house clean. However, it is still better than any one of them trying to keep the house clean on their own or practising on their own, because these choices will lead to zero gain. In other words, the worst outcome is the one where their actions are not matched. The payoffs in that scenario are those of a hi-lo game. Let us represent these outcomes and the preference orderings in Table 4.2, assuming that the two persons are highly morally motivated and aim for the morally optimal outcome:

Table 4.2

		Housemate 1	
		Clean	Play
Housemate 2	Clean	100/100	0/0
	Play	0/0	50/50

Preference ordering
1st Keep the house clean at all times (clean/clean)
2nd Be able to jointly play wedding music piece (play/play)
3rd Be the only one who cleans OR be the only one who practises music (clean/play or play/clean)

At this point, let me briefly point to a problem with using game theoretic approaches to gain insights for real-world moral decision-making. As Bacharach (2006) emphasises, "games are by definition situations in which different players' acts are causally independent. This part of the definition of a game is due to the fact that game theorists want to model decisions made without physical communication" (p. 50). The reality of a situation like *Housemates* or *Hikers*, however, is that both potential collaborators are likely to and, in fact, can be expected to communicate. We have assumed for the sake of argument that in our version of the *housemates* scenario both cannot communicate their choice to the other until after they have made it. This is guaranteed by the fact that they never encounter each other when at home.[23]

In any case, I believe agents would still make the same moral choices in the following modified *Hikers* scenario: in order to free a trapped person who would otherwise die each participant in an experiment has to press a yellow button. Alternatively, if each presses an orange button they win a luxury holiday. Participants cannot communicate with each other or observe the other person's choice. If they press different buttons the trapped person will remain trapped and they will not win the holiday trip either.

Our basic intuition is that both housemates should do their bit in cleaning the house and that the participants in the experiment described earlier should both press the yellow button. But how *do* we make choices in such scenarios? Some authors suggest that in situations like *Housemates* (and also *Hikers* for that matter), individual agents who choose to cooperate do in fact we-reason and that we-reasoning can explain the cooperative choices players make even if it may disadvantage them (Bacharach 1999, 2006; Hakli et al. 2010; Butler et al. 2011; Butler 2012), that is, they frame the problem from the perspective of the group. Once they have established the best outcome for the group they infer their individual strategy.

My hypothesis is that in situations like *Hikers* and *Housemates*, individual agents regularly do we-reason and that they *ought* to so, that is, they ought to reason from the perspective of the group. In the following I will show how I-mode reasoning fails to correspond to our basic intuition.

If we look at the problem the individual housemate in our hypothetical scenario is facing, we can imagine them to reason in the following way:

- Depending on what *B* does, my action towards keeping the house clean will be in vain or not. On my own, I cannot keep the house clean at all times. My attempt at keeping it clean alone will not make a difference to the outcome.[24] If my action does not make a difference, then I have no obligation to perform it.
- Therefore, *if B* cleans, then I have an obligation to participate.
- Furthermore, *if B* does not clean but practises music, then I have an obligation not to clean either, but to practise music (to secure the second-best outcome).

If reasoning in *I*-mode, the individual agent reasons about what is best for her to do given what others do. In contrast, in we-mode reasoning she reasons from the point of view of the group.

The individual housemate (or hiker) may reason in I-mode that if her obligation is to do the best she can, to maximise the good, then what she ought to do depends on what others do. In that case housemate *A* has an obligation to contribute to the joint action *only if housemate B contributes* and vice versa.

Let me now turn to the problems with I-mode reasoning, using the example of *Hikers*. The first problem is that I-mode reasoning only seems to yield conditional obligations for each hiker, which means that it does not support what we earlier called the 'basic intuition' that together the hikers should save the trapped man. If the other hiker embarks on lifting the tree, then I have an obligation to also embark on lifting the tree. And if the other hiker does not embark on lifting the tree, then I have an obligation to not embark on lifting it either, but to go my way to secure the second-best good (perhaps that of finishing the walk that we have been planning for a long time together). The morally optimal action (or outcome) does not have a corresponding moral obligation: there can be no all-out obligation to free the trapped man, only conditional obligations on each to contribute to the joint endeavour.

Using I-mode reasoning, we cannot confirm our *basic intuition* and, therefore, we cannot confirm our *derivative intuition* – that a wrong is committed in failing to save the man – either. If they fail to free the trapped man and continue on their hike, the wrongness of failing to save him would not seem to go over and above the wrongness of failing to contribute to saving him. If there is no obligation to save him (as there is no appropriate subject of such an obligation) then no one can be blamed for having failed to save him. This seems to contradict our derivative basic intuition.[25]

Another problem is that conditional obligations raise the problem of mutual release: if both hikers simultaneously walk away (or just stand there and do nothing), then none of them has an obligation to assist (see Goodin 2012). This is because the inaction of each undermines the possibility of joint action. Hiker 1's walking away undermines hiker 2's ability to make a difference and vice versa. Each can claim that they would have helped had they thought the joint action possible but seeing that the other walked away they (rightly) concluded that it was not possible. Simultaneous refusal will nullify a conditional obligation: hiker 1's refusal nullifies hiker 2's obligation at the same time that hiker 2's refusal nullifies hiker 1's obligation (see also Section 2.2).

Further, and perhaps more controversially, the I-mode approach seems to challenge what I would consider our moral phenomenology. According to studies in experimental game theory, we do in fact sometimes see problems as problems for us, for groups, rather than for us as individuals. Plus, and more importantly, we sometimes start our deliberation from the point of view of what the group might be able to achieve (Butler et al. 2011; Butler 2012).

Also, it seems that we-reasoning can *explain* why we see ourselves as having an obligation. What is it that makes people acknowledge a duty to assist the trapped man in the first place? Is it the fact that the circumstances (the problem plus the fact that someone is there to help me solve it) enable *me* to generate the morally most valuable outcome? Or in other words, is it the gravity of the problem plus my individual difference-making ability? In that case, I have decided that the other's willingness to help is part of the 'circumstances'. And my individual difference-making ability depends on those circumstances.

While our individual difference-making ability does depend on the other in a scenario such as *Hikers*, I believe it would be a mistake to primarily focus on this individual ability in explaining why we consider the option of acting collectively. An awareness of our *collective* difference-making ability explains better why we would consider the option to jointly assist. If we start from our collective difference-making ability, we will not consider the willingness of the other to be merely part of the circumstances. What this means is that most people would think it necessary in situations like *Hikers* to convince the second person to assist if they were unwilling to do so or hesitant, rather than take their unwillingness as a mere given. Most people would also think that we must not wait until the other has signalled their willingness to collaborate but that we each must be proactive in signalling that. This seems to suggest that the starting point of our reasoning process in such scenarios is the collective perspective. In other words, we seem to we-reason.[26]

Such pro-group I-mode reasoning – that is, I-mode reasoning that is group-regarding – will often yield similar results to we-mode reasoning but not always (Table 4.3). As Hakli et al. emphasise, "only we-mode reasoning strictly entails some kind of conclusion" as to how an individual should act in a collective action scenario:

Table 4.3

Pro-group I-mode reasoning	We-mode reasoning
1. I have two options: I can contribute to lifting the tree or not.	1. There are three options: we can lift the tree together, we can each go our way or one of us can try to lift it on their own.
2. The first option produces the morally best group outcome only if the other hiker cooperates.	2. Clearly, the first option is the best from a moral point of view.
3. Choosing the second option, will produce the second-best group outcome, but only if the other hiker also chooses the second option.	3. I should play my part in making it the case that we lift the tree.
4. Therefore, if the other hiker cooperates in lifting the tree, then I should contribute to lifting the tree (if I want to achieve the best group outcome).	
5. If the other hiker does not contribute, then I should not contribute either (if I want to achieve the best group outcome).	

Apart from the problem that pro-group I-mode reasoning is not strictly action-guiding, it also does not eliminate the lower equilibrium. We-mode reasoning eliminates the lower equilibrium entirely. And this seems – again – to correspond to our moral intuitions: we do not usually think it would be ok for the two hikers to go their way.

The advantages of we-mode reasoning become more obvious when we look at our *Commuters* case. In the case of the commuters pushing a 20t+ train aside, there is no strict, but only wide joint necessity: there are more people present than, strictly speaking, necessary to achieve the desired outcome.[27] This means that no individual's contribution or failure to contribute will – taken by itself – make a difference to whether or not the optimal outcome is achieved.

In this case, each individual reasoning in pro-group I-mode is fully justified in thinking the following:

1. I have two options: I can contribute to pushing the train aside or not.
2. If sufficiently many others are willing to (and do) contribute then adding my contribution is not actually helping to produce the outcome. It is superfluous and makes no difference to the outcome.
3. If an insufficient number of people contribute, then:

    *   If even when adding my contribution we still fall short of the required minimum number of contributions then my contribution makes no difference or, in other words, it is not the best response to the choices of others. Or,
    *   If my contribution is the one contribution needed to help cross the threshold of minimally necessary contributions then it will make a difference, or, in other words, it is the best response to the others' choices.

4. Only in the last case does my action secure the best outcome and is the best response to the others' choices.
5. It is not clear whether or not I have an actual obligation to contribute to freeing the trapped man (this is assuming that nothing I could individually do would help him) and it is very difficult for me to find out (because I do not know the exact number of people willing to contribute and the number of those who are necessary). Further, it is unlikely that I will be the difference-maker.
6. Also, because my contribution is not necessary for producing the desired outcome, it would never be *my* failure to contribute which undermines the joint cause. After all, my failure to contribute could always be compensated by any of the other undecided or unwilling agents.
7. There are no strong reasons for me to contribute.

The problem is, of course, that this kind of reasoning is available to every single commuter on the platform. Pro-group I-mode reasoning in wide joint necessity cases cannot guarantee the optimal outcome. This problem is effectively prevented by we-mode reasoning:

1. There are three options: A sufficiently large subgroup of us push against the train together and succeeds in tilting it, or we all go our way, or some of us try to tilt the train even though our numbers are insufficient for making a significant difference.
2. Clearly, the first option is the best from a moral point of view.
3. I should take steps towards realising the first option (e.g. by encouraging others to push against the train with me).[28]

This reasoning schema reflects cases where there is no certainty as to exactly how many people are required to help and decisions have to be made fast. This will often be the case in rescue scenarios, but may be different for other joint-necessity cases. If the circumstances permit potential collaborators may engage in more sophisticated forms of reasoning or *collective* types of reasoning. What type of reasoning is available to them will depend on their epistemic position (for instance, whether or not people can communicate with one another).[29]

We-mode reasoning is reasoning at the individual level. This will be the only kind of reasoning possible in the kind of scenarios we are looking at: urgent rescue cases with very limited opportunity for potential helpers to communicate, discuss options and choose joint strategies. We-mode reasoning can avoid a suboptimal outcome in such cases, but probably not in more complex cases.

We started by assuming that in *Hikers* and *Commuters*, the two helpers present should pick the Pareto-optimal (and morally optimal) outcome (basic intuition). We established that in strict joint-necessity cases, I-mode reasoning can lead to that outcome but only we-mode reasoning guarantees it. Further, I-mode reasoning only yields I-mode, conditional obligations.

We-mode thinking or 'we-reasoning' – in contrast – can yield an all-out, unconditional, collective obligation to assist. In I-mode, the lack of individual capacity to guarantee the morally best outcome undermines the obligation to achieve that outcome: I have no obligation to free the trapped man because I cannot do so. The focus on collective capacity in we-mode reasoning makes room for the possibility that the individual members of the group collectively have this obligation. As Hakli et al. said, in we-mode we can choose outcomes, not strategies (2010: 298).

Should we say that the moral-maximising agents in our two exemplary cases ought to reason in we-mode and to frame the situation as one for the group? I think they do: unless they have reason to believe that the other(s) will defect they should frame the situation as a problem for the group.[30] If they fail to we-frame the situation they make a mistake in moral reasoning (that may or may not be excusable). Flawed reasoning can sometimes still yield the right result. But if agents fail to collaborate as a result of flawed reasoning they violate a moral obligation.

Before moving on, let me briefly point to a related way of explaining we-reasoning in the context of moral decision-making. According to Christopher Woodard, we regularly have group-based (as opposed to individual-based) reasons for action (2003, 2011). He suggests that both types of options can generate reasons for action (which can come into conflict) (2003). When I have a group-based reason to do something – to pick an individual strategy, for instance,

> the idea is not that there is a reason to perform *A* because it will bring about *P*, or make P more likely. Instead it is that the goodness

or rightness of P provides reasons to perform its parts, just in virtue
of their being parts of it.

(2011: 263)

In short, possible patterns of group action can generate reasons – moral
reasons – for individual group members to play their part in the group
action. Importantly, the relationship between individual reasons for an
action *A* and a whole pattern of action P is a part–whole relationship, not
a cause–effect relationship. Woodard argues that

> the idea is not that there is a reason to perform *A* because it will
> bring about *P*, or make P more likely. Instead it is that the goodness
> or rightness of P provides reasons to perform its parts, just in virtue
> of their being parts of it.
>
> (2011: 263)

For the argument in this book I assume that there is a close relationship
between reasons and obligations in that the former can give rise to the
latter.

More sophisticated (and arguably more robust) forms of we-reasoning
include Adam Morton's (2005) solution-based thinking and Robert Sugden's account of team-reasoning (Gold and Sugden 2007b). Both are
types of individual reasoning. This is how Francesco Guala summarises
Morton's account:

> Seen from the point of view of an individual player, solution thinking
> can be reconstructed as follows:
>
> 1. S is the obvious solution to the coordination problem.
> 2. You also think that S is the obvious solution to the coordination
>   problem.
> 3. To achieve S, I must do X and you must do Y.
> 4. You also think that I must do X and you must to Y.
>
> (2016: 97)

Here, each agent or player 'simulates' the other agent's thoughts. That
way agents can coordinate. Guala writes: "[e]ach agent asks: what is the
easiest or the most natural way to tackle this problem? What is the obvious solution? If there is a clear answer, then the same reasoning is attributed to the other player by default" (2016: 96). This type of reasoning is
slightly more sophisticated than the very basic account of we-reasoning
I have been operating with simply because it involves agents making
assumptions about other agents' beliefs.

The same is true for Robert Sugden's account of mutually assured team-
reasoning.[31] Note that on this account team-reasoning is understood as

individual deliberation and that individual deliberation includes beliefs concerning other agents' mental states:

Schema 12.7: Mutually assured team reasoning

(1) I am a member of S.

(2) I identify with S and acknowledge U as its objective.

(3) In S, there is reciprocal reason to believe that each member of S identifies with S and acknowledges U as the objective of S.

(4) In S, there is reciprocal reason to believe that each member of S endorses and acts on mutually assured team reasoning.

(5) In S, there is common reason to believe that A uniquely maximizes U.

I should choose my component of A.

(Gold and Sugden 2007b: 303)

Agents' beliefs are supported by 'reciprocal' and 'common' reasons, which Gold and Sugden explain as follows:

> On the analogue of the definition of common knowledge, there is *common reason* to believe a proposition p in a set of individuals T if: (i) for all individuals i in T, i has reason to believe p; (ii) for all individuals i and j in T, i has reason to believe that j has reason to believe p; (iii) for all individuals $i, j,$ and k in T, i has reason to believe that j has reason to believe that k has reason to believe p; and so on.
>
> (Gold and Sugden 2007b: 302).

Agents have reasons to believe p if p "can be inferred from propositions that she accepts as true, using rules of inference that she accepts as valid" (ibid.). In order to have common reasons then, an agent must have beliefs about which beliefs other agents accept as true. That is, this type of deliberation requires some form of higher-order beliefs beyond shared beliefs. As such, it is epistemically more demanding but also more robust than Morton's solution-based thinking or the account of basic we-reasoning that I have proposed.

I have discussed individual modes of deliberation about our individual strategies and obligations in joint-necessity cases. However, it is clear that most collective moral action scenarios are more complex than the ones used as examples earlier. Most importantly, many of them do not have one Pareto-optimal or otherwise salient solution. Further, as indicated in Chapter 3, there may be many different possible combinations of individual contributory actions and agents may have to get it exactly right: collective outcomes are often multiply realisable. Also, as indicated earlier, agents may start out with different moral preferences such that we-reasoning is not likely to yield the optimal result.

In scenarios where individual deliberation cannot reliably yield optimal action recommendations, group-based forms of reasoning may be required. I will not rehearse the various models for group-based reasoning here (Hakli et al. 2010). Note that the epistemic requirements on group-based reasoning are greater than on we-reasoning (as I understand it), because it requires direct communication between group members and is often feasible only where the group is clearly defined.

Hakli et al. (2010) exemplify how a group preference matrix, that is the process by which a plurality of agents agree on a common preference ordering, can be formed. Arriving at a common goal or shared preference matrix is something that agents do at least in part together; it is the result of a joint deliberative (epistemic) effort.[32] Joint-necessity cases do not generate collective obligations whenever individual we-reasoning does not yield clear results and group-based reasoning is not possible.

Finally, what needs to be said about the moral deliberation process discussed in this chapter is that often or even most of the time agents will not go through these steps one by one, but instead perform them simultaneously. Such judgements will be more reliable where the joint task is a regularly performed collective action or previously rehearsed.

4.5 Group Knowledge

In order for a plurality of agents to have a collective moral obligation, does some form of group knowledge have to exist in the group? Are there facts that the members of the group have to know in common, or, at least, facts that they each have to know in order for them to have a joint obligation?

This question can only be addressed in the context of the process of moral deliberation described previously. But before I can do so, let me briefly explain the different types of group knowledge.

The most basic type of such knowledge is *shared knowledge*. A proposition p is shared knowledge in a group consisting of x and y if x knows p and y knows p. Knowledge of p is fully shared in a group where p is known by every member of the group. Partially shared knowledge of p obtains where some proportion of group members knows p.

A proposition p is first-order common knowledge in a group $[x, y]$ if

 (i) p is shared knowledge, and
(ii) all group members know (i).

It is second-order common knowledge if all group members know (ii), and so on.

Public knowledge is weaker than common knowledge: a proposition p is publicly known in a group if it is generally the case that people in that group know p and that fact itself is generally known. For instance, that high levels of GHG emissions are causing climate change is generally known and the fact that this is generally known is itself generally known. I know that you (are very likely to) know about climate change and its causes without having ever spoken to you about it and vice versa. Propositions can be public knowledge to varying degrees.

In order to have collective moral obligations, then, do agents need to have some kind of group knowledge? The upshot of the preceding discussion is that agents need to at least have shared knowledge (or beliefs) in cases that resemble Hilo, such as the *Housemates* or the *Hikers*. They need to share a belief concerning the morally optimal outcome and the individually required actions that produce it. This is likely to obtain where such options are salient.

More complex cases, with various equilibria or cases where no morally optimal outcome is salient will usually require that agents jointly come to an understanding of what they want to achieve and in the process of establishing such an understanding agents will often form some kind of higher order beliefs that are characteristic of public and common knowledge.

Note that in such circumstances the mere existence of a collective obligation does not depend on the prevalence of a certain type of group knowledge *before* the joint-necessity case arises. Rather, such obligations depend on whether or not the required kind of knowledge – shared (as a minimum), public, common or other[33] – can be achieved at acceptable cost, where agents are faced by joint-necessity problems.

Group knowledge such as shared, common or public knowledge can be often established by an individual person where she deems it necessary (for instance, as a result of her 'we-framing' a particular situation). She can establish such knowledge merely by informing others of her views and engaging in an exchange over the best course of action.

Note also that while common knowledge is hard if not impossible to attain in large, dispersed group, this does not apply to shared and public knowledge, which are fairly undemanding. Within the global community, there is close to fully shared knowledge of some propositions – for instance, concerning the anthropogenic climate change. We can have global public knowledge to a degree. This means that with regard to some very specific morally relevant issues humanity may have global joint ability and (what I will call 'massively shared') moral obligations. I will come back to this issue in Chapter 8.

4.6 Simplicity, Complexity: Additional Factors for Collective Moral Obligations

Certain background and circumstantial factors will diminish or add complexity to our collective moral action problems. The scenarios we have analysed so far – *Hikers*, *Commuters* and *Housemates* – what did they have in common? In each of the examples given, the individual members of the group were in the same place at the same time: in the first two scenarios, they were also in a position to communicate, observe each other, and have a grasp of the situation – its seriousness and urgency. They were furthermore individually capable of performing the necessary contributory actions. The scenarios described so far had characteristics that only apply to a narrow selection of cases:

(i) *Moral simplicity* describes a bundle of features that I believe impact on the kind of obligations we will hold jointly in a given scenario: a concrete aim/goal; a concrete beneficiary; a concrete addressee of the duty (or group of addressees); a concrete place/location; the action is limited in time and is one-off (except *Housemates*). In particular, I believe that the criteria bundled under moral simplicity mirror the criteria for so-called perfect duties or duties without (much) latitude, as opposed to imperfect duties or duties with (more) latitude. In fact, all the collective obligations we have discussed so far were obligations with little latitude. Further, in *Hikers* and *Commuters*, the need for assistance is immediate and urgent. They are emergencies and one-off scenarios: this aspect contributes largely to making the case for all-out collective duties to assist compelling. To what extent collective obligations in cases that are not emergencies (but perhaps recurring problems) are less likely to become all-out duties will yet need to be determined.

(ii) *Epistemic simplicity* obtains where it is clear what needs to be done; it is clear what each individual needs to do; it is clear when the goal has been accomplished; it looks like there is a good chance of achieving the outcome. I already discussed epistemic simplicity to some extent. If a scenario is epistemically too complex, collective moral obligations may not arise, as I argued earlier. One aspect of this is the exclusivity to assist: non-exclusivity to address the problem can complicate ascriptions of obligations. In all the scenarios examined, there was exactly one plurality of agents available and responsible for addressing the problem. In those cases, it would be obvious to the reasonable agent that if they do not help then no one will. If, however, multiple (sub-)groups are available to address a certain scenario or problem then it will be less clear who should act. In those cases, all are under an obligation to act unless or until others act. However, such cases may be further complicated if additional contributions are detrimental to collective success, i.e. when the problem is worsened by too many agents attempting to assist. In short, a group's (or agent's) exclusive ability to address a problem can deliver greater epistemic simplicity and certainty with regard to their obligations. And – to the extent that one's obligations depend on one's available evidence – epistemic simplicity can in fact have an impact on whether or not a plurality of agents have obligations at all.

(iii) *Cooperative simplicity:* As to the third aspect, the kind of action(s) required in order to solve the problems discussed so far were either distributive or fairly straightforward cooperative collective actions (Schwenkenbecher 2020). Roughly, distributive collective actions are those where individual contributory actions can be performed more or less independently. For instance, keeping the kitchen clean together is something that we can each contribute to whenever we wish to do so. It need not be done at the same time or place, and it need not be done considering the exact contributory actions of the other. For cooperative collective actions, in contrast, individual contributions are interdependent, interwoven, and often mutually responsive. Performative collective actions are often like that. Lifting the tree off the trapped hiker is also a cooperative collective action. Pushing the train off the trapped commuter is has features of both, but is – by and large – still a cooperative action because all agents must push against the train in the same place and roughly at the same time. Other things being equal, the less complex a required collective action, the more likely are agents to acquire collective obligations to perform it.

An issue that I do not address here is collective obligations that may arise cases without joint necessity. Where one group (or one agent) can in principle solve a problem, usually, the burden on them will be eased if other groups or agents are helping them. Here, collective obligations may arise for reasons of fairness and just distribution, in addition to reasons for assisting (or addressing the respective problem).

One of the most important upshots of the discussion in Chapter 3 is that joint-necessity cases where we-reasoning does not yield clear results and team-reasoning is not possible do not generate collective obligations. This has produced the following:

Conditions for collective moral obligations

Agents *a, b* and *c* have a collective moral obligation if[34]

(i) There exists a specific morally significant joint-necessity problem *P*, such that agents *a, b* and *c* can collectively, but not individually, address *P* [joint necessity + joint ability].[35]

(ii) Conscientious moral deliberation leads all of them (or a sufficiently large subset of them) to believe that some collectively available option *O* is morally optimal[36] with regard to *P* [they have reason to we-frame *P* and to consider *O*].

(iii) *A, b* and *c* (or a sufficiently large subset of them) are in a position to determine individual (or joint) strategies to realize *O* and to achieve *P*.[37]

These are the conditions for pro tanto collective obligations. It is clear from this that not just any plurality of agents will be able to address some problem together. Whether or not they can will depend on the kind of group they are, including group cohesion.

Let me add a brief comment on more complex collective action problems. Pluralities of agents may themselves not collectively solve P but have reason to see themselves as part of second-order collective endeavour(s) that form part of first-order collective endeavour(s) to solve P. That is, they can see themselves as forming part of polycentric clusters of activity. Both collective action and obligations would be layered in such cases. In such cases, the *individuals' collective obligations are indirect* or *second-order collective obligations*. Again, the relationship between the second-order and the first-order endeavour may not be a cause–effect relationship but a part–whole relationship, such that a second-order collective endeavour may be obligatory even where it is not a difference-maker. An example of this would be individual employees' obligations to participate in improving their organisation's environmental record with a view to contributing to the entire industry's efforts to improve theirs.

The idea of secondary obligation, again, is nothing new, I believe. An individual agent may be under an obligation to look after her friend's cat because she promised to do so. This will give rise to all kinds of secondary obligations: she will not only have to buy cat food but she should also make sure she has enough money to buy cat food, and so on. Such indirect obligations usually come with significant latitude as to how they need to be discharged.

Let me return to the above-mentioned criteria for collective obligations, particular the requirement that agents be in a position to determine individual strategies towards addressing the problem in question. Importantly, public information campaigns can devise individual strategies for O and P.[38]

We should also keep in mind that collective (pro tanto) obligations can and will regularly conflict with individual obligations and with other group-based obligations. This tension cannot be completely resolved by the approach defended here, but perhaps it encourages us to see group-based obligations as on a par with individual obligations.

Finally, note that what I have defended so far seems to be an account of so-called perfect duties, or duties without latitude. That is, I have talked about collective duties that arise with regard to a *specific problem* and most examples feature specific duty-bearers. However, several authors (Murphy 2000; Cullity 2004; Schroeder 2014) who have endorsed some version of collective obligations have framed these as (arising from) a collective principle of beneficence that is better understood as a collective *imperfect duty*. I think the account I have defended so far should in principle work for both types of duties. This becomes more clear when we replace talk of imperfect duties with talk of duties with latitude, as I prefer. A duty can have latitude along several different dimensions: act type or token, place, time, or manner in which it needs to be discharged and whether or not it is owed to anyone in particular (Rainbolt 2000). Naturally, where *specific* actions are required it will be easier to devise a shared strategy or to have one salient solution known by all.

Notes

1. We need not worry about using game theoretic terminology here because the notion of 'payoff' as it relates to preferences can perfectly well reflect moral preferences. For the morally motivated or conscientious agent the payoffs are ranked according to moral criteria with the highest payoff being the one that is morally best.
2. I am not claiming that all these accounts are the same or even very similar. But because they all require some form of common knowledge or beliefs (or reasons) they are significantly different from 'we-framing' and 'we-reasoning' as these are understood here.
3. One might think of this as a type of epistemic obligation.
4. I explain how public knowledge differs from common knowledge in Section 4.5.
5. This thought experiment is modelled on Frank Jackson's 'Drug Example' (1991).
6. Note, again, that Zimmerman speaks of 'acts', but he has made it clear that he applies this term loosely to performing actions and producing outcomes alike.
7. The order roughly indicates the ordinal ranking of these options within their category.
8. There may be cases where I cannot be sure as to whether an option is collectively available to me and the other person(s). I may rank an option highest that is in fact not available to the other. In such cases, we may or may not succeed in establishing joint action or producing a joint outcome. If we can communicate we can fix these flawed rankings. Otherwise, if there is no way of establishing which collective options are available to each and should be pursued, the agents may not hold a collective obligation.
9. Further, Zimmerman is concerned with all-out obligations, while my concern here is with pro tanto obligations. In order to establish pro tanto obligations it seems to be sufficient to assess the probability of a collective option given that the respective agents try. It is only when we try to establish if there is an all-out obligation that the *likelihood of collaboration* should be taken into account.
10. See also Michael Zimmerman's defence of possibilism in *The Concept of Moral Obligation* Zimmerman, M. J. (1996). *The Concept of Moral Obligation*. Cambridge: Cambridge University Press.
11. Further, there may be hybrids between the two resulting in some kind of imperfect team-reasoning.
12. Hakli et al. (2010) argue that collective reasoning comes in three stages, with individual we-mode reasoning occurring at the first stage, followed by what I call 'team-reasoning' at the second and third stages of collective reasoning.
13. Some of the material in this and the following sections has previously been published in Schwenkenbecher, A. (2019). Collective Moral Obligations: 'We-reasoning' and the Perspective of the Deliberating Agent. *The Monist*, 102(2), 151–171.
14. Robert Sugden explains the origin of the concept on p. 153 in Sugden, R. (2015). Team Reasoning and Intentional Cooperation for Mutual Benefit. *Journal of Social Ontology*, 1(1), 143–166.
15. This is different, for example, from Sugden's notion of 'team reasoning' as a "structure of belief, intention and action" (2015: 152). The notion of 'we-reasoning' I employ here is much less demanding. Further, according to Hakli

et al., 'we-mode reasoning' corresponds to what Michael Bacharach calls 'team reasoning' and pro-group I-mode reasoning to 'functioning as a bene-factor to the group' (2010: 299).

16. The concept of we-reasoning is meant to improve classic game theory in at least three ways: (1) it redefines what a 'rational' choice is for individual players, allowing the cooperative choice in one-shot prisoners' dilemmas to be rational, (2) it allows us to better predict players' choices and (3) it explains why players make those choices.

17. Gold and Sugden do not use the term 'group agency' here in the sense it is used by List and Pettit (2011). Their account of team-reasoning is compat-ible with the latter but perhaps is best understood as showing how formerly unstructured groups can achieve a greater degree of collective agency in the process of team-deliberation.

18. For how their terminology relates to Bacharach's, see Hakli et al. 2010: 299f and 302f.

19. Hakli et al. say that "a group agent can in a sense select outcomes" (2010: 298). I think this is misleading, we-mode reasoning – as I understand it – is, or can be, employed by individuals. Their framing the situation as one for the group and choosing their individual actions accordingly will not require a group agent. Nor does acting together make them a group agent (Pettit, P. and D. Schweikard (2006). Joint Actions and Group Agents. *Philosophy of the Social Sciences*, 36(1), 18–39.).

20. Another difference between my notion of we-reasoning and that of Hakli et al. (2010) is that they consider we-mode reasoning to involve forming a collective intention – an intention with regard to the action (to be) performed by the group as different to the intention concerned with the action (to be) performed by the individual – whereas I do not.

21. Hein Duijf challenges the thesis that agency transformation is fundamentally distinct from preference transformation (see Duijf, H. (forthcoming). Coop-eration, Fairness, and Team Reasoning. *Economics and Philosophy*).

22. I suspect that this case will be counter-intuitive to some. I, for one, would always prefer playing music to cleaning. But let us simply assume that some-thing morally important is attached to the house being clean. And that while the musical performance is a nice gesture, it is less important.

23. Or else, I think participants would still make the same moral choices in the following modified *Hikers* scenario: in order to free a trapped person who would otherwise die each participant has to press a yellow button. Alterna-tively, if each presses an orange button they win a fantastic holiday trip. Par-ticipants cannot communicate with each other. If they press different buttons neither will happen.

24. This is assuming that the outcome is a so-called fixed-sum case: the house either is clean at all times or it is not. My cleaning alone cannot secure that outcome or in fact produce some benefit. I will talk more about fixed-sum and other cases in Chapter 5.

25. I have made a similar point in Schwenkenbecher 2014b. See also Chapter 6.

26. It is possible that from a third-person perspective we are tempted to ascribe collective obligations and obligations to team-reason more frequently, but I am only discussing the perspective of the agents who find themselves in such situations.

27. I thank Matthew Kopec for pointing out the importance of this case for my argument.

28. This reasoning reflects the case of the commuters where there is no certainty as to exactly how many people are required to help and decisions have to be made fast. This will often be the case in rescue scenarios, but not in other

collective assistance contexts. Where there is the opportunity to discuss decisions yet other, more sophisticated, forms of collective reasoning may occur instead.

29. Some accounts of team-reasoning require members to have common knowledge or beliefs (see Gold and Sugden 2007b). However, for what I am proposing, here weaker types of group-based knowledge should suffice.

30. In contrast, Derek Parfit seems to have suggested that we only have reason to act as a member of a potential group if we know that enough other are contributing (Parfit, D. (1984). Five Mistakes in Moral Mathematics. In *Reasons and Persons* (Vol. 1, pp. 55–83). Oxford: Clarendon Press.)

31. For the differences between solution-thinking and team-reasoning, see Guala (2016); Guala, F. (2016). *Understanding Institutions: The Science and Philosophy of Living Together*. Princeton, NJ: Princeton University Press. For a critical discussion of Guala's work, see Pacherie, E. (2018). Solution Thinking and Team Reasoning: How Different Are They? *Philosophy of the Social Sciences*, 48(6), 585–593.

32. On their view, agents will thereby form we-intentions. For more on plural intentions, see Section 2.1.

33. Olivier Roy and I described yet another type of group knowledge – pooled knowledge – in Roy, O. and A. Schwenkenbecher (2019). Shared Intentions, Loose Groups, and Pooled Knowledge. *Synthese*, online first.

34. Note that this does not say 'iff' because collective moral obligations will also arise in cases that are not joint-necessity cases. This means that the present criteria are necessary and sufficient as far as joint necessity cases are concerned, but not as far as all kinds of cases are concerned.

35. This leaves open whether we are facing a wide or a strict joint necessity case, that is, whether or not a subset of two would suffice in resolving P.

36. There may be several optimal options and it may be possible to pursue several of them simultaneously. That is, options may not be mutually exclusive. In that case all that is required is that the deliberators overlap in the options identified as optimal.

37. That is, they can perform the right kind of actions, too, for instance distributive or non-distributive joint actions.

38. Some authors have argued that imperfect collective duties are 'perfected' through regulation and legislation and only then become stringent or enforceable Buchanan, A. (1996). Perfecting Imperfect Duties: Collective Action to Create Moral Obligations. *Business Ethics Quarterly*, 6(1), 27–42; Ashford, E. (2013). Severe Poverty as a Systemic Human Rights Violation. In G. Brock (Ed.), *Cosmopolitanism Versus Non-Cosmopolitanism: Critiques, Defenses, Reconceptualizations* (pp. 129–155). Oxford: Oxford University Press; Goodin, R. E. (2016). Duties of Charity, Duties of Justice. *Political Studies*. However, I am not convinced that this can only be brought about by such institutionalization.

5 What Collective Obligations Mean for Individual Agents

Contributory Obligations, Non-compliance and Joint Blameworthiness

Let us imagine that the hikers, the commuters, or the housemates have deliberated about the problem they are confronted with and their respective obligations. Let us assume they make no mistakes in moral reasoning – they get it all right: they consider all their options and they rank the options correctly.

Either agents arrive at their decision via we-reasoning, that is, they reason independently about what each of them should be doing. Or they reason about their obligations together and engage in team-reasoning. This will depend on the specific scenario – on what it requires and on what it allows for. In *Hikers*, the two helpers may have to briefly communicate about how to lift the tree. In *Commuters* and *Housemates* it may be obvious enough which individual contributory action they should pick, even without joint deliberation.

But at what point exactly do the group members have a joint duty? If we were objectivists about moral obligation then the duty would fall on them the very moment they are in a position to generate a morally optimal outcome by combining their actions in the right way, whether they know that or not. But I earlier argued against objectivism and in favour of prospectivism. Based on our discussion in Chapter 4, they have a collective duty to do x if it is the case that a reasonable person who has conscientiously availed herself of the evidence would come to the conclusion the jointly doing x is the best option available to them.

Obviously, agents regularly fail in their epistemic duties. If they have failed to avail themselves of evidence, and therefore do not rank the collective option highest, can they still have a collective obligation? I think we should answer this question affirmatively. If there is evidence they should have availed themselves of then failing to do so should not undermine their obligation. Zimmerman argued that in order to have an obligation it is not necessary that we know that we have it or that we even know we can do the thing required of us (1996). Epistemic due diligence is crucial to acting morally. In any case, the problem of failing to avail oneself of information and (deliberately or negligently) remaining ignorant of morally important facts is a problem that is not unique to collective ethics; it arises in the same way for individual obligations (Rosen 2003; Miller 2017).

Further, it is possible that agents facing joint-necessity scenarios mistakenly assume that they have joint ability when in fact they do not. In that case, they may wrongly pursue or start pursuing a collective option only to find out after having failed that they were not jointly able to do whatever they set out to do. In such cases, finding out that they have no (or insufficient) joint ability may mean finding out that they have no collective duty, depending on whether or not the evidence suggested that they could have established joint ability at acceptable cost. On the other hand, if they attempted (and failed) to pursue a collective option even though their evidence suggested that they did not have joint ability, then they really had no collective obligation in the first place. In pursuing futile collective options, agents may be forgoing other collectively or individually available optimal options. This may mean that they fail to do what they really ought to have done.

5.1 Individual (Contributory) Obligations

If agents facing a joint-necessity scenario do have a collective obligation – what exactly does such an obligation imply? At this point let me return to the beginning of our discussion and to the suggestion that a collective obligation attaches to the group members jointly.

What this means in practice is that once conscientious agents have established that they have a collective obligation they will have to find out what it is they individually (and collectively) need to do to discharge that obligation. Group members' contributory obligations may go beyond the performance of their individual contributory tasks. Moreover, they may not be required to perform any task at all, for instance, when it is clear that other group members are already doing what is required to secure the joint good. It may also require them to do one thing, figure out the next step, then do the next thing, and so forth. That is, it may require them to perform a series (or sets or patterns) of actions, only the first of which may be known to them at the beginning.

As I mentioned earlier, when it comes to distributive actions, agents would often be in a position to infer their individual contributory obligations independently, as is the case in the *Housemates* scenario and in the aforementioned modified *Hikers* scenario where participants in an experiment must decide independently whether or not to press a button that will release the trapped man (provided both participants choose to press it).

At this point it is important to return to our between different types of joint-necessity cases (Table 5.1). To remind the reader: a joint-necessity case is a case where in order to produce what is morally optimal the actions (or omissions)[1] of at least two agents are required.

- Let x be the minimal number of agents necessary for achieving the required outcome or performing the collective action.
- Let y be the number of available agents who can contribute to the action or the outcome.
- Let z be the maximum number of agents who can contribute to the action or the outcome.[2]

Table 5.1

Strict joint necessity		Wide joint necessity			No joint necessity				
$x > 1$					$x = 1$				
$x = y$		$x < y$			$x = y$		$x < y$		
$y = z$	$y < z$	$y < z$	$y = z$	$y > z$	$y = z$	$y < z$	$y < z$	$y = z$	$y > z$

A version of Table 5.1 was previously published in Schwenkenbecher, A. (2017). Gemeinsame Hilfspflichten, Weltarmut und kumulative Handlungen. *Zeitschrift für Praktische Philosophie*, 4(1), 123–150.

Strict joint necessity is present where an outcome need not only be established jointly by several agents but where the number of available agents (y) equals the number of minimally necessary agents (x). Hikers, for instance, is a strict joint-necessity case: it takes at least two agents to lift the tree and there exactly two agents available. For strict joint necessity it is the case that the success of the collective action (or of producing the collective outcome) is counterfactually dependent on each individual agent's cooperation. This means that each individual agent is unilaterally able to undermine the collective effort.

Wide joint necessity is present where there are more available agents (y) than minimally necessary agents (x). *Commuters* is a wide joint-necessity case: not every single one of the commuters on the platform has to push against the train for it to tilt. Likewise, if in *hikers* there where three potential helpers, then we would be facing a wide joint-necessity case. Characteristically, in such cases the success of the collective endeavour is not counterfactually dependent on the cooperation of *each* agent. No agent can undermine the collective effort single-handedly, but agents can jointly undermine the collective effort.

Most of our real-world, large-scale collective action problems are in fact wide joint-necessity cases.[3] However, it is important not to confuse such cases with those where the threshold for success is merely vague. What I mean by that is cases where we are not sure exactly how many people it takes in order to achieve a collective outcome (epistemic vagueness) or where it is simply not possible to establish how many people *exactly* it takes (genuine or metaphysical vagueness). I take it that mitigating climate change and limiting the global temperature increase to a maximum of 2°C is a problem that displays both types of vagueness. The *commuters* example, in contrast, will only be epistemically vague: individual commuters do not to know how many people it takes to tilt the train. In any case, I am assuming that in addition to that figure being unknown to the individual commuter, she may well be unaware of whether or not she is facing a wide or a strict joint-necessity scenario. If agents have reason to believe that they are facing a strict joint-necessity case, then they each have contributory obligations.

Further, we need to also distinguish cases according to how many agents can maximally contribute to an action or outcome. Imagine that in *Hikers* maximally two people can jointly lift the tree at a time. If there are two people present, then there is strict joint necessity $(x = y = z)$. If there are three or more agents available to assist, some of them need not contribute: $x < y > z$. Necessarily, in such cases, two agents bear the entire cost of the operation while the third need not do anything. The fact that more agents are available than are able in principle to contribute will usually increase coordination cost, especially if it jeopardises the collective endeavour when too many agents try to contribute. Perhaps surprisingly, then, collective endeavours may be more likely to fail when there are more potential contributors.[4]

I have included a third column for cases without joint necessity for completeness' sake. Where a case does not strictly require cooperation (i.e. where it is no joint-necessity case), individual agents may still be morally required to contribute, but for reasons of fairness: it may be required to ease the burden on the other agent rather than leave them to shoulder the whole burden of producing a morally desirable outcome. In other words, where more agents are available than minimally necessary to produce an outcome or good a principle of fairness may require 'surplus' agents to contribute in order to spread the burden more evenly.

Take as an example a variation of *Hikers* where I am able to lift the tree on my own. You may still be required to do a part in the lifting. This may be because, naturally, the duty to lift the tree in such a case would simply fall on both of us and by default we should distribute that burden evenly. I will not discuss these types of obligations here, however, and restrict myself to pointing out that the collective approach to our obligations in such cases is intuitively appealing. Everyday examples of duties that are held in common while lacking joint necessity include co-parenting or sharing housework. Thinking that such duties are collective by default can justify and explain individual duties to contribute to these collective endeavours, while an individualist approach would fail to do so.

Image 5.1 Mountain Lodge

But issues of fairness and just distribution also arise in strict joint-necessity cases. It may be difficult to separate shares in cases like *Hikers* or *Commuters*, but take the following case:

> [*Mountain Lodge*] Five people are staying overnight at a remote lodge in the mountains. They were dropped there by helicopter and they will be picked up by helicopter the next day. They are cut off from the rest of the world (no phone, no internet). At the dinner table, one of them pulls out a knife and threatens to kill another lodger unless the other three pay her $1,000 on the spot. Attempting to disarm her would very likely result in the death of her hostage and is therefore not an option. None of the three remaining lodgers has $1,000, but between the three of them they do. They pay the demanded sum to the aggressor and she lets her victim go.

This is a strict joint-necessity case (all three need to pitch in) and arguably one where three of the lodgers have a collective obligation to hand over the demanded sum. How much should each of them contribute? Assume for simplicity's sake that each has $450 on them. Should two of them hand over all they have and the third gives $100? Does it matter?

This question is ultimately about how the burden of individual contributory duties should be distributed among group members should the question of distribution arise, that is, should there be an opportunity to adjust and perhaps negotiate the burdens' distribution. In many urgent joint-necessity cases there may be no such opportunity.

I think that the question of burden-distribution, while morally relevant, is subordinate here.[5] By that I mean that an unjust distribution of burdens need not undermine a collective obligation (Miller 2011; Schwenkenbecher 2013a; Karnein 2014). In her work on responsibility and social connection, Iris Marion Young has made some headway towards how to distribute contributory duties for combating (structural) injustice, identifying a set of parameters for determining these responsibilities, while also leaving open the question of how much weight to give each of them. In her earlier work (2004), there are three parameters: connection, power and privilege (pp. 385ff). In her 2011 book, *Responsibility for Justice*, there are four: power, privilege, interest and collective ability (pp. 144ff). I will not discuss these parameters in detail but merely add that, arguably, one's competing obligations and (prior) commitments ought to play a role as well.[6]

Unfairness in the distribution of individual burdens may sometimes permit unilateral withdrawal from the collaboration, but not where one's defection would result in an injustice (Schwenkenbecher 2013a). For instance, it may be overall permissible to withdraw (or decrease) one's contribution to a collective farewell present for a colleague in case other colleagues are not contributing their fair share. But this move seems less permissible where someone's life is jeopardised by my refusal to shoulder an unfair share, as would be the case in *Hikers* or *Mountain lodge*. In other words, if agents jointly hold an obligation then they may sometimes be required to take up the slack left by other agents – be it because these defect or because they take on less than their fair share. I see it as an advantage of the collective obligations approach that it makes sense of slack-taking in a way that the individualist approach would not. The reason why I sometimes have to take up the slack left by others is that we shared an obligation to do something together in the first place. Just because the other does less than they should does not get me off the hook. The willing group members may still have to ensure that the desired outcome is produced (Schwenkenbecher 2013a; Karnein 2014). That is, I disagree with Liam Murphy's view that we only ever have to contribute our 'fair' share to collective endeavours (Murphy 2000).

Let me once more return to membership obligations in wide-necessity cases. The discussion so far has made it clear that the collective obligations approach will yield the following result in cases of wide joint necessity: if there are more agents available than minimally required to perform the desired action or to produce the morally optimal goal then those who need not contribute are not off the hook. Rather, they have the same obligation to see to it that the collective outcome is achieved just like every other agent who is covered by the collective obligation. This may require them to act or to refrain from acting, depending on the circumstances. Further, if several agents together hold a duty the default should be that whatever burden the duty imposes should be distributed fairly or else agents should be compensated for unavoidable unfair burden distributions (Schwenkenbecher 2013a).

Take the following variation of *Hikers:* you and *two* of your friends encounter the trapped man. Now there are three available helpers and only two are required to lift the tree. In this case it would be arbitrary to ascribe the collective duty to assist to any dyad of helpers. Or, in other words, assuming that all three are similarly situated and able to help, there is no reason to ascribe the obligation to any sub-group of two. Because every reason to do so would be arbitrary, we should ascribe the obligation to all three. The three have to establish how to distribute that obligation and they may or may not decide that all three or only two of them should help. Importantly, if it is the case that maximally two can help, the third person may have a duty to compensate the other two for their efforts. In fact, we regularly compensate others in this way. Say you go camping as part of a group of four – if two people prepare meals for everybody, the other two could reasonably be expected to take on other tasks such as doing the dishes, roughly equivalent in cost. By taking on a share of the burden we acknowledge the collective nature of our activity.

Our discussion shows that our individual contributory obligations are highly context-dependent and are not necessarily fixed by the collective duty. That is, there is a sense in which the collective nature of a duty generates a particular kind of latitude with regard to individual contributory duties.

Let me now move to a feature of collective obligations that has not been explicitly discussed yet. So far, most of the cases I have presented are *fixed-sum cases*. What I mean by that is the following: in each of these cases, the good (or the outcome) to be achieved has a binary success criterion. Either the good is produced or not. There is no partial production of the good or outcome in question – it cannot be supplied in degrees.

For instance, the hikers or the commuters either free the trapped person or they do not. In *Housemates*, either the house is clean at all times or not. And in *Mountain Lodge*, either the $1,000 ransom is paid or not. Or take a real-world example: the outcome of a referendum about a certain political decision, such as the 2016 Brexit referendum, is a fixed-sum good. Either a certain outcome (a majority vote to leave the European Union or to remain part of it) is achieved or it is not achieved. Having 49% of people vote in favour of remaining within the EU did not achieve the outcome of remaining in the EU *to some extent*. It did not achieve that outcome *at all*.

But many (collectively and individually producible) goods are not like that: they come in degrees. Take this variation of the mountain lodge ransom case: perhaps instead of paying $1,000, the three lodgers are told by the kidnapper that the more they pay the less will the victim suffer. In other words, the more money is handed over, the sooner will her tormentor release the victim. Here the desired outcome comes in degrees: it is best if the victim be released instantly, but there is still value in her being released after a short while. In contrast, the person attempting to lift the tree on her own in *Hikers* produces no value whatsoever. Her individual efforts are in vain unless she is supported by the other hiker. While joint necessity concerns *the manner in which* an outcome needs to be produced, namely jointly, the distinction between fixed-sum good cases and incremental cases concerns *what kind of outcome* needs to be produced.

It would seem that it is easier to determine the appropriate level of individual contribution to a fixed-sum good because there is a clear limit as to what must be jointly produced. In contrast, when we need to jointly produce a good that comes in degrees, it will usually be harder to establish how much we need to contribute to that good. However, this need not especially worry us here, because this problem is not unique to collective obligations.

There is another aspect of collective obligations, which is relevant to determining contributory obligations: whether they are strongly or weakly collective. All collective obligations are characterised by normative primacy of the collective level. The more strongly collective our obligations are, the greater are what I call *normative links between group members*.

Normative primacy of the collective level: In proposing that moral obligations can sometimes be collective in nature, several scholars suggest that the collective level is to be considered primary and the question of individual obligations as secondary (Isaacs 2011; Schwenkenbecher 2014b; and Wringe 2016). This reflects the fact that collective obligations are regularly multiply realisable (Tamminga and Hindriks 2020). It is the collective obligation that gives rise to the individual contributory obligations (Wringe 2016). Framing the idea of normative primacy of the collective level in terms of reasons for action, one might say that a collectively optimal pattern of action can give individuals group-based (or pattern-based) reasons for action even where their individual actions make no direct causal contribution to the realisation of that pattern, for instance when the outcome is overdetermined (Woodard 2003, Woodard 2011). Alternatively, one might say that an obligation is collective when individual agents have reason to deliberate from the point of view of the group (Schwenkenbecher 2019). In other words, the normative primacy of the collective level could be interpreted as metaphysical, logical, functional, or deliberative.

Normative links between agents: Another way to understand the importance of the obligations' collective character is to point to special normative links between members of such collectives. For a set of agents to collectively have an obligation may require them to take responsibility for the success of the collective action, for instance by coordinating the joint activity and generating the kind of group knowledge required for the group members to be able to fulfil their contributory actions. Further, it may mean that group members have to pick up the slack left by others. All this, however, presupposes that certain epistemic conditions hold within the group, for example, that information is shared in the right way. Finally, group members may also be linked by considerations of fairness in the distribution of contributory roles.

Normative links between group members will add strength to our obligations. Small-scale joint-necessity cases will regularly feature such links. This may be crucial in putting both rational and psychological pressure onto agents to actually discharge those duties. Such links will strengthen moral reasons and moral resolve, potentially turning pro tanto into all-out duties and making certain collective actions not just epistemically salient but normatively salient. In turn, they change our contributory obligations within the group. In contrast, our obligations to perform distributive actions would usually be weakly collective only.

5.2 Failures to Comply With Collective Obligations

What does it mean to violate a collective obligation? Note that if we adhere to the prospective view of obligation, this can only mean that we did not do what our best bet was in the circumstances. This could be because we did not choose the best option or because we did nothing at all and ignored the problem we were faced with. Failures to comply with a collective obligation may be due to mistakes in moral reasoning, deliberate defection, or collective inaction. I will not discuss mistakes in moral reasoning here in any detail. Suffice it to say that these can be manifold and they can arise at both the individual and the collective level. They may be excusable or not. Further, agents can try to do what is best but fail to achieve the desired outcome. Such collective failure may or may not be their fault. If they are not at fault, this means that they either discharged the obligation by trying (albeit failing) or else that the task was too difficult to warrant a collective obligation in the first place.

Defection by individual agents (or groups thereof) may render collective efforts impossible: because it takes two people to lift the tree off the hiker, one hiker's defection will unilaterally prevent the rescue. Perhaps she simply refuses to help without having a good reason. What happens to the hikers' collective obligation in such cases? We might be tempted to say that because they now no longer have joint ability to assist, the hikers no longer have an obligation to assist. This would imply saying that they are unable to assist if (and because) one of them is unwilling to contribute. Is one's own willingness to contribute a necessary condition for having the ability to contribute? I should not think so. This is different if an agent has in fact removed herself from the scene in ways that make it actually impossible for her to contribute. In that case they no longer have joint ability. But if potential helpers are present at the scene and simply refuse to help (for lack of caring appropriately) they are nonetheless able to assist.

However, if one is stubbornly refusing to participate, it becomes unreasonable for the other to continue we-framing the scenario and to take the collective option of lifting the tree seriously. The willing agent may try to persuade the defector to do her share. Once she is certain that the collective option is not available she is required to do whatever is the best of her individually available options.

But is the defector off the hook? By refusing to help she has made the option of collectively assisting the trapped man unavailable. It might seem then that the hikers are not in violation of a duty precisely because they no longer have joint ability. Consequently, the defector is not in violation of a duty to contribute, or is she? She is, in fact, no more off the hook than an individual agent is off the hook for refusing to discharge her individual duty. For as long as she is able to reverse her refusal and to take part in the joint action she is still failing in her duty if she refuses to contribute. Further, she is in violation of a duty as soon as she refuses (i.e. assuming, of course, that she has good reason to rank the collective option highest and no good reason to refuse to contribute). However, the question is *which* duty does she violate with her refusal: *her* duty to contribute or *their* collective duty to free the trapped man? It seems odd to suggest that one agent can be in violation of an obligation that is collectively held. Rather, she would be in violation of her contributory duties, therewith undermining the collective obligation.

In sum, when an agent unilaterally defects they violate their contributory obligation. We can distinguish two cases:

1) Strict joint necessity, as in *Hikers*: her defection is sufficient for undermining the group effort. She is then responsible (and arguably morally blameworthy) for the failure of producing the collective outcome, even if she does not, strictly speaking, violate the collective duty, because it was not hers.

2) Wide joint necessity as in *Commuters*:

   a) Her defection does not undermine the group effort. In fact, the group effort goes ahead. In this case she violates her contributory duty as a duty to make an appropriate contribution consistent with the success of the collective effort unless or until sufficiently many others take actions that guarantee collective success.

   b) Her defection does not *uniquely* undermine the group effort. However, a sufficiently large number of agents in the plurality defect, too, so that the group effort fails. In this case each defecting agent is in violation of her contributory duty and if their subset is large enough that they could have ensured the success of the collective outcome then they are jointly in violation of their collective obligation, too. They are also, arguably, jointly blameworthy for the failure of the collective endeavour and each is individually blameworthy for failing in her contributory duty. I will say more about blameworthiness in a moment.

It may be the case, though, that one agent's evidence differs from another's and as a result they do not rank the (same) collective option highest. In that case, did they have a collective obligation to assist in the first place? If they conscientiously availed themselves of the evidence and on that basis ranked the available options differently (or deliberated over different sets of options) then my view commits me to saying that they had no collective obligation in the first place. This is because their moral deliberation was unlikely to produce the same result. Or, to put it differently, if epistemic circumstances differ sufficiently between agents, no collective obligation arises. However, keep in mind that we can often influence the other person's epistemic circumstances. We can signal willingness, we can share evidence, and we can engage in joint deliberation. We can thus generate collective obligations where previously there were none.

5.3 Joint Blameworthiness

We regularly blame individuals when they fail to contribute to collective endeavours without a valid excuse or other mitigating circumstances. If you refuse to help me lift the tree, for instance, then you are responsible and blameworthy for our failure to assist the trapped man, because your defection unilaterally undermines our joint ability. But even in a wide joint-necessity case where their contribution is not, strictly speaking, necessary, agents may still attract blame if they refuse to contribute. Suppose that three hikers encounter the trapped man, but one of them categorically refuses to contribute but the other two lift the tree together. What has the defector done wrong and what would we blame her for? It seems that we are blaming her for failing to display the appropriate kind of willingness to contribute.

But consider a further variation where a maximum of two people can contribute to lifting the tree such that the third person (whoever it is) need not or perhaps must not participate. If one of them categorically refuses she still fails in her duty to be disposed to contribute even though that refusal does not undermine the success of the collective endeavour. The defector – in unilaterally exempting herself from the group endeavour – fails to display the right kind of impartiality (Cullity 2004) and to be appropriately responsive to the demands of the situation (Björnsson 2014). That *one of them* must not contribute does not condone *her* unilateral withdrawal. It does not seem right that she should unilaterally decide that she is the one who will not contribute while the other two do.

Imagine now that all three refuse to contribute. It seems that we would want to blame them for more than merely for failing to display an appropriate willingness to contribute. Rather, if all three defect they all are blameworthy for failing to assist the person in need. But what if two out of three defect? Their combined defection undermines joint ability and as such guarantees collective failure. Who is the appropriate object of blame and other reactive attitudes in such circumstances? I argue that group members can be *jointly* blameworthy. If all three hikers in the previous example fail to lift the tree when they easily could have and arguably should have collaborated then they have jointly violated their collective obligation and individually violated their individual (contributory) obligations. If no mitigating reasons apply they are jointly to blame for their collective failure and individually for the individual failure. Naturally, the two types of blame – collective and individual – can come apart. That is, agents can be jointly blameworthy for having failed to discharge a collective obligation even if not every agent in the group is individually blameworthy – they may have done their part. This is the case where only two of them defect and so the group effort fails, even though the third person was willing to contribute and tried.

I believe that this approach has an advantage over the individualist approach to obligations (and blameworthiness). Individual defections in strict joint-necessity cases unilaterally undermine the success of the collective endeavour, which makes allocations of blameworthiness straightforward. However, in wide joint-necessity cases it is not true that any particular individual's defection would frustrate collective success. Individualist accounts struggle to account for the defector's wrongdoing in such cases, because individual defection – taken by itself – does not undermine the collective goal. This is true of every single agent in the plurality, so to absolve individual defectors from wrongdoing and blame in wide joint-necessity cases is equivalent to condoning collective defection. However, collectivists can point to the collective obligation as giving rise to individual contributory obligations and unilateral defectors are in violation both. On my view, when violating collective obligations, agents may be collectively blameworthy, that is, they share the blame.

An additional difficulty arises where agents differ in their assessments of the available options and therewith fail to acquire a collective obligation. If this is due to differences in evidence, agents may well be in a position to resolve this in the course of interdependent team-reasoning, but not in the case of independent we-reasoning. If it is due to different value judgements this may be rectified in the course of team-reasoning. Otherwise, blame should lie with the person who failed in her epistemic obligations or who grossly misjudged the value of available options. An agent may further become aware that the other agent(s) are not in a position to rank the same collective option highest. In that case there is no collective obligation; however, the knowing agent may be able to generate one by sharing her information. If she fails to inform others, she may – again – be blamed for failing in her epistemic duties. Finally, there will be cases of reasonable moral disagreement. Agents may be excused for joint failure resulting from such disagreement and remain blameless.

5.4 The Knowledge Condition

In order for two or more agents to share an obligation, do they have to be fairly certain that the other(s) will do their part? If I think it unlikely that others contribute (perhaps because they ranked options differently or because they are not morally motivated agents), would I have an obligation to contribute regardless? If not, then that would seem to severely limit the cases where we have collective obligations.

Let us take a closer look at the role of probability considerations in moral deliberation. It appears that most collective obligations ultimately depend on individual agents' assessment of the probability of establishing the joint endeavour. And if so, would this not make the notion of collective obligations almost irrelevant for large-scale collective action scenarios because agents would usually lack the certainty that others will contribute? I argue that this question is imprecise. An initial assessment of probability takes place in the course of we-framing, that is, in the course of considering available options. Where evidence suggests that collective options are (most likely) not available, a reasonable agent has no grounds for we-framing.

In some cases there is no instant feedback concerning others' willingness to contribute. Agents may therefore be excused for failing to contribute where the stakes for unilateral contribution are high. In repeat scenarios they may be excused for opting out down the track. Where agents can communicate and instant feedback as to others' willingness to contribute is available this problem is less severe.

The idea that in order for us to have obligations to contribute to a collectively available option we need to hold the belief that others will contribute was, for example, defended by Derek Parfit, one of the first moral philosophers to think about collective moral action problems. In *Reasons and Persons*, Parfit puts forward a collective principle of beneficence:

When (1) the best outcome would be the one in which people are benefited most, and
(2) each of the members of some group could act in a certain way, and
(3) they would benefit these other people if enough of them act in this way, and
(4) they would benefit these people most if they all act in this way, and
(5) *each of them both knows these facts and believes that enough of them will act in this way*, then
(6) each of them ought to act in this way. . . . Even if each of them benefits no one, they together can greatly benefit these other people.
                                                              (1984: 77, my emphasis)

Parfit's suggestion is that duties to contribute to cooperative endeavours can arise even where each contribution makes no difference or benefits no one directly or perceivably as is the case in large-scale wide joint-necessity cases, for instance. Rather, we are obligated to contribute where we know that there is an existing cooperative or collective endeavour, which will produce the best outcome out of a range of alternative options. Parfit defends the view that failing to contribute is wrong even if our contribution or lack thereof does not improve or diminish the good, for instance, when we free-ride on an existing collective good.

According to Parfit, we only have obligations to contribute if we *know* that enough other people will (condition 5). But can we ever motivate obligations to contribute when there is no such certainty as to how others will act? Take the question of reducing one's individual carbon footprint: as a matter of fact none of us know whether enough other people will reduce their emissions. In fact, we have reason to assume that they will not. Or return to the commuters: they may not have any beliefs about whether or not enough of their fellow commuters are taking action. If Parfit is correct, it is unlikely that there could ever be large-scale collective (or, as I will call them, 'massively shared') obligations in loose groups with fairly weak epistemic links between members. In principle, there are two ways around the problem that Parfit's conditions pose for our argument concerning obligations to mitigate climate change: a weak and a strong solution. Their availability depends on whether or not the conditions are necessary or merely sufficient. Let me start with the weaker assumption and then move to the stronger one.

The claim made by Parfit is a conditional claim. If conditions (1–5) apply then each member of a group has a duty to contribute to the best outcome. If the conditions are jointly sufficient, rather than necessary, we can argue that even if condition (5) – the condition that we believe that enough others will act in the required way – does not obtain, we may still have obligations to act in the way that collectively produces the best outcome.

However, if Parfit's conditions are individually necessary – and that is what I understand them to be – a failure to have the right beliefs results in a cancellation of the duty to act in a way that is collectively optimal. On this reading, then, individual agents would not be required to reduce their carbon footprint, contribute to global poverty relief, or maintain social distancing while there is uncertainty about others' actions and they may also be off the hook for failing to contribute in cases like *Commuters*.

It follows from what I discussed in earlier chapters (in particular in Chapter 4) that we should reject Parfit's knowledge condition as too strong. Pattern-based moral reasons for action apply even in the absence of strong beliefs concerning others' contributions. A weaker, and in my view more plausible, condition would release agents from collective (and contributory) pro tanto obligations if they believe that *not enough others* will act.

But let me provide additional reasons for why it might not be desirable to have such a strong epistemic condition as part of our account of collective obligations, using the example of collective carbon footprint reductions. Individual acts of mitigation may well have no (discernible and direct) impact on the overall concentration of GHGs in the atmosphere, but they could well have an indirect impact by making a difference to *other people's actions*. The same would apply to the individual commuters in our previous example. Parfit's condition demands that each individual potential contributor believe that enough of them will contribute before she is required to act. Even if we think that a strong knowledge condition is warranted such a condition will be more plausible if requiring that each group member (have reason to) believe that if she herself contributes enough of the others are likely to act in the same way. For instance, individual agent's carbon footprint reductions are most likely to have an impact on whether other agents reduce their carbon footprint if those who implement them are trend-setters or otherwise public figures who share information widely and are able to inspire people to change their behaviour.[7] In other words, we need not take other agents' mitigation efforts simply as a given. Our individual contributory actions may well influence their willingness to contribute and indirectly persuade them to follow our example. And *if* one's actions are likely to influence the actions of others, then by our very contribution to solving the collective action dilemma we can make it more likely for them to contribute and more likely for the dilemma to be solved. The greater an agent's potential impact on public opinion and other people's attitudes and actions, the greater their reason for contributing to a collective endeavour even in the absence of any certainty concerning other agents' contributions. Further, the extent of such influence rather than being fixed can be increased by one's own efforts: there are ways of contributing to the collectively best outcome that make others' compliance more likely. And, last but not least, there may be situations in which we are permitted to coerce others into compliance (Øverland 2009). In sum, even where we believe that not enough others will contribute towards a collective endeavour we may still share an obligation to produce the corresponding outcome provided that we are in a position to effect (or increase) others' compliance.

To sum up, agents who are under a collective obligation have derivative individual obligations to establish and promote the collective endeavour. They may even permissibly use force to get other agents to comply. They can be *jointly blameworthy* in case of collective defection. For collective moral action problems with strict joint necessity the number of agents available to address the problem equals the number of agents minimally necessary to address it. For example, there is strict joint necessity if it takes at least two people to operate a particular machine and there are exactly two people available to do so. One agent's defection suffices to thwart the collective endeavour. An example from International Relations is the sanctioning of humanitarian interventions by the UN Security Council. Each member must vote in favour ("contribute") in order for an intervention to be sanctioned. Wide joint necessity exists where the number of available agents exceeds the minimally necessary number of contributors and most large-scale collective action cases are wide joint-necessity scenarios. Importantly, collective obligations give rise to individual contributory obligations for all agents in the respective group, even for those who need not (and also those who must not) take action.

Notes

1. Omissions are intentional refrainings, as opposed to inactions, which are unintentional. I will ignore the discussion on whether or not omissions are actions (see, e.g., Talja, J. (1985). On the Logic of Omissions. *Synthese*, 65(2), 235–248.)
2. It might be that it is not feasible for more than z number of agents to contribute to the outcome or it might even undermine the success of the joint action.
3. One of the notorious exceptions is the sanctioning of humanitarian interventions where each member of the UN Security Council must vote in favour (or contribute) in order for the intervention to go ahead: a strict joint-necessity case.
4. Importantly, this is different from the so-called bystander effect, where the presence of other agents and potential helpers sometimes jeopardizes people's willingness to assist someone in need.
5. Though I should say that it may play a role for converting pro tanto into all-out obligations. If I have two competing obligations, one of which requires me to make a disproportionate sacrifice (disproportionate in relation to the contributions of others), then this may be reason to discharge the other obligation instead (provided I cannot discharge both).
6. I have argued in the past that *capacity*, *moral correlation* and *commitments of oneself and other agents* should play a role. Schwenkenbecher, A. (2011). Punishing Collective Agents. Non-Compliance with Moral Duties by States (Response to Toni Erskine). *Ethics & International Affairs*, online exclusive.
7. See Cristina Bicchieri's work on trendsetters in Bicchieri, C. (2017). *Norms in the Wild: How to Diagnose, Measure, and Change Social Norms*. New York: Oxford University Press.

6 A Comparison of Existing Accounts of Collective Obligations

How are we to judge whether any particular theory of collective obligations is a good one or is, in fact, preferable to another? In the following, I give an overview of current approaches, discuss their merits and explain how they differ from mine.[1]

6.1 Meta-Criteria for a Theory of Collective Moral Obligations

What exactly should we expect from a theory of collective moral obligations apart from a general level of plausibility? Should it equally cover small-scale and large-scale collective action scenarios? Should it help us solve collective moral action problems?

I briefly discussed some of these meta-criteria in Chapter 1. There, I suggested that our theory would ideally confirm our moral intuitions for those cases where these are fairly strong – in simple small-scale joint-necessity cases. It should *harmonise with our basic and derivative moral intuitions*. I appreciate that the use of moral intuitions in ethical theorising is somewhat contested but will nonetheless assume that, ideally, our account should confirm these intuitions.

I also mentioned previously that a theory of collective moral obligations must be *practically action-guiding*. It must clearly indicate the right course of action for a given agent or sets of agents in a given collective action scenario.

Further, such a theory should to some extent *explain tension* between collectively available options (e.g. climate change mitigation) and individually available options (e.g. the enjoyment of activities that produce GHG emissions). It should go some length towards explaining why we feel on occasion torn between the two.

One might further think it desirable that an account of collective obligations harmonises with generally accepted principles of moral theory, in particular, the *agency principle* and the *capacity principle*. While some scholars argue that there are good reasons to give it up (Wringe 2010), an account of collective obligations that does not violate the agency principle would have the advantage that it could be endorsed even by those who would like to hang on to the principle.

The capacity principle states that if an agent ought to do x, this implies that she can do x, and if she cannot do x, then she need not do x. Again, the principle that 'ought implies can' is perhaps less clear than it appears at first glance (see, for instance, Lawford-Smith 2015). A plausible account of collective obligations must engage with this principle.

Further, we might prefer accounts that are ontologically as frugal as possible (*ontological parsimony*).

Finally, there are several desiderata for accounts of collective obligations and responsibility that their advocates, sometimes implicitly and sometimes explicitly, endorse.

Also mentioned previously are the following two desiderata. First, there is the *unification desideratum*. Scholars often defend collectivist approaches as a way of unifying our obligations to act towards collective endeavours (Ashford 2013; Schroeder 2014; Wringe 2016). The idea is that collective obligations (usually) give rise to members' obligations. Understanding the collective level as primary furthermore helps to make sense of individual obligations of the members, and it can solve coordination problems.

The second is the *moral improvement desideratum*. This is one of the main motivators of proposals to understand some duties as collective: it helps overcome the *individual impotence objection*, which is the view that I do not have a duty to contribute to a collective endeavour where my contribution makes no perceptible difference (Parfit 1984; Pinkert 2015). An account of collective obligations is meant to resolve collective moral action and deliberation dilemmas.

Finally, there is an aspiration which one might call the *moral phenomenology desideratum*. Though this criterion is less frequently expressed, it hints at something important. Bill Wringe suggested that considering some obligations to be collective better corresponds to how we perceive our obligations than a purely individualist account. In fact, he claims, "It is a virtue of a view within theoretical ethics that it vindicate a large amount of the phenomenology of actual situations, and views which do so are to be preferred, *ceteris paribus*, to views which do not" (2016: 477).

Here is the complete list of desiderata:

- Action-guidance
- Explanatory power
- Harmony with moral intuitions
- Harmony with existing moral principles
- Ontological parsimony
- Unification of theory
- Moral improvement
- Moral phenomenology

Now that we have established along which lines we may compare different theoretical approaches; we can look at those on offer in a bit more detail. At this point let me offer a rough categorisation of the different theories of collective moral obligations that have been put forward to date. Take the earlier-mentioned scenario of the two-person shallow-pond case. Let us assume that we agree with the basic intuition that the passers-by should rescue the child and that none of them can do it on their own.

Whose duty is it, then, to rescue the child? The difficulty to answer this question in a straightforward way is what motivates the need for a theory of collective moral obligations in the first place. The duty to rescue the child cannot be the duty of any of the individual bystanders, because none of them is capable of rescuing the child on her own. It is furthermore obvious that the two bystanders are not a so-called group agent. That is, they do not meet the criteria so far put forward as necessary conditions for group agency by the aforementioned authors such as Peter French (1984), Christian List and Philip Pettit (2011), or Toni Erskine (2003). They seem to be a different kind of group. And yet they can act together, and, intuitively, we would like to ascribe to them the obligation to rescue the child. Similarly, some would like to ascribe the duty to mitigate climate change (or, at least, to close the emissions gap) to the global affluent, as several authors have done (Blok et al. 2012; Schwenkenbecher 2013a, 2014a; Wynes and Nicholas 2017; Björnsson forthcoming).

This problem of ascribing the moral obligation to do what is only collectively possible to some suitable agent or group of agents is solved by different theories in different ways. I will start by discussing so-called individualist theories, according to which collective obligations are just obligations of individuals to do something individually, such as contributing to a shared goal or to forming a group agent, provided that (an)other person(s) cooperate(s) in some way. According to the authors defending this view, joint-necessity cases like the two-person shallow-pond case will trigger duties for each individual passer-by to enable, promote or foster collective action towards rescuing the child in some way. I take Stephanie Collins (2013)[2] and Holly Lawford-Smith (2015) to put forward a view of this kind.

The second group of theories advocates collective moral obligations as obligations *of* collective entities: that is, as obligations of certain groups. According to these authors, the passers-by *as a group* hold an obligation to rescue the child. They are some kind of putative group agent, or potential group agent, and that agent holds the obligation. I take Virginia Held (1970), Larry May (1992), Bill Wringe (2010, 2016), Tracy Isaacs (2011), David Killoren and Bekka Williams (2013), Toni Erskine (2014) and Sean Aas (2015) to hold views of this type. In a sense, these theories postulate the existence of a group agent (or something akin to a group agent) that is capable of holding duties despite failing to show the structural elements of collective moral agency as defended by authors such as List and Pettit (2011) and Toni Erskine (2003).

Finally, I will address theories that advocate the idea of 'joint' duties – the view that individual agents can hold moral obligations jointly (Pinkert 2014; Schwenkenbecher 2013b, 2014b). According to this kind of view, the two passers-by hold the obligation to rescue the child jointly or together. My own view, which falls into this category (as does Felix Pinkert's), construes the 'ought' as a joint imperative or a plural normative property. Or else, as Gunnar Björnsson (2014) puts it, agents can "share" an obligation. I will then briefly sketch how my own view avoids many of the shortcomings of the other views portrayed here.

6.2 Reductionist Accounts

One might think that the most obvious way to spell out the obligations involved in cases like the two-person shallow-pond scenario, climate change or global poverty is as *individual duties* to make a contribution to solving the respective problem, or else as duties to team up with others or to act in a way that is morally optimising. There are several such approaches which predominantly spell out moral obligations vis-à-vis collective action problems as conditional obligations of individual agents.

According to Stephanie Collins (2013), we can have *duties to collectivise*. In our example, the two passers-by each ought to work towards forming a group agent, which can rescue the child (in Collins' original example it is indeed a group of bystanders who must collaborate to rescue a drowning person). Or, put differently, *a* and *b* ought to each do *y* (form a group agent) with a view to the group agent doing *x* (rescue the drowning person).

This proposal seems to operate within the constraints of commonly accepted principles. It does not breach the agency principle – only agents have duties on this account, for instance. However, there are two possible ways of spelling out the duty to form a group agent: what is meant is that each passer-by ought to do what she deems necessary in order to form a group agent or else both ought to form a group agent. The latter action cannot be performed individually but only jointly. The former interpretation does not breach the capacity principle – and I assume that this is how Collins meant her case to work – while the latter does. However, note that on the former reading, which is in harmony with existing principles, the bystanders do not have a duty to assist the child (as this would be in breach of the capacity principle). If they fail to assist, they each have failed in taking the relevant steps towards forming a group agent. They have not failed (in a moral duty) to save the child. In fact, they had no obligation to save the child. The former reading, therefore, contradicts our basic intuition. If we think that one can only be retrospectively blamed for what one had a duty to do, then there is no blame to be apportioned for failing to assist the child, which contradicts our derivative intuition. The bystanders are only blameworthy for having failed in taking the required or appropriate steps towards forming a group agent. I think this makes Collins' view unsatisfying.

Further, it is at least unclear why the passers-by should form a group agent to save the drowning child. The presumption behind this requirement seems to be that only a group agent could save the child; that is, whenever agents intentionally collaborate in the way the passers-by do, if they rescue the child together they do in fact form a group agent. Now we may well call any plurality of agents who spontaneously collaborate (me and my colleague lifting a table together, for instance) a 'group agent', but why? Several authors have argued that such collaboration is best described as 'joint' or 'shared' action (Pettit and Schweikard 2006; Bratman 2014) and have distinguished it from the actions of incorporated (or constituted) agents as, for instance, described by List and Pettit in *Group Agency*. Why lump these two categories together? Why assume that a novel agent is formed when two people spontaneously collaborate? The motivation behind this could be a bias towards agency monism: any action that takes place must be clearly ascribable to *one* agent. But apart from a certain desire for tidiness in our social categories, little speaks in favour of agency monism. Also, individualist accounts that insist on describing the rescue as an action of a group agent add an ontological layer that is not needed. This is at odds with the desideratum of ontological parsimony.

Else, we might think of the bystanders' duties as conditional. One might think that each has an obligation to contribute to saving the child if she has reason to believe that the other one will contribute, because only in that case will her contribution make a difference for the better (as the example assumes that there is nothing she can individually do to make things better).

According to the simple conditional obligations view, each has an obligation to participate in rescuing the child if the other participates (or is willing to participate) in rescuing the child. Each passer-by has an obligation if the other makes an effort towards rescuing the child.

> [a] ought to x_a only if [b] x_bs and
> [b] ought to x_b only if [a] x_as.

While I am not aware of any scholar who put forward such an account of collective duties, it seems to be implied by individualist maximising act-utilitarianism. After all, you can maximise the good only if your friend contributes and vice versa.[3] I limit my commentary to pointing to a number of problems with conditional obligations, generally. First, all individualist accounts share the same problem – namely that they cannot motivate a duty to actually rescue the child (or to mitigate climate change or stop global poverty for that matter). So they fail to meet the 'moral improvement' desideratum and are at odds with the basic intuition. If you are willing to bite that bullet,[4] then these views may nonetheless be attractive to you.

Second, there is the problem of mutual release: if both agents simultaneously refuse to act, each makes it the case that the other has no duty to contribute. Hence, surprisingly, in that case none of them seems to have done anything wrong. Bob Goodin came up with a solution, which, while maintaining the conditionality of the obligation, avoids the mutual release problem (Goodin 2012). He proposes that each needs to make a commitment of the following kind: "I will if you will" and "I will if (you will if I will)" (ibid., p. 24). While I cannot discuss this proposal in detail here, one might wonder if complex conditionals fare well on our moral phenomenology desideratum, that is, whether or not agents perceive their commitments in joint-necessity scenarios as conditional.

Further, it is unclear whether conditional views are really action-guiding. If I have an obligation to assist only if you are willing to assist, then what do I do in scenarios when it is hard for me to find out if you are willing to assist? Take a two-person joint-necessity case that resembles a so-called hi-lo game. Let us assume, as we have assumed so far, that the best outcome is achieved if both passers-by rescue the child. There might be a second-best collective outcome though: both walk past the pond to their respective destinations and, as a result, arrive in time at their scheduled meetings. Surely, such an outcome has some value, even if it is significantly lower than that of rescuing the child. Now suppose that the worst cases are those where either passer-by attempts to rescue the child on their own. Not only will they not succeed, but they miss their meeting as well. Faced with this scenario, they may deliberate on what it is they should be doing: clearly, *if* the other person tries to rescue the child they, too, should try to rescue it. However, if the other one walks on, they too should walk on, at least from the point of view of maximising utility. What should they do? A conditional theory simply will not answer this question.

Finally, let me point to an argument against *logical* reductionism advanced by Allard Tamminga and Frank Hindriks. In "The Irreducibility of Collective Obligations" (2020), they argue that statements about collectives are not logically equivalent to conjunctions of statements about individuals. Therefore, group obligations do not reduce to member obligations. They provide a formal analysis of how fulfilling an individual obligation is neither necessary nor sufficient for fulfilling a member obligation.

6.3 Collective Moral Obligations as Obligations of Groups

Many of the problems of individualist accounts can be avoided if we are open to the possibility that the requirement to provide collective assistance in our exemplary case does not simply reduce to individual obligations. Let me turn to one of the earliest and most influential contributions to this debate: Virginia Held's discussion of the moral responsibility of random collectives. She argues that where "the action called for in a given situation is obvious to the reasonable person" (1970: 476) and the action must be performed jointly, then those who are in a position to jointly perform it can be held retrospectively morally responsible (and blamed) – as a group – for failing to do so. While her view is coined in terms of retrospective responsibility, I think we can treat it as making a point concerning forward-looking responsibility or obligations, too.

The problem is that when holding that a plurality (or 'random collection') of agents ought to do x together, as Held does, the underlying assumption seems to be that such pluralities of agents can hold moral obligations. That is, Held's view seems to be that groups of agents who do not form a group agent can hold moral duties.

Held's view then violates the *agency principle*. According to the agency principle, only moral agents can hold moral duties. The random collection consisting of the two passers-by (a conjunction or plurality of agents) is not in itself a moral agent. If the agency principle in this form is correct, then Held's view is thus problematic. Now one might think that the agency principle is false or else requires modification. I will not discuss this issue here but simply point to Bill Wringe's argument in favour of dropping the principle (Wringe 2010).

Held[5] has an alternative proposal for cases where the best course of (joint) action is not obvious to the reasonable person or salient. It is worth noting that Collins' approach is very similar to Held's alternative proposal. According to Held, in cases where a group agent or group action *proper* is required and the action called for is less obvious, the individual group members can potentially be held responsible for failing *to form a group*. That is, Held acknowledges that collective obligations may persist in cases where it is not immediately obvious what needs to be done. Note that there is also some ambiguity in the phrase "the action called for", for it can refer to the collective action or the individual contributory actions or both. I assume that Held refers to both.

In any case, Held argues that the *group itself* is responsible if its individual members fail to jointly act in the kind of collective assistance scenario she has in mind, though she does not seem to think of the 'random collection' in her example as a group agent in the strict sense. Toni Erskine writes: Held's

> argument and the particular time-sensitive, life-and-death examples that she invokes actually point toward an intermediary type of association that the members of her random collection have an obligation to form themselves into: an informal association, loosely organized

and capable of some deliberation leading to coordinated action, but lacking the organizational or decision-making trappings of structured institutions.

(Erskine 2014: 130)

Reflecting on this comment, we can see that for the kind of cases Held focuses on – namely bystanders overwhelming an attacker or rescuing someone from a collapsing building – no group agent in the strong sense is indeed required. However, there may be cases where the formation of such a group agent *is* necessary in order to prevent something morally bad from happening.

In any case, it is this intermediary type of association that Toni Erskine's position attempts to capture in her own work. In the context of international relations, Erskine has defended the view that so-called coalitions of the willing can have moral obligations. Its members are "temporarily united in pursuit of a common purpose, but the coalition itself lacks an established organisational and decision-making structure" (2014: 121). She argues:

If there is a duty to perform a particular action, and if individual agents can come together to perform this action when they could not have performed it individually, then they each have an obligation to contribute to establishing the type of group necessary for this duty to be discharged.

(p. 133)

It should be noted that Erskine's view refers to coalitions of states and non-state organisations but not to individuals. Here is how I – liberally – would adapt her approach to the realm of individual agents. On Erskine's account, if there is a duty to rescue the child and the passers-by can come together to do so, then they each have an obligation to contribute to establishing the kind of group needed for rescuing it. Put differently: the passers-by ought to each contribute to transforming their group so that they become capable of doing x.

Note that this view requires a certain kind of group to be formed – not a group agent – but a goal-oriented collective. Erskine thinks that all that is required of the individuals here is to act jointly. They need not form a – structured – group agent. This difference is reflected, for example, in the different way in which the coalition of the willing can be held responsible: responsibility ultimately distributes between the members of the group but does not sit at the level of the group as such, according to Erskine.

On this view, then, each of the passers-by has an obligation to each do what it takes to collaborate in assisting the child. In this sense, Erskine's is a version of the view that the individual agents need to take steps towards establishing joint ability.

However, to the extent that joint ability is all that is required, talking of 'groups' seems quite superfluous. Rather, it seems to be sufficient to say that the passers-by ought to each see to it that they are jointly capable of doing x.

Note, however, that there is a form of circularity in Erskine's proposal. She argues for a conditional: that *if there is a duty* to perform a particular action and that action cannot be performed individually then the individual agents have to transform the 'group' they constitute. However, there is obviously a problem with the antecedent of the conditional – the claim that there would be a duty to perform that action in the first place. Whose duty is it at the point in time where the individual agents have not yet formed a group capable of addressing the problem – or have otherwise made it possible that they could jointly act upon the problem? Erskine seems to be saying that if the group has a duty to do x, then the individuals in the group have a duty to enable joint action with regard to x. This would suggest that the loose group of individuals, or else the plurality or the conjunction of individuals, has a duty. Again, as with Held's position, this one violates the agency condition. And it seems to contradict Erskine's own view that the group as such is no appropriate addressee of such obligations. If we grant that, then there can be no duty to perform a certain action, even if the action (or outcome) may be morally desirable.

In short, I think Erskine's view is most plausible where it defends a duty on the individuals to collaborate and coordinate their actions. She rightfully says that this is a 'shared' or distributed responsibility – it rests on each of the participating individual agents. Her work partly draws on Larry May's works on collective responsibility: *Sharing Responsibility* and, especially, *The Morality of Groups*. However, most of May's discussion in both works is coined in terms of retrospective responsibility, rather than prospective responsibility or obligations, which is what I am concerned with here.

In *The Morality of Groups*, May emphasises that in mobs – large and unstructured collectives – it is the relationships between individuals that matter for determining their collective responsibility:

> My own view is that social groups should be analysed as individuals in relationships. Groups themselves do not exist in their own right; but the individuals who compose groups also are often not understandable as acting in isolation from one another.
>
> (May 1987: 9)

According to this kind of approach, the relationships in which individuals in loose groups stand to each other are crucial not only in determining the nature of the group but also for discussing the possibility of such groups having obligations.

In his later work, *Sharing Responsibility*, May discusses another type of collectivity: putative groups. These are groups that have enough leadership (or cohesion) to convert themselves into groups that act. According to May, when a group fails to prevent a harm that it could have prevented, the group may be held collectively responsible for that failure. This collective responsibility is distinct, according to May, from the individual responsibility of its members. May calls the sum of individual responsibilities of the individual members 'shared' responsibility. Importantly, it is possible that a group is collectively responsible for harm without any of the group members sharing responsibility for the harm (May 1992: 107). That is, in our *collective shallow-pond* case, May's position would hold the passers-by collectively responsible as a group if they failed to assist the child. In addition, one or both of them could be individually responsible. In any case, because May's view is formulated negatively and focuses on collective harm, mainly, the following is merely an attempt at a potential reconstruction of his view, in terms of positive duties, rather than being a view that he has explicitly expressed.

May's view on collective responsibility for a group's inaction – if applied to our case – would be as follows: the putative group consisting of the two passers-by is retrospectively collectively responsible for the harm to the drowning child if they fail to rescue it. Put in terms of positive duties, the putative group consisting of the passers-by ought to do x.

Provided that the forward-looking and backward-looking cases are parallel, on May's account, putative groups as such can hold moral obligations. Again, to the extent that such groups are collections *of* agents rather than collective or groups agents in their own right, such a view would violate the agency principle. Note that so far I have not suggested that the agency principle should necessarily be upheld. At this point, I am merely noting that several of the existing views on collective obligations violate that principle.

Finally, Tracy Isaacs briefly discusses the idea of putative agents (in May's sense) having forward-looking obligations in her book *Moral Responsibility in Collective Contexts*. In it, Isaacs claims that there can be no collective obligations without a collective agent, but she allows for 'putative obligations' to attach to groups that are not yet formed as agents. What this means depends on whether there is clarity as to the collective action required – whether it is obvious to the reasonable person "what the potential agent will be and what it will do" (Isaacs 2011: 152). If this *clarity condition* is met, putative collective obligations function in the same way as collective obligations of proper group agents (and goal-oriented collectives). According to Isaacs, this means that there exists an obligation at the collective level that orders and mediates but does not reduce to (or is the aggregate of) individual obligations. Rather, putative obligations serve as 'mechanisms' for determining individual actions and duties (ibid., 149–151). She adds that when a putative collective obligation becomes 'actual', then "the relevant obligation will be that of an organization or a goal-oriented collective" (ibid., 152). The putative group is therewith transformed into an actual agentive group.

The clarity condition invoked echoes the 'reasonable person standard' put forward by Held and the salience condition proposed by Felix Pinkert (see following). Isaacs suggests that where the clarity condition is not met, there is no putative obligation of the loose (putative) group. That is, whatever obligations group members have in such cases, they are not obligations to contribute to a collective endeavour and cannot be explained (or justified) with reference to a group obligation. However, Isaacs does not consider the possibility of an obligation on the members of the group to establish clarity, which is what Pinkert proposes.

With regard to our example, Tracy Isaacs' view then amounts to the following: the putative group consisting of the two passers-by has a putative obligation to do x (rescue the child).

In other words, Isaacs, too, defends a view that violates the agency principle. Or at least her view appears to violate it because she *does* argue that the group changes in the course of carrying out the joint action – it becomes an organisation or else a goal-oriented collective. I take it that Isaacs is trying to say that the group becomes an agent capable of holding duties, and in becoming this agent, the putative obligation becomes an actual obligation (2011: 152).

However, if a putative obligation is something like a potential obligation, an obligation that is not quite yet a proper – or actual – obligation, then it remains to be discussed why such a potential obligation should function as an ordering mechanism in the same way as an actual obligation for determining individual contributions. In a way then, Isaacs circumvents the problem of ascribing obligations to collectives that are not agents by introducing the idea of putative obligations. However, it is not quite clear what putative obligations are. Are they a weaker form of obligation? And what would that mean? Alternatively, if they really only convert to actual obligations once the plurality of agents has transformed into an actually group agent, why are they binding obligations in the first place before that happens? Or, if they are merely potential obligations, why ought you and your friend to do something that will turn a potential into an actual obligation? In other words, where does the binding character of this individual contributory obligation come from? In short, Isaacs' approach does leave crucial questions unanswered; yet, to be fair, her book only briefly touches on these issues and was not meant to give an exhaustive account of joint or collective obligations.

Similar to Isaacs, Bill Wringe (2010, 2016) proposed that in being the subject of an obligation an unstructured collective may turn into an agent: "[I]t is not that certain entities are morally obligated in virtue of the fact that they are agents; rather we should take them to be agents in virtue of the fact they are the subjects of moral obligation" (2010: 221).

He refines this view in a later article, in which he argues that only those collectives that are capable of becoming agents can be the subject of obligations. However, Wringe departs from Isaacs when he claims that even when a collective is a potential agent, it can still be subject to an actual duty (2016). According to Wringe, the bearer of collective obligations is a collective or group and such obligations supervene on individual obligations. Individuals acquire contributory obligations by virtue of being members of a group with a collective obligation.[6]

According to Wringe's view on collective obligations, the (potential) agent consisting of the two bystanders ought to rescue the child. So according to Wringe, our passers-by, by virtue of being a potential agent, acquire a collective obligation to rescue the child, which then gives rise to the individual obligations to contribute.

The aforementioned authors are all trying to capture the same basic idea: that sometimes it is required of agents to transform themselves into the kind of group that can successfully address a certain problem. In other words, sometimes we ought to generate immediate joint ability (in Pinkert's terms, see following). However, these authors do not want to let go of the idea that even prior to having such joint ability there is an obligation on the members of the group to address the problem as such. That is, they do not want to let go of the basic intuition and the improvement desideratum. But at the same time, they need to solve the problem of moral agency: who holds the obligation? Some come down on one side of the fence: Erskine claims that it is ultimately the individuals who are responsible; some come down on the other side: May, Wringe and Held think that it is the groups. Others, like Isaacs, sit somewhat on the fence.

Finally, Sean Aas presupposes that unstructured collectives can have putative obligations as collectives and argues that whether or not they do depends on their ability to act (Aas 2015), which in turn depends on its members' joint willingness to do their part. He proposes the following necessary and sufficient conditions for collective obligations:

> A collective is obligated to ϕ if and only if (a) its members are obligated to: be prepared to do their part in ϕ-ing, if they become sufficiently certain that enough others will as well and (b) if the members live up to this obligation, then (it is sufficiently likely that) the collective will ϕ.
>
> (p. 19)

It seems that Aas is defending a view according to which the members' obligations take precedence over the group's obligation. In our case, then, the passers-by are only obligated to rescue the child if each of them is sufficiently certain that the other will contribute. Now, of course, we tend to assume that each tries to communicate with the other when she comes across the drowning child. In that case, they each will (or will not) reassure each other of their willingness to contribute, and in case they do, the group acquires an obligation.

On Aas' account of members' obligations, the group consisting of the passers-by ought to rescue the child *iff* it is the case that

> *if* they each are certain as to the other's willingness to be prepared to do their part, they each acquire an obligation to be prepared to do their part, and
>
> *if* it is the case that each is prepared to do their part it is sufficiently likely that together they will succeed rescuing the child.

In other words:

> $[a\ b]$ ought to x iff
>
> a. a ought to x_a if a is certain that b will x_b, and
> b ought to x_b if b is certain that a will x_a, and
> b. a and b are likely to succeed in doing x if they x_a and x_b.

Condition (b) is obvious: a plurality of agents only has an obligation to do something only if its members are likely to succeed in doing that something given they each do their part. In other words, we are never collectively obligated to pursue the impossible (or unlikely).

Condition (a), however, generates a few problems and reveals the weakness of biconditionals generally: they are not very informative. Aas' conditions may reduce to a mere explication. What it means to have a collective obligation is simply what is stated in (a) and (b). And indeed, we are none the wiser for knowing Aas' conditions as to when such collective obligations arise. If we ask how the conditionals in (a) can be fulfilled, then we must ask how such individual contributory obligations arise in the first place. When is it the case that if I am certain that others are prepared to do their part in a collective endeavour I have an obligation to (be prepared to) contribute? Different answers are possible. Some will be circular; for instance, we have an obligation to (be prepared to) contribute to a collective endeavour if we are part of a group that has a collective obligation to undertake that endeavour. Others seem too narrow; we have an obligation to be prepared to do our part if we are a difference-maker – that is, if without us the collective undertaking would fail. And still others too wide: whenever there is something morally valuable that we could collectively produce we have an obligation to produce it provided enough others contribute.

At this point, and in keeping with the aim of this section, it is important to note that on the basis of Aas' conditions we cannot decide whether or not he thinks that the group obligation boils down to a conjunction of individual members' obligations or whether there is a group obligation in addition to the members' obligations. It seems though he has the former in mind. Namely, what it means to say that a group or plurality of agents ought to do something is the same as saying that each ought to do their part if they are certain that others do their part and together they can succeed in performing that action. This, ultimately, appears to be an individualist and conditional account of the duties involved, even though Aas set out to defend collective duties. I have already discussed the problems of individualist (conditional) accounts.

Let me very briefly mention two other approaches: Liam Murphy in his book *Moral Demands in Nonideal Theory* used the notion of 'collective beneficence', arguing that the duty to contribute to poverty relief (and similar global duties) is to be understood as a collective duty which needs to be fairly distributed among the members of the global community. Murphy's notion of collective beneficence is that of a distributive collective duty, where saying that a group has a duty of collective beneficence means that each has a (fair) share of that duty. However, in such distributive cases, according to Murphy, there exists no duty to take up the slack left by others: that is, no duty to contribute more than one's fair share. Similarly, in *The Moral Demands of Affluence*, Garrett Cullity assumes that beneficence is a collective duty and illustrates this claim with precisely the collective rescue case I am using. However, he does not develop this idea further in the book.

In summary, one could say that each of the theories in this category either violates the agency condition (in that they attribute obligations to pluralities of agents who do form a 'novel' agent in its own right) or postulates superfluous entities (in that they claim that a group agent needs to act when really the individual agents just act jointly) or else begs the question against what it means to be a group agent (by assuming that whenever individuals intentionally cooperate they are in fact forming a group agent). It is in particular the last point that seems to be at odds with our moral phenomenology. Presumably, to the individual agent, being part of (and act as part of) a constituted group agent (for instance, a university) feels very different from acting jointly with others by joining forces for a particular (often short-term) purpose.

6.4 'Shared' and 'Joint' Obligations

Let me now turn to proposals that suggest spelling out collective obligations as 'joint' or 'shared' obligations. Pinkert's account of joint duties centres on the notion of 'joint ability', distinguishing between mediate and immediate joint ability. Immediate joint ability to x is only present where there is one salient possible collective pattern of actions that would constitute x-ing and every relevant agent believes what is in fact her part to be her part (2014: 194). In our modified shallow-pond case, this means that if there is one combination of actions that would save the child and it is salient and both passers-by have true beliefs concerning these actions, then they have the joint ability to rescue the child. Pinkert would argue that in our case the passers-by have a joint obligation to rescue the child.

Pinkert also considers the possibility of joint duties in cases where there is no such salient pattern and the individual parts are not immediately known to the members of the group, or else, they do not (yet) have true beliefs concerning their parts in x. In such cases, the members of the group are jointly able to do x if there is a preliminary action y_x that they are jointly able to perform (and that meets the salience criteria as per above-stated) and that if taken will enable them to perform the action x. In other words, if there is some preliminary step to doing x, which establishes their immediate joint ability to do x, which is obvious to them and which they have the ability to take, then they have mediated joint ability to do x. If there is to be a joint obligation, there must be mediate or immediate joint ability. Or, in other words, joint ability is a necessary criterion for collective obligations.

I will not provide a detailed critique of his argument here, because I do not have the space. I think Pinkert's approach fares really well on a number of desiderata; it allows for our basic intuitions to be confirmed, aligns with our moral phenomenology and debunks the impotence objection. Yet, because it does not give us the full picture on collective obligations (nor does it aspire to do so), it falls short of ultimately telling us *under what circumstances* we have collective obligations. It is not action-guiding – it only gives us one necessary criterion. As such, it can do little to unify moral theory. Further, and this is a problem for all approaches in this category – we might think that it is not parsimonious: it introduces a new 'type' of obligations that are 'joint' and a new plural moral property.

Gunnar Björnsson encounters the same issue when he argues that individual agents can *share* moral obligations (2014, forthcoming). 'Sharing' an obligation is different from how holding an obligation is standardly conceived. On Björnsson's account, if the group members have the motivational sensitivity required of moral agents, they will find out what to do and get others to participate where possible. An essentially shared obligation of two agents a and b to do x exists where

> their failure to do x would be morally bad and their doing x would be ensured, in a normal way, by a's and b's caring appropriately.[7]
> (Adapted from Björnsson forthcoming)

Björnsson's main example is a shared obligation not to pollute a lake, where no individual agent's contribution would lead to the lake's pollution, but together their contributions do. If applied to our modified shallow-pond case, I believe that Björnsson's account would imply the following: the passers-by share an obligation to rescue the drowning child if and only if their failure to do so would be morally bad and it is the case that if they cared appropriately – that is, if they showed the right kind of moral motivation – they would rescue the child.

If we unpack this biconditional, the following conditions emerge: a shared obligation to do x exists where x is objectively morally right or morally optimal (and not doing x is objectively morally wrong) and appropriately motivated agents are able to both recognise the moral status of x and to secure x. Note that this is the strongest possible interpretation of Björnsson's account, but I believe it to be what he has in mind. Now the main problem with this approach (or my take on it) seems to be that it is too strong. We do not always recognise what is morally optimal even if we are morally highly motivated agents. To demand that moral obligations – collective or individual – only exist where we are in a position to establish what is morally optimal (or suboptimal) undermines most of our moral obligations.[8]

However, a more plausible interpretation of Björnsson's proposal is available. The condition that the failure to do x be morally bad could also be interpreted as meaning that failing to do x is prospectively or subjectively suboptimal. In that case two agents would have an obligation to do x if they believe x to be optimal (subjective view), ideally on the basis of evidence (prospective view).

I believe that this proposal has several advantages over Pinkert's: it gives us necessary and sufficient conditions for collective obligations and as such can be potentially action-guiding. It aims at unifying our theory of moral obligations in that it shows how the same general theory of obligations covers both individual and collective cases. It does, however, in its current shape fail to explain the tension between our individual and collectivist inclinations in situations where we are not sure if collective action is taken. Further, it is (still) a little light on the detail: what does it mean to 'care appropriately', and how does such caring prevent collective action dilemmas?

6.5 Collective Moral Obligations From the Perspective of the Deliberating Agent

Let me conclude by explaining how my own proposal satisfies our desiderata while avoiding some of the pitfalls discussed earlier. In developing an account of collective moral obligations, a recurring problem was how to accommodate the idea that our obligations can sometimes be directed at collective endeavours and sometimes at things we could individually achieve. I found that starting from the perspective of the deliberating agent at the centre of the account is the best way to reconcile the tension between the individual and the collectivist pull, while still providing action-guidance. I am suggesting that a plurality of agents a, b and c have a collective moral obligation if:[9]

(i) There exists a specific morally significant joint-necessity problem P, such that agents a, b and c can collectively, but not individually, address P.[10]

(ii) Conscientious moral deliberation leads all of them (or a sufficiently large subset of them) to believe that some collectively available option O is morally optimal with regard to P.

(iii) A, b and c (or a sufficiently large subset of them) are in a position to determine individual (or joint) strategies to realise O and to achieve P.

For a plurality of agents *a*, *b* and *c* to have a collective moral obligation means that they jointly hold that obligation. It is essentially a shared duty from which derivative individual duties arise. It is clear from this that not just any plurality of agents will be able to address some problem together. Whether or not they can will depend on the kind of relationship between the individuals, including what they know about the problem and about each other, as well as on the problem at hand and the complexity of its solution. My proposal also covers cases where there is no direct communication between individuals but where instead they have the same true beliefs concerning the facts surrounding P or else there is a salient, publicly known solution, as Pinkert, Held and Isaacs suggested (in their respective terminology).

Let me focus on the requirement that agents be in a position to determine individual strategies towards O and P. Importantly, public information campaigns can devise individual strategies for O and P. As such, we – members of a capable plurality – can have collective obligations to address large-scale problems, even on a global scale, without having (*de re*) knowledge of the members of the plurality (their identity or actions).

Further, the requirement of moral optimality (2) allows for more than one optimal option, and it may be possible to pursue several such options simultaneously. That is, options may not be mutually exclusive. In that case all that is required is that the deliberators overlap in the options identified as optimal. Note what moral optimality consists in is not spelled out in the proposal – what exactly is morally optimal would depend on which substantive moral theory is true.

This proposal explains how as moral deliberating agents we come to feel torn between individually available and collectively available options: it is often unclear whether or not others recognise the collective option to be optimal and whether or not they are conscientious deliberators. The proposal is action-guiding in that it identifies one morally obligatory course of action in scenarios like the two-person shallow-pond case. It is what must appear morally optimal to the agents involved, given their evidence and provided that they are conscientious. As such it confirms our basic intuition and satisfies the moral improvement desideratum without violating the agency and capacity principles.

With regard to more complex, large-scale collective moral action problems, the proposal can hold its ground, I believe. As mentioned before in Section 4.6, even where pluralities of agents do not collectively solve P they may have reason to see themselves as part of second-order collective endeavour(s) that form part of first-order collective endeavour(s) to solve *P*. They can thus be partaking in polycentric clusters of activity, with layered collective action and obligations. Therefore, the *individuals' collective obligations would become indirect* or *second-order collective obligations*. The relationship between the second-order and the first-order endeavour may not be a cause–effect relationship but a part–whole relationship. As such, some second-order collective endeavour may be obligatory even where it is not a difference-maker. In sum, the proposal can be action-guiding not just in small-scale joint-necessity scenarios but also for large-scale collective action problems. Crucially, it draws attention to the fact that our obligations in such cases depend on our knowledge of individual strategies and of other people's attitudes and beliefs.

Finally, research from experimental economics, social psychology and evolutionary biology suggests that we regularly see ourselves as part of groups that can or ought to act.[11] This propensity to see ourselves variously through individual and collective 'frames' – while highly context-dependent – lends further support to the idea that some of our obligation should be conceived as collective obligations. One might object that the so-called bystander effect poses a challenge for that claim.[12] According to that well-studied behavioural pattern, the presence of another person (or several other people) will often reduce the likelihood of someone intervening to help another in a critical situation (Latané and Darley 1970; Fischer et al. 2011). At a second glance, though, the research on the bystander effect does not undermine the point presented here for a number of reasons. First is that research does not focus on joint-necessity cases (even if some of the scenarios presented to subjects in experiments could be interpreted as such). Second, there is some indication that the bystander effect reduces when the action called for clearly *is* one of joint necessity. Fischer et al. (2011) suggest that the bystander effect is reduced if the other bystanders are perceived as potential co-helpers ('a competent service group' versus 'an unspecified social group'). Importantly, this is only for situations where the person intervening is endangered by helping the victim and would need other bystanders to protect her – so it still does not quite address the question of whether or not *in general* the bystander effect is less pronounced when the action called for is a joint action or the outcome is one that is only collectively achievable.

6.6 In What Sense Is This Still a Collectivist View?

One might wonder whether the proposed view does not end up being suspiciously close to an individualist view. Let me begin with a more general comment on reductionism in collective ethics. In part, how we conceptualise collective obligations depends on whether or not we believe that collective social phenomena reduce to individual phenomena. Many collective action scholars in philosophy are not reductionist in this sense;

their approaches are *explicitly* collectivist (Schweikard 2008; List and Pettit 2011; Wringe 2016; Himmelreich 2017).[13] In contrast, in political science and economics the term 'collective action' is often understood in a reductive sense – the dominant theories are individualistic. Importantly, metaphysical reductionism is different from explanatory reductionism. An individualist approach to collective action may be compatible with explanatory collectivism – the view that in explaining social phenomena we need to make reference to groups, sets of agents and collective action.[14] Further, metaphysical reductionism is distinct from logical reductionism (Tamminga and Hindriks 2020).

It might seem that in principle the deliberative approach to collective obligations defended here (mainly in Chapter 4) could be paired with a reductionist, individualist view, according to which agents have obligations to be responsive to others in joint-necessity cases but where collectives that are not (group) agents cannot hold moral duties. So what is the advantage of combining it with a notion of *jointly held* obligations?

As pointed out repeatedly, I believe that the individualist approach – while not without its merits – falls short of providing the full picture. It is only where we assume a joint obligation that the individuals who form the plurality actually have an obligation to produce the optimal outcome (where they can and where it is obvious to them). We established that a collective obligation exists where a plurality of conscientious agents rank a specific collectively available option highest. Doing so implies believing that one ought to produce that optimal outcome together with the other agent(s). A belief that one ought to produce an outcome together with others goes far beyond the requirement to be responsive to other agents as an individual agent. Rather, it implies an awareness of oneself as part of a plurality that needs to address the problem in question, with an implicit acknowledgement that the obligation is on several agents together.

I am not claiming that there is anything wrong with arguing that in joint-necessity cases agents need to be responsive to other agents. This applies on my view, too. But it follows as a requirement of *rationality rather than morality* from the acknowledgement that the obligation is on several agents, not on individual agents alone. It is the result of the individual agent's reasoning along the following lines: I really think that we should do *x*. *Therefore* I need to figure out how to do *x* together with you.

But note that responsiveness to the other is not the only thing that follows from the acknowledgement of joint obligations: if I am convinced that we should do *x*, and you are not, then I will try to convince you. I will not just respond to your actions and decisions but also actively try to influence them. We know that this often works, especially when we can directly communicate with someone.

In fact, where an individual agent knows that the other(s) in the plurality has the same evidence as they do concerning a joint-necessity case, they tend to expect them to rank their options in a similar way and to be similarly promoting the joint option. In other words, as individual agents we expect others to recognise that duties can be 'on us'. And if they fail, we will tell them that they ought to be responsive *because* we need to do this together. I cannot see how the individualist view explains the requirement of responsiveness without reference to a group or joint requirement (in particular, for wide joint-necessity cases).[15] But what is more, I doubt that they can give a better explanation than the joint duties view.

Another indication that my view is not reductionist is that the collective obligation is ontologically distinct from the individual contributory obligations. That this is the case can easily be seen from the fact that collective obligations (and corresponding actions) are multiply realisable. Or, in other words, the individual obligations can change even if the collective obligation remains the same. Joint obligations both depend on individual agents' epistemic positions vis-à-vis the collective action problem and give rise to individual agents' (contributory) obligations.

Notes

1. This chapter contains an updated and abridged version of Schwenkenbecher, A. (2018). Making Sense of Collective Moral Obligations: A Comparison of Current Approaches. In T. Isaacs, K. Hess, and V. Igneski (Eds.), *Collectivity: Ontology, Ethics and Social Justice* (pp. 109–132). London: Rowman & Littlefield.
2. In her 2019 book *Group Duties*, Collins develops a different, more comprehensive view.
3. While he did not put forward a view of this type, David Estlund recently constructed an example with this structure to illustrate what he calls the 'normativity gap'. My point here is precisely that such a gap can (sometimes) be avoided. Estlund, D. (2017). Prime Justice. In K. Vallier and M. Weber (Eds.), *Political Utopias* (pp. 35–55). Oxford: Oxford University Press.
4. As Holly Lawford-Smith is happy to do, for instance (Lawford-Smith, H. (2015). What 'We'? *Journal of Social Ontology*, 1(2), 225–249.)
5. Held says: "But when the action called for is not obvious to the reasonable person, a random collection may not be held responsible for not performing the action in question, but, in some cases, may be held responsible for not forming itself into an organized group capable of deciding which action to take" (1970: 476).
6. He thinks collective (CO) and membership obligations (MO) have three connections:

   > Explanatory connection: CO can be used to explain MO
   > Ontological connection: CO give rise to MO
   > Supervenience connection: CO supervene on MO (2016: 473).

7. Adapted from Björnsson, G. (forthcoming). On Individual and Shared Obligations. In M. Budolfson (Ed.), *Philosophy and Climate Change*.
8. For an argument to that extent, see Michael Zimmerman's critique of objective moral obligations in Zimmerman, M. J. (1996). *The Concept of Moral Obligation*. Cambridge: Cambridge University Press.
9. Note that this does not say 'iff' – collective moral obligations will also arise in cases that are not joint-necessity cases. This means that the present criteria

are necessary and sufficient as far as joint-necessity cases are concerned, but not as far as all kinds of cases are concerned.

10. This leaves open whether they are faced with a wide joint-necessity case (the number of available contributors is greater than the number of minimally necessary contributors, which means it is not strictly necessary that all contribute in order to guarantee the success of the joint effort) or a strict joint-necessity case (the number of available contributors equals the number of minimally necessary contributors), that is, whether or not a subset of two would suffice in resolving P.

11. These are just a few examples from economics, psychology and evolutionary biology: Louis, W. R., D. M. Taylor, and T. Neil (2004). Cost-Benefit Analyses for Your Group and Yourself: The Rationality of Decision-Making in Conflict. *International Journal of Conflict Management, 15*(2), 110–143; Bacharach, M. (2006). *Beyond Individual Choice: Teams and Frames in Game Theory*. Princeton, NJ: Princeton University Press; Butler, D. (2012). A Choice for 'Me' or for 'Us'? Using We-reasoning to Predict Cooperation and Coordination in Games. *Theory and Decision, 73*(1), 53–76; Thomas, E. F. and W. R. Louis (2013). Doing Democracy: The Social Psychological Mobilization and Consequences of Collective Action. *Social Issues and Policy Review, 7*(1), 173–200. Tomasello, M. (2014). *A Natural History of Human Thinking*. Cambridge, MA; London: Harvard University Press.

12. I would like to thank Hein Duijf for pressing me on this point.

13. There are different types of collectivists. The ones mentioned here are weak collectivists – they mostly see their approach as continuous with what is generally assumed about individual action and intentions.

14. Christian List and Kai Spiekermann argue that 'supervenience individualism' and 'causal-explanatory holism' are compatible (List, C. and K. A. I. Spiekermann (2013). Methodological Individualism and Holism in Political Science: A Reconciliation. *The American Political Science Review, 107*(4), 629–643.)

15. See also Tamminga, A. and F. Hindriks (2020). The Irreducibility of Collective Obligations. *Philosophical Studies, 177*(4), 1085–1109. They make a formal argument to the extent that member obligations *essentially* refer to a group.

7 Massively Shared Obligations and Global Poverty

Hopefully, at this point the reader of this book will consider the proposed theory of collective moral obligation to be at least plausible. They may even grant that this theory can help us better understand some of the conundrums we are facing in an ever more complex, interconnected world. Despite greater than ever exposure to information concerning the impacts of our actions and unprecedented opportunities for collaboration across national and cultural boundaries, we might be growing ever more uncertain about what it means to be doing the right thing. One of the most difficult issues to assess is whether we can have what I will call *massively shared obligations*. In other words, is the theory proposed here significant beyond small-scale and medium-scale scenarios? What can it tell us about our obligations to reduce global poverty, to protest structural injustice, to mitigate climate change, to stop antimicrobial resistance or to cooperate with public authorities in the face of a global pandemic?

7.1 Differences Between Small-Scale and Large-Scale Joint-Necessity Problems

Even if one considers the view presented so far to be plausible, one may nonetheless remain doubtful as to its applicability in large-scale collective action scenarios. In this section and the following one, I will show that these doubts are partially justified. Not only are there morally significant differences between groups of different sizes and types but also these differences have been systematically underestimated in some of the literature on global obligations.

Take, for example, the view according to which just like two individuals can have obligations to jointly rescue a drowning child from a pond if it takes both to do so, we can also have collective obligations to help those suffering from poverty globally. Variations of this view have been defended by Garrett Cullity and Bill Wringe.[1] In *The Moral Demands of Affluence*, Cullity writes that

> we stand under a collective moral requirement of beneficence to help needy people through aid agencies, and there is an individual moral

requirement of fairness upon each of us to contribute towards meeting that collective requirement.

(2004: 65)

Though Cullity does not give a conclusive argument for the collective nature of this requirement, he claims that the life-saving analogy for donating to poverty relief as first put forward by Peter Singer (Singer 1972) should be understood as grounding a collective rather than an individual requirement 'given the way that contributions to aid agencies are cooperatively pooled' (Cullity 2004). In arguing against Singer's view of obligations to assist the global poor as direct individual obligations to save lives, Cullity provides his own variation of Singer's original shallow-pond case – the two-person winch scenario:

Image 7.1 Joint rescue

A collective requirement of beneficence can exist when it is possible for us to help someone together, even if none of us could have helped on her own. . . . If someone is drowning in front of you and me, and can be rescued only by using a winch mechanism that requires two people to operate, then it is obvious that we are morally required to help him, even if neither of us could do so single-handedly.

(Cullity 2004: 61)

Similarly, Bill Wringe defended the idea of collective obligations by using small-scale collective action scenarios (Wringe 2016): two tenants have to alert the owner of their building of worsening damage to the roof and they can only do this together; only one of them can type the email and only one of them knows the technical details to describe the damage accurately. Wringe extrapolates that the same kind of collective obligations arises with regard to global poverty (Wringe 2010, 2016). His main argument is that members of collectives that are not agents – such as the two people in the building with the leaking roof, but also the 'global collective' – can organise themselves to become an agent or agentive. On his view, this is enough to ascribe collective obligations. While I share Wringe's and Cullity's assessment of the small-scale scenarios, I do not think it is obvious that we can extrapolate from them to large-scale cases. Can we really assume that collective ability and therefore also the kind of collective obligation are the same for small groups as for extremely large groups? I should not think so.

Here are four reasons as to why. Firstly, massively shared (pro tanto) obligations are less likely to turn into all-out obligations. In the small-scale scenarios invoked, where agents come face to face with the problem and where they can interact directly, several simplifying factors make it the case that pro tanto collective obligations become all-out obligations. These factors are missing largely in massive collective action scenarios. I have already discussed these factors (see Section 4.6), so they will only receive a brief mention here: *moral simplicity, epistemic simplicity* and *cooperative simplicity.*

Secondly, because epistemic conditions differ greatly between small and large unorganised groups, their collective abilities differ greatly. In particular, so-called cooperative collective actions will rarely be available to the latter kind of group. Therefore, massively shared obligations will usually be *weakly collective* only. I give a detailed argument for this claim in Section 7.3.

Thirdly, and relatedly, large-scale joint action, which is usually distributive, is phenomenally distinct from small-scale joint action. It feels very different to the agent whether they are involved in face-to-face cooperative interaction (or at least a scenario where direct communication is possible) or in somewhat anonymous distributive action with unknown collaborators. There is a sense of 'we' that emerges effortlessly and naturally in face-to-face interaction, and the presence of so-called joint attention can facilitate joint action.[2] Further, common knowledge proper is not present (or not even possible) in large-scale collective action scenarios and so are weaker and more ephemeral forms of interdependent knowledge. This, in turn, has an impact on those beliefs that are fundamental to the forming of plural intentions and people's willingness to contribute to joint endeavours.

I argued that three agents *a, b* and *c* have a pro tanto collective obligation to address some problem *P* if conscientious moral deliberation leads all of them (or a sufficiently large subset of them) to believe that some collectively available option *O* is morally optimal with regard to *P* (they have reason to we-frame *P* and to consider *O*) (see 4.6). Agents will be less likely to we-frame large-scale, distributive action scenarios compared to small-scale scenarios due to the absence of conditions that promote we-framing such as common knowledge and shared attention.[3]

Fourthly, where large-scale, perhaps even global problems are concerned, collective solutions are rarely available to large, non-organised (or minimally organised) groups of agents. In other words, agents are less likely to be in a position to determine individual (or joint) strategies to realise a collectively available option and to achieve a joint outcome. This can be a result of the problem's epistemic or moral complexity,[4] or it may be because the kinds of actions required to solve it are not available to non-organised groups (cooperative complexity) or all of the aforementioned.

Having said that, we might say that *some* large-scale collective action problems really are *not* too complex to be addressed by large and dispersed groups with no significant level of organisation if agents are in a position to produce desirable outcomes by way of aggregating individual actions or their effects.

Here is one example: herd immunity against an infectious disease – that is, the absence of the pathogen causing it – is a public good that is only produced if in a given population the vaccination rate is above a certain minimum threshold. Where herd immunity is undermined by low vaccination rates, those who cannot be vaccinated because they are too young, old or ill are at risk of contracting the respective disease, which – in the worst case – may lead to death. Protecting these vulnerable groups from the respective disease is only collectively possible: a sufficiently high percentage of people in that population must be vaccinated. Here it seems easy to stipulate a collective obligation, at least for those groups to whom these causal links are known. Again, public information campaigns can further increase public knowledge of the interrelation of vaccination behaviour and outbreaks of (sometimes) archaic infectious diseases. The collectively optimal pattern of action and individual contributory actions are obvious, and they are generally not too costly.

Or take the problem of climate change mitigation. Do we have collective obligations to address this problem through the combined effect of individual action choices? Clearly, climate change mitigation is much more complex a goal than, for instance, herd immunity. Let me, therefore, make a conditional claim: if climate scientists are correct in assuming that aggregate individual behavioural changes can have a significant if not decisive impact on closing the global emissions gap[5] (Blok et al. 2012; Wynes and Nicholas 2017), then I see no reason why we (capable citizens around the world)[6] should not in principle have an obligation to make those behavioural changes with a view to contributing to large-scale collective action on climate change. However, I believe that public knowledge concerning the gap and the measures to reduce it is currently insufficient for grounding an all-out collective obligation to reduce or eliminate the emissions gap.

The crucial role that *direct* interaction and communication play in coordinating spontaneous collective endeavours (such as the joint rescue of an injured motorist) and establishing the epistemic conditions for we-framing (and agency transformation) can potentially be fulfilled by other means, such as public information campaigns, blogs, social media and so forth, when it comes to large-scale collective action. However, the latter will usually require greater levels of organisation and leadership, and where these are absent we – members of large, non-organised but potentially efficacious groups – may lack the prerequisites for holding collective moral obligations to address these issues. In sum, the case for massively shared moral obligations is rather weak. The next section will show this in detail, focusing on the problem of global poverty. The upshot is that we can have global obligations to address global moral problems, albeit in a fairly limited sense.

7.2 Global Obligations to Combat Poverty

Most people agree that *we*[7] ought to eradicate global poverty or stop global warming, but many are unsure about just how and how much each of us ought to contribute towards these goals. Seeing that, individually, the vast majority of us do not seem to be able to make a significant difference to the problem, several scholars suggested that duties to assist the poor are some kind of *collective obligations* or *collective responsibility* (Cohen 1981; Murphy 2000; Cullity 2004; Nussbaum 2006; Young 2006; Schlothfeldt 2009; Wringe 2010; Young 2011; Schroeder 2014; Beck 2016; Schwenkenbecher 2017, 2020). Others make similar claims for obligations to mitigate climate change (Cripps 2013). However, the authors defending such views have employed fairly different notions of 'collective duties' – some of which are more plausible than others. Other authors reject the view that poverty relief, for example, is a collective duty for a number of reasons. Some do so, because they reject the idea of collective obligations of non-organised collectivities altogether (Lawford-Smith 2015). Others accept the view that duties can in principle be collective but have argued that in this case they are not (Schwenkenbecher 2013b; Pinkert 2014). In the following I argue that most of our obligations with regard to global poverty (and arguably other global action problems) are at the most *weakly collective*.[8]

Before we continue several clarifications are due. First, the aforementioned authors and the following discussion focus on collective obligations that 'ordinary citizens' can have. There are three different ways in which individuals can take action vis-à-vis these large-scale problems. We may:

- Take direct action where we can individually make a difference; or
- Act as members of organised groups; or
- Act as constituents of unorganised collectives.

Few of us have the power and influence to unilaterally make a direct difference to the kind of problems I am focusing on here. Many more of us can play a role as members of organised groups, such as universities, corporations, governments and their agencies, and other organisations. But I am interested in the third type of action, which is available to all of us and which can potentially be very impactful.

As such, my focus is on collective obligations that ordinary citizens can have qua constituents of unorganised collectives (as opposed to group agents). I take it for granted that group agents such as states, national and international organisations, and corporations (and, therefore, their members) have duties to address global challenges. The same applies to individuals in powerful positions. However, not only do these agents regularly fail to act on their obligations, ordinary citizens can still effect change in the world, albeit only collectively, for instance as constituents of unorganised collectives. These are agents who can perform coopera- tive joint actions or distributive actions – more on these terms later – but who are not united by a formal, enduring decision-making structure.

For those who are not in positions of power and influence we can usu- ally make a real difference only collectively. One might further narrow down this group by only covering the 'global affluent' – that is, those ordi- nary citizens who can easily afford to make monetary contributions. Iris Marion Young thinks that even those who are victims of injustice have some responsibility to fix the problems they are facing (Young 2011). I will not take sides in this debate but instead simply speak of 'ordinary citizens' keeping in mind that obligations are not evenly distributed among us.

Because we can only make a significant difference together, or collec- tively, it is no surprise that many believe the obligations to improve exist- ing large-scale problems are collective in some sense. But how exactly can large numbers of moral agents who are geographically dispersed (such as the global affluent) have a collective obligation?

Earlier, I put forward the following conditions for (pro tanto) collective obligations:

Agents a, b and c have a collective moral obligation if:

(i) There exists a specific morally significant joint-necessity prob- lem P, such that agents a, b and c can collectively, but not indi- vidually, address P [joint necessity + joint ability].

(ii) Conscientious moral deliberation leads all of them (or a suf- ficiently large subset of them) to believe that some collectively available option O is morally optimal with regard to P [they have reason to we-frame P and consider O].

(iii) A, b and c (or a sufficiently large subset of them) are in a position to determine individual (or joint) strategies to realise O and to achieve P.

Could these conditions ever be satisfied with regard to global moral problems, in particular global poverty? Is global poverty a problem that we – 'ordinary' citizens, that is, agents in no special position of power or ability to foster collective action – could collectively address?

Let me start by asking what kind of problem global poverty is? We need to be aware that it is not *one* problem but rather the result of a series of more fundamental problems that contribute in different ways to producing global poverty. The underlying economic and political causes are extremely diverse. They include factors such as unjust international trade regimes and the imposition of unsustainable economic management through global organisations such as the International Monetary Fund, World Bank and World Trade Organisation. Other frequent serious external interferences include foreign powers supporting (or worse installing) corrupt domestic elites. There often is a lack of solid public infrastructure paired with dysfunctional bureaucracies. Lack of education, health care and social security as well as massively unequal distribution of wealth in many of the most affected countries are other factors contributing greatly to poverty. Violent conflict and oppression are ripe in many of the poorest countries. Civil wars have rendered many of them politically very unstable. Finally, there are environmental factors, extreme droughts or flooding, ever more frequent because of a warming climate, which hit those regions hardest that are already most disadvantaged. This list is not meant to be exhaustive. It is merely meant to convey the fact that we are facing a very complex set of problems.

Can we address these underlying problems collectively? As ordinary citizens who do not form an organised group, we surely cannot do so directly in the way the hikers or the commuters can directly address the problems they are faced with. But remember that we may have second-order or indirect collective obligations (see 4.6). Where complex problems are concerned, agents may themselves not collectively solve *P* but have reason to see themselves as part of second-order collective endeavour(s) that form part of first-order collective endeavour(s) to solve *P*. Agents can form part of polycentric clusters of activity where individuals' collective obligations are indirect or second-order collective obligations. In other words, we can have obligations to back activities that contribute to or are constitutive of larger morally important collective endeavours. We can address large-scale and even global problems indirectly by lending support to organisations that have a more direct impact on these problems. Indirect obligations usually come with significant latitude as to how they need to be discharged.

We can contribute positively, for instance, by volunteering for or donating money to such organisations. Or we can refrain from acting in ways that interfere with the aims and work of these organisations, for instance through ethical consumerism (where this is proven to be effective). Further, we can support the right kind of political action – through voting, rallying and lobbying. Oftentimes, our individual contributions of either kind will not have an impact if taken in isolation but only if taken together. In sum, it seems that the first of the three criteria can be at least partially met where global poverty is concerned: it is a specific morally significant joint-necessity problem, such that a plurality of agents can collectively, but not individually, address it.

What about the second criterion? Is it the case that were we to conscientiously deliberate, we would come to believe that some collectively available option O is morally optimal with regard to the problem of global poverty? On my view, the fact that any people donate money or otherwise support existing endeavours to combat the root causes of poverty demonstrates that they choose to pursue a collectively available option. As a moral choice, their actions only make sense if viewed in the context of the collective endeavour they are contributing to, and such choices are usually accompanied by de dicto beliefs in contributions by others.

But *should* a conscientious deliberator rank (some of) these collective options highest? Let me briefly explain how the second condition should be understood with regard to such complex problems. As I said, the complex of problems that constitute (or produce) global poverty cannot be reduced to a single problem. Only some of these can we as an unorganised group collectively help improve. So what condition (ii) requires is that conscientious deliberators when faced with P should find *some* collective option to be optimal. Naturally, there is no single optimal collective option with regard to this particular problem; rather, there is a class of collectively available options. Deliberating agents may well find several of these to be optimal (perhaps each with regard to different sub-problems). They need not all pick the same option for this condition to be satisfied. Rather, in order for there to be a collective obligation, there would have to be sufficient overlap in the collectively available options agents choose.

It is important to note that some conscientious deliberators may rank an individually available option highest. This could be due to three things: they have bad evidence, or they made a mistake in deliberation, or they are indeed in a position to produce a better result through individual action. The latter group of people are not covered by the collective obligation. And indeed this makes perfect sense: there are influential and powerful individuals who can unilaterally have a decisive impact on some of these problems. Where this is the case, their obligation is individual, not collective, according to my account. This seems to be the intuitively correct result. In contrast, only agents who recognise that their best bet is to be part of a collective endeavour have a collective obligation (provided the other criteria are met).

Finally, are we – ordinary citizens – in a position to determine individual (or joint) strategies to realise O and to achieve P as condition (iii) requires? The short answer is 'yes'. I believe that we – or a sufficiently large number of us – are in such a position, at least to the extent that we are concerned with the sub-problems and sub-options described earlier.

In fact, it seems that movements such as *Effective Altruism* are aimed at generating individual strategies to jointly realise these objectives and sub-objectives.[9] Where agents are not in a position to determine an individual strategy, they are not covered by our collective obligation. Further, many people will not be able to afford contributions to these endeavours. Our substantive theory of morality should exempt these people from contributions. That is, they may be covered by a pro tanto duty but should not be covered by an *all-out* collective duty once all the relevant aspects of the situation have been taken into account.

In sum, a collective obligation to combat global poverty binds all those for whom it is the case that conscientious moral deliberation implies that their efforts are most efficient where they are part of a collective endeavour aimed at combating poverty, provided they are in a position to know *how* to be part of such an endeavour and they have no reason to assume that there are not enough similarly placed others. Note that different individuals (or individual group agents) will have different options for discharging such obligations. Finally, it should be added that states, too, can have collective obligations (together with other states).

7.3 Large-Scale Distributive Action

In her work on global justice and collective responsibility, Iris Marion Young argued that we ought to fight structural injustice by "joining together with others in collective action" (2006: 123). While I share the sentiment, which, as we have seen, has inspired many philosophers to make related claims, her statement needs qualifying. In order to get a better sense of what massively shared obligations might be like, we need to return to a distinction made earlier regarding the different ways in which sets of agents can collectively bring about outcomes (or perform actions). *Genuine collective* action is not to be confused with the *aggregation* of actions. Let me explain each in turn: the latter describes outcomes produced by the *aggregation* of independent individual actions where these actions are *not intended* to produce that outcome, such as causing climate change through cumulative GHG emissions. My focus is on what I call *genuine collective action*.

Genuine collective actions are either

(a) cooperative (interdependent) *joint actions* (Pettit and Schweikard 2006; Bratman 2014), or
(b) *distributive actions* resulting from cumulative individual contributions towards a shared goal (Ludwig 2016),[10] or
(c) actions of *group agents* or incorporated groups, where the group's agency is not reducible to the agency of its individual members or the group has an identity over and above that of its members (Erskine 2001; List and Pettit 2011; Tollefsen 2015).

Because I am interested in obligations that individuals outside incorporated groups hold, I will leave (c) aside. The remainder of this section clarifies the difference between cooperative joint actions (a) and distributive actions (b). Let me stress that I am not suggesting that these two types of action exhaust the whole spectrum of genuinely collective action in unorganised collectives nor that they will always occur in the pure form described here. Rather, in their pure form they represent two opposite ends of a continuum. There will be hybrid forms, too. What I am aiming to show in the next section is that these different types of collective action have very different implications for potential collective obligations to address structural injustice. But beforehand, let me give a more detailed account of the differences between them.

Dancing tango, playing a duet and lifting a table together are instances of what I call *cooperative joint action*. In contrast, people donating one million dollars to a charity for disaster relief, or neighbours keeping a local beach clean by taking turns in collecting rubbish, would count as *distributive actions*.

Cooperative joint action is highly interdependent collaboration between individuals, and many joint actions cannot be performed by an individual agent as a matter of principle, such as aforementioned duet playing or tango dancing. More importantly, however, individual contributory actions cannot be performed in isolation, even though they may be performed consecutively, as in co-authoring a book or an article, where co-authors take turns.

Distributive collective action results from the individual actions of two or more agents that are intended as contributions towards a joint endeavour (or shared goal). Such actions can in principle – though often not literally – be performed by one individual agent. A group (or set) of agents' cumulative ability to produce distributive action merely requires that a sufficiently great number of individual agents have the ability to perform individual actions towards a shared goal and that they each have reason to adopt that goal, or, as I put it earlier, they must be able to carry out their respective individual actions with a view to combining them.[11]

Naturally, it will more often be the case that a group (or set) of agents have the ability to perform a distributive collective action than a cooperative joint action, because conditions for joint ability will be more demanding in the latter case. For instance, for cooperative action, agents must usually have second- or higher-order knowledge of a shared plan[12] and others' intentions. This will often be the case where agents can directly communicate with one another, and these facts are 'out in the open', so to speak. The strongest form of interdependent knowledge of this kind is common knowledge, but weaker forms of interdependent knowledge may suffice, depending on the action in question. For many

types of cooperative action, for instance, it may be sufficient that plans
and intentions are public knowledge among agents:

A proposition *P* is public knowledge among agents *x*, *y* and *z* if it is
true that

(a) most of them know *P*, and
(b) most of them know (a).

For distributive collective action, shared knowledge of the joint plan
suffices:[13]

A proposition *P* is shared knowledge among agents if each of them
knows *P*.

Distributive actions will be those where people intend to contribute to
some joint outcome but do not necessarily communicate with other people
who could potentially work towards the same outcome or where they do
not necessarily know anything about those people's intentions. If I stop
eating meat because current animal husbandry practices are bad for the
environment, then this may form part of a distributive action to reduce
global meat consumption. Similarly, people may be reducing their carbon
footprint in order to contribute to mitigating climate change (Dietz et al.
2009). Importantly, where distributive actions take place, there is often
some kind of shared, publicly available plan, which ascribes individual
roles to secure the collective end. Public health campaigns may promote
distributive action on important issues: for instance, increasing vaccination
rates in order to produce herd immunity. Where distributive action is concerned, individual contributions are usually straightforward and simple.

Many collective actions, however, are significantly more complicated
than that. They require precise levels of (often sustained) interaction
between participants. People in unstructured groups can perform such
cooperative joint actions to a point. Usually, organised (or structured)
agents will be best at performing such tasks and unorganised groups
might transform into structured group agents when confronted with such
challenges. The more intricate the level of organisation in such a group is,
the more closely will it resemble a group agent. (But I am not concerned
with that part of the spectrum of genuine collective action here.)

The two types of actions discussed – joint action and distributive
action – are ideal types. Some collective actions may fall in between these
categories or display features of both. However, roughly, they represent
two fundamentally different ways in which agents in unstructured groups
can jointly produce outcomes (or perform actions). The important thing
to note is that many instances of structural injustice will require a variety
of agents and groups of agents to take various forms of remedial action.

The aforementioned distinctions are important because they will ulti-mately help us better understand the kind of collective obligations we may have to address complex, large-scale problems. To illustrate this, let me have a quick look at some of the arguments made in relation to our (collective) responsibility to address global poverty. In my view, authors rarely give enough credit to the diversity of collective actions required to address this problem. As such, arguments for collective obligations to address poverty tend to be too general.

One observed tendency is to focus predominantly on distributive action solutions to global poverty, for instance, when it is discussed as a problem of individual donations towards charity (Murphy 2000; Cul-lity 2004; Singer 2009). However, I think it is misleading to characterise the problem of global poverty primarily in this way. Far from being a distributive action problem, it is better interpreted as a *combination* of multiple distributive action problems and multiple genuine cooperative action problems. For instance, a significant part of the problem of global poverty are unjust global trade agreements and unjust global financial institutions (Pogge 2005). Taking action on both issues requires genu-ine cooperative action at a global level, ideally by institutional agents. Short-term poverty and disaster relief, in contrast, can be achieved by dis-tributive collective action. Cumulative donations to charities (and other contributions to their work) may count as distributive actions in support of existing cooperative action. Arguably, both types of action are required in addressing this problem. In my view, the topography of obligations concerning complex, large-scale problems is complex and multifaceted, rather than neat and tidy.[14]

Therefore, I also want to caution against approaches that portray 'our' duty to address global poverty mainly as a duty to perform a cooperative action. Just like the previously mentioned view, these approaches paint an unrealistically simplistic picture of the moral landscape. One of the overly simplified approaches, in my view, is what I have called the *joint-rescue-analogy view*. As discussed in Section 7.1, according to this view, just like two individuals can have obligations to jointly rescue a drowning child from a pond if it takes two people to do so, we can also have collective obligations to help those suffering from poverty globally. 'We' usually means 'the global community' or 'the affluent'. Variations of this view have been defended by Garrett Cullity[15] and Bill Wringe, for instance (see Section 7.1).[16]

Neither Wringe nor Cullity give an account of what it means for a group to have collective ability, but both implicitly assume that the kind of collective ability (and therefore also the kind of collective action and obligation) involved must be the same or at least similar enough in the global and the small-scale scenario.[17] This is surprising, because a number of factors influencing the group's ability to organise itself and to jointly act that are present in the small-scale scenario are lacking in the global case (as discussed in Section 7.1).

But we need not approach the question of collective ability of unorganised groups of individuals (passers-by, commuters, the global affluent, ordinary citizens, etc.) in this narrow sense of cooperative action described earlier. Many of those who defend collective obligations assume very different – much weaker – criteria for collective ability and also a weaker concept of collective action.

The notion of collective action underlying Felix Pinkert's view of joint duties is more closely aligned with what I have called 'distributive action'. Just like Wringe and Cullity, Pinkert thinks that unorganised groups of agents can hold moral duties, provided they have joint ability. Pinkert distinguishes between mediate and immediate joint ability to do *x* (Pinkert 2014).

Immediate joint ability to do *x* exists where there is one *salient* possible collective pattern of actions that would constitute *x*-ing and every agent in the relevant group believes what is in fact her part to be her part (Pinkert 2014: 194). In cases where there is no such salient pattern and the individual parts are not immediately known to the members of the group, or where they do not (yet) have true beliefs concerning their parts in *x*, they could still hold joint duties if they have *mediate* joint ability – that is, the capacity to establish immediate joint ability: "agents can already be jointly able to perform actions which first require them to coordinate" (ibid, p. 197). In other words, if there is some preliminary step to doing *x*, which establishes their immediate joint ability to do *x*, which is obvious to them and which they have the ability to take, then a group of agents have mediate joint ability to do *x*. This means that they may have a joint duty to do *x* even if there is no salient pattern of action to start with. On Pinkert's account, then, immediate joint ability (and a joint duty) can be present even if there is no communication between the different members of a group, let alone something akin to interdependent, interlocking intentions (Bratman 2014).

Pinkert's criteria will often be met where simple, distributive actions are concerned. Interestingly, though, he does not think that the global affluent (or humanity as a whole) are under a collective obligation to remedy global poverty, for example. This is because he believes that it would take us too long to establish immediate joint ability to actually save people from dying. That is, we would take too long to coordinate in order to save all the lives that could be saved. I believe that this conclusion, too, falls prey to an overly simplistic view of our obligations vis-à-vis large-scale injustice: global poverty is a complex problem, and as such the obligations to remedy it will be diverse and complex, held by different kinds of agents. It seems misguided to assume that there could be only *one* all-encompassing collective obligation and one set of conditions triggering that obligation. And while we may not be able to address 'the' problem of global poverty, we are well capable for addressing some of the sub-problems that make up global poverty.

As mentioned, the root causes of global poverty are best addressed by organised group agents. Still, the unstructured global collective of 'ordinary' citizens can play a supporting role and take up some of the slack left by those agents. Contra Pinkert, I argue that we can have multiple collective obligations to address large-scale (even global) injustice. With regard to global poverty, there do exist salient patterns of collective action and there is some shared and public knowledge as to how we can individually contribute. One of the ways to discharge our obligations is via financial or other contributions to existing organisations that fight the causes and mitigate the impacts of poverty.[18] Through their activities and information campaigns, these organisations make certain patterns of group action and individual contributory actions supporting their work salient. Arguably, there is less public knowledge concerning (how to fight) the roots of structural injustice and poverty than there is concerning mitigating its impacts. But to the extent that information on either type of goal is readily available, ordinary citizens are under a duty to jointly support existing efforts to fight poverty and to therewith perform collective actions in the distributive sense. Donations, for example, can be seen as cumulative contributions towards a collective goal.

One particularly important factor for a group of agents' collective ability is the knowledge or beliefs that group members share. Even though I do not agree with Pinkert's ultimate conclusion regarding our obligations vis-à-vis global poverty, he – correctly, in my view – highlights the significance of epistemic conditions for joint ability. Pinkert emphasises that it must be 'obvious' to the agents how to play their part or that a collective solution must be 'salient' for them to have immediate joint ability, but he does not provide much detail on these epistemic requirements.[19,20]

Scott Shapiro's account of massively shared agency – collective agency of very large, loose groups – is more concrete: he emphasises that "shared intentional activity is activity guided by a shared *plan*" (p. 277). Shapiro's notion of a plan in some sense mirrors Pinkert's concept of a 'pattern' and corresponding 'roles': a 'plan' contains a specific end as well as specifying how to achieve that end, that is, which actions individual group members are to take in order to achieve that end. So, what does it mean for a plan to be *shared*?

> A plan is shared by a group to J when (1) the plan was designed, at least in part, for the members of the group so that they may engage in the joint activity J and (2) each member accepts the plan.
>
> (2014: 278)

Accepting a plan does not entail that each member know the full content of the plan, but the content is publicly accessible for those who wish to find out. Further, according to Shapiro, shared activity requires that each member intentionally follows their part of the plan and that this fact – as well as the fact that there is a shared plan – is common knowledge (2014: 277).

I believe that Shapiro's proposal is best understood as an account of distributive action.[21] But, depending on what exactly Shapiro means by 'common knowledge' (and he does not specify in the text), his epistemic condition may well be too strong to capture the kind of massively shared agency that he is after and which we are focused on here. According to the so-called iterative definition, "a proposition *P* is common knowledge in a group if and only if everyone in the group knows that *P*, everyone knows that everyone knows that *P*, and so on for any iteration of 'everyone knows that'" (Roy and Schwenkenbecher 2019). Clearly, if we adopt the iterative definition of common knowledge, we have to accept that the global affluent, or members of loose and dispersed groups more generally, cannot engage in shared activity of this kind. Group members may be justified in having first- or even second-order (de dicto) beliefs about others' knowledge of the shared plan and their respective intentions. But if there is no direct communication between group members, the iteration will stop somewhere.

Shapiro's account is more plausible with a weaker interpretation of the common knowledge condition. Perhaps all we need in order to jointly follow a shared plan is *public knowledge* of the shared plan. As mentioned before, public knowledge obtains where most people (or a large enough subset of those who can contribute to the shared end) know the plan and most people (or a large enough subset) are aware of that fact.

Yet even with this modification, Shapiro's account is more demanding than Pinkert's in terms of what beliefs and attitudes group members need to share (or have in common) in order to jointly act. Rather than arguing that one account is preferable to the other, I suggest that different types of collective action problems will require different types of joint ability and differing levels of shared beliefs of the group members. Further, as I will indicate later, stronger normative (including epistemic) connections between group members have implications for the obligations they can have in common.

In sum, I have discussed three issues so far: (1) the different *kinds* of actions that are required in the fight against large-scale moral problems, focusing mainly on the problem of global poverty, (2) what it means for large, unorganised groups of people to have the ability to perform a distributive collective action, and, in particular, (3) what group members need to know in order to be able to act. The upshot was that in order for such unstructured groups to have the required collective ability, there needs to be at least one collective pattern of action, which, if realised, will fix the problem in question, and this pattern is salient (or obvious) to group members. This includes that they have accurate beliefs with regard to the role that they need to play in order for the collective action to succeed. This pattern can take the shape of a 'publicly known shared plan'.

The public nature of the plan will make it the case that group members have some reason to believe (de dicto) that there are indeed other agents sharing that plan and collective end. I will come back to this issue in the next section, when discussing the relevance of normative links between group members.

However, so far I have said little about what it means to share obligations on a massive scale. This will be discussed in the next section.

7.4 Massively Shared Collective Obligations

To start with, let me locate our discussion within the larger context of the debate on collective obligations. Ultimately, most moral agents will hold a variety of different obligations – individual and collective – to contribute to addressing large-scale collective moral action problems. Some of these obligations will focus more narrowly on cooperative actions, some on distributive actions and many on actions that will fall in between these two types. I would add, though, that our obligations also depend on the type of problem we are attempting to address, the kind of action that is required to remedy it and the kind of contribution we can make to it. Many of us will not be in a position to initiate collective action but merely to contribute to existing endeavours. This, too, is a way of discharging our collective obligations.

Our moral obligations vis-à-vis complex moral problems are best understood as a polycentric cluster of collective and individual obligations, I believe. My focus, however, is on a particular subtype of our obligations to address those problems, namely those that are most easily had – obligations to contribute to large-scale distributive action. I have already shown that large and dispersed collectives can meet one necessary criterion for such obligations – cumulative ability – provided there exists a publicly known shared plan or an otherwise salient pattern of action.

With regard to concrete, clearly circumscribed distributive action problems, can members of large, dispersed groups such as the global community have 'massively shared' collective obligations?

Examples of the kind of distributive actions I am interested in include donations towards charities that aim at sustained political and economic change, and individual behavioural change where our standard practices cause collective harm to those who are already disadvantaged (as in reducing our carbon footprint or purchasing certain consumer goods). They also include political mass movements such as Black Lives Matter or collective compliance with public health recommendations in a global pandemic, such as the COVID-19 crisis. Yet in what sense would obligations to contribute to these causes or to cooperate in such circumstances be *collective*?

Normative primacy of the collective level: As mentioned earlier, one reason for construing obligations as collective is to account for the fact that, with regard to problems of structural injustice (or, more generally, large-scale collective action problems), no individual's actions taken in isolation will fix the problem (joint necessity). Rather, it is the collective ability of a set of agents to produce an outcome or perform an action that is seen as grounding such obligations. Further, in many cases, an individual's omission or inaction may not even make a difference for the worse, namely where there are more potential contributors to solving a problem than minimally necessary, that is, when we are then faced with a *wide joint-necessity* case. If our obligations depended on our unique ability to make a difference to an outcome, then none of the bystanders in this case would have an obligation to intervene. After all, if they fail to act, there are still others who could help the drowning person. This dilemma is avoided if, as several scholars proposed, the collective level is considered primary and the question of individual obligations as secondary (Isaacs 2011; Schwenkenbecher 2014b; Wringe 2016). Note that this move is not available to the third interpretation of collective duties mentioned previously.

Normative primacy of the collective level can be understood in several ways: as metaphysical, logical, functional or deliberative. If couched in terms of moral reasons for action, a collectively optimal pattern of action can give individuals group-based (or pattern-based) reasons for action even where the outcome is overdetermined (Woodard 2003, 2011). Normative primacy of the collective level can also be understood as a requirement on individual agents to deliberate from the point of view of the group about their obligations in a given scenario that requires their intervention (Schwenkenbecher 2019). Collective obligations can be understood as giving rise to individual obligations and as being ontologically more fundamental (Wringe 2016). Further, a formal argument can be made that individuals' member obligations *essentially* refer to a group (Tamminga and Hindriks 2020). I suggest to call obligations that display these kinds of normative primacy of the collective level 'weakly collective' obligations.

Normative links between agents: Another way to understand the *collective* character of moral obligations is to think of them as generating special normative links between members of said collectives. I suggest calling this a 'strongly collective' understanding of such obligations.[22] For a set of agents to collectively have an obligation in the strong sense may require them to take some responsibility for the success of the collective action, such as coordinating the joint activity and generating the kind of group knowledge required for the group members to be able to fulfil their contributory actions. Further, it may mean that group members have to pick up the slack left by others (Schwenkenbecher 2013a). Finally, group members may also be linked by considerations of fairness in the distribution of contributory roles (Cullity 2004). Normative links of this kind require that certain epistemic conditions hold within the group, for example, that information is public or shared in the right way.

Our obligations to perform the kind of distributive actions that I have been mainly focusing on would be weakly collective, in that the collective level has normative primacy. However, normative links within the group will bolster and strengthen the collective character of obligations by exerting both rational and psychological pressure to discharge those duties onto agents. They can strengthen moral reasons in favour of collective options by making collective patterns of action salient over individual patterns of action. When facing collective action problems, individual deliberating agents are regularly torn between individually efficacious actions and collectively available options. In other words, there is a tension between choices that make a direct difference and those whose success depends on how others choose (Schwenkenbecher 2019). Adequate information flow within groups concerning other agents' choices can make specific group patterns salient as well as lower the risks involved with picking collectively available options generally. Group members who can directly communicate can jointly work out strategies for optimal action via team-reasoning (Gold and Sugden 2007b; Hakli et al. 2010). In epistemically more tightly knit (and yet unstructured) groups, compliant members are more likely to know about others' defections, giving them an opportunity to pick up the slack left by the defectors in order to secure the group goal. Arguably, under certain conditions, group members, even in unstructured groups, have obligations to take on more than their ideal fair share of costs when discharging obligations (Cullity 2004; Miller 2011; Schwenkenbecher 2013a; Karnein 2014).

The greater a group's epistemic cohesion, the more likely is there to be a robust sense of group membership and identity. We have learned from research in social psychology that a sense of group membership will enhance cooperative behaviour (Thomas 2009b; Thomas et al. 2009; Bicchieri 2017). It is therefore desirable, from the point of view of combating structural injustice via large-scale collective action, to distribute information in the right way so as to generate a stronger sense of group identity and mutual accountability.

In sum, I suggest that ordinary citizens' obligations to address large-scale moral problems will often be collective only in a very weak sense, in that the collective level has normative primacy in determining the content of their individual obligations. Against that backdrop, it is easy to see that strengthening normative and epistemic links between agents in unorganised groups may change the nature of their obligations and may, in fact, increase normative pressure to contribute to collective action. Importantly, though, strengthening those links is an action that may not readily be available to agents in large and dispersed unorganised groups.

7.5 Three Objections: Claimability, Enforceability and Action-Guidance

Perhaps, the reader is in agreement with what has been said so far about collective obligations to address global poverty. But what implications does it actually have for each of us? That is, does the argument made here change anything with regard to any particular person's obligation towards combating global poverty or other cases of large-scale injustice?

One way to answer this question is to ask whether the argument in favour of framing duties to address global poverty as collective duties can deliver on what I will call the 'claimability desideratum', meaning whether it can neutralise the so-called claimability objection, which – as far as I am aware – was first and most forcefully made by Onora O'Neill (2013). According to this objection, which was originally levelled against a human right to subsistence, because a human right to subsistence is not claimable against any specific duty-holder, we should reject it as a universal human right. O'Neill argues that "we cannot tell who violates a right to goods or services unless obligations have been allocated" (2013: 428) and bemoans

> an international human rights culture that is replete with claims about abstract rights . . ., but often muddled or vague, or both, about the allocation of the obligations without which these rights not merely cannot be met, but remain undefined.
>
> (ibid.)

While my argument is not couched in terms of human rights, we can nonetheless see how it is vulnerable to the objection. Because I am suggesting that there is a collective duty to address poverty, who are the concrete duty bearers?[23]

Can our argument in favour of collective obligations neutralise the claimability objection? I can see two strategies for doing so. The first employs an argument by Wringe (2010) that an obligation to secure the means of subsistence worldwide need not be held by particular *agents*. That is, non-agents can (and do) hold this obligation. I have already discussed Wringe's view before (Section 2.3), so I will not do it again here.

A second argument is that there are in fact countless agents who can bear an obligation to secure the right to subsistence *together* or *jointly* – these agents include states, non-state organisations, companies and corporations, and individual agents. In short, they include all currently existing moral agents (bearing in mind that not all of them may have the capacity to contribute). It is an empirical question whether or not these agents can *in fact* secure that right collectively. I take it that people like Peter Singer argue that together we can make sure that everyone has the basic means of subsistence, not just in the sense of a remote possibility but in the sense of an actual option available to us (2009). If he is correct, then it seems that the notion of collective moral obligations defended here can indeed debunk the claimability objection.

One might disagree with that conclusion by saying that it is too difficult for individual agents to figure out what needs to be done in order to provide the basic means of subsistence. In fact, Jesse Tomalty argued that there is no collective duty of humanity to secure the human right of subsistence because there is *no joint mechanism* such that each individual knows what to do with regard to securing that right (2014). Tomalty argues that due to the complexity of the problem "it is not obvious to the reasonable person what is required of them in order to do their part in fulfilling the joint duty" (p. 12). Further, she believes that "every individual performing what he or she reasonably takes to be his or her duty will not necessarily result in producing the desired outcome of poverty eradication worldwide" (ibid.). In short, Tomalty denies that my condition (iii) is met – that we can devise individual strategies towards a morally optimal outcome.

I take it that securing the right to subsistence is not the same as eradicating poverty but is, in fact, more easily secured. Tomalty's view, therefore, misfires when she argues against our duty to secure the former by showing how we are not capable of producing the latter. But, more importantly, it is not obvious that we should be unable to do our part in a joint duty to secure the means of basic subsistence or combating poverty. I agree with Tomalty that we – 'ordinary citizens', individual agents – cannot jointly eradicate poverty without any type of coordinated and structured action. But I do not think that we are in a situation where such action is fundamentally lacking. Rather, there exist countless coordinated endeavours to address poverty and provide for basic needs, and we can contribute to these efforts in multiple ways, supporting and enabling them. I do not think it is too hard for each of us to determine individual strategies towards improving the situation even if the morally best outcome, the complete eradication of poverty, is not available to us as an unstructured group. Naturally, there are many different possible strategies for improvement and many optimal sub-outcomes. But we need not design our collective endeavour from scratch, like Virginia Held's random individuals who had to figure out quickly how to jointly rescue somebody, an example Tomalty invokes (Held 1970).

Further, I take it that Tomalty operates with an objective view of moral obligation because she cautions that what reasonable persons would do may not be actually best for eradicating poverty by way of adding plausibility to her view that there cannot be a collective obligation to do so. I think the prospective view of moral obligation which I adopted earlier in my argument protects the claimability advocates from this conclusion. In the end, we – moral agents worldwide – 'only' have a collective obligation to do what our evidence suggests is best. Does this mean that the right to subsistence reduces to a right to having capable agents do what appears best to them with regard to subsistence, given their evidence? This seems to follow from my argument, but note that my view is not couched in terms of rights and corresponding duties. All I have tried to show here is that in principle we need not reject a right to subsistence *on the grounds that it is not claimable*. Note that because I do not commit to any substantive ethical view I am not saying that we – or most of us – do in fact have an all-out obligation to secure that right nor that there even is such a right. Again, I am merely saying that there could be such a duty given that there are agents who can hold the duty collectively.

One might counter that my account of collective obligations still faces some of the same problems that O'Neill decried when she rejected the right to subsistence. One of her complaints was that if a duty is unallocated we cannot point to someone violating it. This problem seems to persist with my account of global obligations to combat poverty. It is fair to say that currently we – ordinary citizens across the world – do not do enough to reduce poverty. On my account of collective obligations, are there any concrete agents we point to? Earlier, I argued where agents jointly violate a duty they are jointly to blame. However, because joint blameworthiness does not reduce to individual blameworthiness, this does not allow us to conclude that any particular person has individually failed in their contributory duty (or deserves blame). After all, specific individuals may have done their share or even more than that.

Some might argue that because we should be able to enforce duties of justice and we are not justified in enforcing *this* collective duty it cannot be a duty of justice but is merely a – less stringent – duty of charity (Miller 2011; Goodin 2016). In other words, the kind of collective obligations I have been defending are merely some weak type of obligation – one that we can violate without repercussions. In order to address this claim it is important to ask what exactly enforcing a moral duty amounts to? It is usually taken to mean that it may be permissible to impose some cost on non-compliant agents in order to force them into compliance. For instance, imagine that there is a third person in the *Hikers* scenario such that she cannot contribute to the joint action herself, but she can impose cost on the two hikers if they fail to assist. She could threaten them with physical or other harm should they not help the trapped man. It seems to me that she would be permitted or even required to do that if that were the only way of getting the two hikers to assist the trapped man. How much force and how great a cost are permissible would depend on what is at stake. Gerhard Øverland (2009) argued that it should depend on the agent's contribution to the problem and the likely effect of imposing such cost:

> Given that thousands of people are dying from poverty-related causes each day and we live in affluent societies with ample means to help a substantial part of this world's needy population, the permissibility of using force against ourselves to get us to assist the global poor cannot be easily dismissed. Its permissibility will depend on the extent to which we have contributed to their unfortunate situation, and/ or failed to assist at low cost to ourselves, and, of course, the likely effect of applying such force.

(pp. 231–232)

Further, Christian Barry together with Gerhard Øverland (Barry and Øverland 2016) argued that "when people fail to assist, this can significantly increase the cost others could permissibly impose on them in the future to help the person in need" (p. 31).

Suppose that we could agree on how great a cost it is permissible to impose on agents who fail to assist others when they could do so at relatively little cost. And suppose that imposing such cost would potentially force unwilling agents to shoulder their fair share of a collective obligation to combat global poverty. Is the collective duty to combat global poverty, which I have defended here, a duty that is thus enforceable?

The short answer is "yes", but we need to be careful what this means. On the view that I have been defending many of us will have collective pro tanto obligations to address global poverty. A moral duty is only violated when there is an *all-out* obligation. Whether it is the case for any particular individual agent that they were part of such an obligation is a matter of individual assessment (and here, I believe, I part ways with Barry and Øverland, who appear to take for granted that all affluent people have all-out obligations to combat poverty). Where an agent has an all-out obligation, it seems to me that this justifies imposing some cost on her if that will make her discharge the obligation. In that sense a duty to combat global poverty and individual contributory duties are in principle enforceable.

Admittedly, though, the sense in which we – the global moral community or, more narrowly, the global affluent – are collectively obligated to reduce poverty may appear much weaker and looser than the sense in which we are collectively obligated to help the man trapped under the tree or the commuter caught between the platform and the train. I have accounted for this impression by arguing that our massively shared duties are usually only weakly collective.

Further, I believe that certain features of small-scale rescue scenario make it the case that we find it more plausible to ascribe ad hoc all-out duties to the agents involved. These features include the urgency with which agents need to address the problem, their direct unmitigated exposure to the problem, the singularity of the event (meaning that it is not a recurring problem) as well as their exclusivity to assist and the ease with which the circumstances incite agents to we-frame the problem. Moreover, it is easier for the individuals in our rescue cases to discern individual and joint strategies to overcoming the problem. Global poverty and the ways in which we can jointly address it are a messy, confusing affair. Moral deliberation will not yield clear-cut answers and produce singularly optimal joint and individual strategies even for the conscientious agent.

But, as Ami Harbin has argued, fighting injustice is regularly disorientating, and we should not see epistemic uncertainty as an indication of moral ambiguity (Harbin 2014). Or, in other words, having moral obligations does not require complete certainty as to what needs to be done. Here, again, I think the prospective view of moral obligation will help us overcome the puzzlement caused by complex collective moral action problems. We are obligated to do what is our best bet given the evidence we have (availed ourselves of) while being aware that this may not be the objectively best choice (see also Zimmerman 1996).

Finally, does my view not result in exactly the kind of proliferation of collective duties which I initially criticised and which Lawford-Smith (2015) justifiably worries will render such duties impotent? In order to address this worry we need to know more about it: what does it mean for a duty to be impotent? Lawford-Smith writes: "[a]ttributing obligations to such [unstructured] groups makes those obligation statements impotent: it requires action from something that cannot act" (2015: 226). This worry is easily countered: as I – and many other scholars have argued – agents can *jointly act* even where they do not form a novel agent (see Chapter 3). Further, a (collective) obligation does not necessarily require agents to perform an action as such (Chapter 2). However, there is more to Lawford-Smith's worry. Further down, she adds:

> But it is also bad because it does not get us any further along in doing what the claims were presumably meant to do, namely, explicating the normative implications of large-scale harms such as threatened by climate change, or present in global poverty. We should get our story straight, so that we can actually give useful advice that, if acted upon, would see those problems actually being addressed.
>
> (pp. 226–227)

Her point here seems to be about action-guidance on the one hand and effective collective action on the other. Let me address the second issue first: the idea is that our account of collective obligations should be such that if everybody met their obligations with regard to some problem *P*, then *P* would in fact be resolved. This suggests to me that Lawford-Smith thinks that our obligations should reflect what is *actually* best. That is, it seems that she holds an objective view of moral obligation – a view we have grounds to reject, as I have explained in Section 4.3.

Further, her comments suggest that there is a problem with action-guidance if we ascribe duties to groups that are not agents. If we do so, Lawford-Smith argues, we cannot give useful advice to people as to what their moral obligations are. Though her claim is not directed at my account in particular, it is worth asking whether it is the case that the account proposed here is worse at guiding agents in their moral deliberation than the alternatives. Some of the alternatives have already been discussed (throughout the book and in particular in Chapter 6). It was shown that conditional accounts of obligations to contribute to collective endeavours and corresponding I-mode reasoning do not yield clear results with regard to individual strategies and as such are worse at guiding action than accounts based on we-mode reasoning.

Lawford-Smith's is not a conditional account. Instead, she suggests that in joint-necessity cases individuals are obligated to create collective agents because these are the "kinds of groups that can reliably produce desirable outcomes" (2015: 244). The worries I have with proposals of this type have already been made explicit. But let me reiterate: to say that we always need a group agent to reliably address a joint-necessity problem is either wrong (if we are using a notion of group agency that is roughly similar with List and Pettit's) or it begs the question (if we stipulate that every time agents act or intentionally produce an outcome together they are in fact a group agent). Note that a fixation on action or acting as what moral obligations require of us combined with an undisputed acceptance of the agency principle may explain this approach. But – as I have said repeatedly – we need not view obligations as requiring actions in the narrow sense nor need we accept that only agents can act. Remember the *housemates* in one of our previous examples: they can perfectly well keep the house clean at all times without forming a group agent or without performing a collective action in the narrow sense.

Further, note that approaches that primarily advocate for the formation of group agents might struggle to motivate duties to contribute to large-scale collective endeavours. First, we can hardly estimate whether or not we will succeed in forming a group agent together with others if we tried. In fact, it looks like most of the time we will not be likely to form such an agent. Second, there exist countless collective endeavours which we are able to (and arguably should) support. On my account of collective obligations, for some of us the best choice is to contribute to (existing) collective endeavours while for others establishing such endeavours – collectivising – will be the best bet. Such a conclusion does not render the notion of collective obligation impotent by any measure. That it does not generate clear-cut answers to the question of what each of us ought to do then is because this question cannot be answered in a general way.

My view accounts for the natural messiness of our obligations. It is tempting to think that for every problem there is a suitable moral obligation which, if discharged, would actually solve the problem. I worry that it is this way of thinking about our obligations that actually renders these obligations impotent: if we really ought to fix everything that is suboptimal we might end up resigning to moral inertia for feeling overwhelmed. Instead, I think we ought to do the best we can while accepting that – given our manifold limitations – it will never be everything we could have done.

Notes

1. A version of this view seems to also be present in Schroeder, A. (2014). Imperfect Duties, Group Obligations, and Beneficence. *Journal of Moral Philosophy*, 11(5), 557–584.
2. For a discussion of the role of joint attention in joint action, see, e.g., Seemann, A. (2007). Joint Attention, Collective Knowledge, and the "We" Perspective. *Social Epistemology*, 21(3), 217–230; Fiebich, A. and S. Gallagher (2013). Joint Attention in Joint Action. *Philosophical Psychology*, 26(4), 571–587.
3. The presence of a coordinator or a coordinating plan can mitigate these impacts and increase the likelihood of we-framing for large-scale distributive action scenarios. See, e.g., Roy, O. and A. Schwenkenbecher (2019). Shared Intentions, Loose Groups, and Pooled Knowledge. *Synthese*, online first.
4. Ami Harbin argued that fighting injustice will often leave us disorientated (Harbin, A. (2014). The Disorientations of Acting against Injustice. *Journal of Social Philosophy*, 45(2), 162–181.)
5. The emissions gap is the gap between the level of emission reductions required for limiting global warming to maximally 2°C (with a high probability) and the emission reductions states have currently committed to (UNEP 2017)
6. A fully fledged argument for this conclusion would need to specify who counts as 'capable' in this regard. My first instinct would be to suggest that anyone who has the economic, intellectual and epistemic capacity to make such behavioural changes without incurring disproportionate costs. Obviously, this should not be tied to someone's nationality – it may well be that a rich person from Zambia is more 'capable' in this sense than a poor person from the United States.
7. I will leave open who is meant by 'we' for the time being.
8. My own view has shifted on this since my 2013 paper in *Ratio*, where I argued against global moral obligations.
9. See, for instance, Pummer, T. and W. MacAskill (forthcoming). Effective Altruism. In H. LaFollette (Ed.), *International Encyclopedia of Ethics*. Wiley Blackwell.
10. To be clear, Ludwig's account of collective agency (2016) is inclusive of cooperative joint actions as portrayed by Bratman (2014) and Pettit and Schweikard (2006). However, his examples more closely resemble what I call distributive actions.
11. This last condition excludes cases where agents are ignorant of either the shared goal or other facts that might lead them to adopt that goal. For instance, a group of agents who have never heard about climate change do not have the ability to perform some distributive collective action aimed at reducing global warming. They can, of course, still take actions to that effect. But these would be aggregate actions, not genuinely collective actions.
12. A 'plan' specifies the steps necessary for achieving an 'end' or 'goal'.
13. One might think that some knowledge of others' intentions (concerning the shared goal) is required for this action type: how can I intend to reduce my carbon footprint *with a view to the shared end of mitigating climate change*, for instance, if I do not know whether others also intend to reduce theirs? After all, for mitigating climate change it is necessary that a large number of agents reduce their emissions, not just me. I suggest that we need not know that *specific* others share our intention in order to form our own, but we merely need to have some belief that it is likely that *some* persons share our intentions (i.e. have the same intentions as we do). Obviously, the more certainty we have about others' intentions to contribute, the stronger our reasons to also adopt such intentions.

14. In this regard, I believe, my discussion complements and further develops Young's approach.

15. One might wonder why I object to Cullity's work both for focusing on distributive solutions *and* because it portrays our collective obligations as requiring cooperative action. My point is that in *The Moral Demands of Affluence*, Cullity mainly focuses on distributive action (donations) but at the same time defends his 'collective requirement' to engage in distributive action by appealing to a cooperative joint action scenario.

16. A version of this view seems to also be present in Schroeder, A. (2014). Imperfect Duties, Group Obligations, and Beneficence. *Journal of Moral Philosophy*, 11(5), 557–584.

17. This problem is also present in Young's work, in my view, for instance, when she claims that we need to fight structural injustice by "joining together with others in collective action" (2006: 123).

18. There may also be options for ordinary citizens to fight injustice by making discerning consumer decisions en masse. I will not discuss this option, but merely point to the complexity of the issue as debated for instance in Jacobsen, Eivind, and Arne Dulsrud (2007). Will Consumers Save the World? The Framing of Political Consumerism. *Journal of Agricultural and Environmental Ethics*, 20, 469–482.

19. Agents have to mediate joint ability if they can easily produce a salient solution (Pinkert 2014).

20. Along similar lines, Tracy Isaacs invoked a 'clarity condition' for ascribing obligations to members of loose (in her terminology: putative) collectives: "Only when the course of action presenting itself is clear to the reasonable person is it accurate to think in terms of the collective obligations of putative groups" (2011: 152).

21. In fact, he criticises the way most philosophers of action approach collective agency as having "largely concentrated on analyzing shared activities among highly committed participants. . . . This restriction, however, has rendered these theories inapplicable to instances of massively shared agency" (2014: 258).

22. I believe that Margaret Gilbert's account of joint commitment is primarily focused on these group-internal normative links (Gilbert, M. (2006). *A Theory of Political Obligation: Membership, Commitment, and the Bonds of Society*. Oxford: Oxford University Press.)

23. Wringe has argued in favour of global collective obligations with a view to fending off the claimability objection (which he calls the 'agency objection'). His argument is – as we saw earlier – that the bearer and the subject of an obligation can come apart. We also saw that he operates with a different notion of collective obligations than the one defended here (Wringe, B. (2010). Global Obligations and the Agency Objection. *Ratio*, 23(2), 217–231.).

Conclusion

Many things have happened since I started writing this book. While the world was by no means a perfect place back then, it seems that the need for bottom-up, grassroots collective action beyond the actions of government is greater than ever.

Right now, the world is in the grip of a global pandemic caused by a highly contagious and often deadly virus. Different countries' responses to COVID-19 are telling – not just of the political aptitude of their leaders but of the communal spirit they invoke or fail to invoke. The 'each-to-their-own-approach' is failing abysmally while those leaders and officials who appeal to the collective nature of the task at hand and encourage people to think of health as a public rather than a private good (which is, of course, nothing else but we-framing and we-reasoning in practice) show impressive results in beating the pandemic.

This example also shows that even large-scale collective action and global change are ultimately not successful without, and, in fact, partly consists in, action at the local, communal and interpersonal levels. Combating the pandemic requires coherent government action as well as people actually making everyday sacrifices, changing their behaviour, looking out for others and – where necessary – taking action beyond what is legally required of them should their governments fall short of showing appropriate leadership.

One of the other large social and political movements that are dominating the news – *Black Lives Matter* – demonstrates this even more perfectly. Overcoming structural racism is neither solely a bottom-up nor top-down endeavour. It requires social activism at the macro- and micro-levels. It is overcome in changing interpersonal relations, direct interaction and communication between individuals, as well as changing the structural conditions within which discrimination and chauvinism thrive.

I set out to find an answer to the question when we should 'get our act together' to effect change in the world. Using the tools of philosophy, the book showed that this question is much more easily answered for small-scale, one-off problems than for systemic injustice. Still, I believe that an answer to the question has been found even if that answer is less clear-cut than one might hope. Most of us are not morally required to be 'first movers' of large-scale collective action, but all of us can be expected to do their share of scaling back social injustice. Even if our actions are but tiny drops in an ocean of change, it is the tiny drops that make the ocean. Our collective moral obligations to effect change in the world, to combat injustice, to resist oppression really are a complex cluster of duties to act on a variety of levels.

Perhaps this sort of conclusion means that the book fails to give an entirely satisfying answer to the initial, motivating question. But at least this would be an informed failure as it points to the limits of moral theorising in a way that is – I believe – fundamentally instructive: there is no set of necessary and sufficient criteria to tell us how to act in the real world when collective action problems arise. Morality is messy, inconclusive and tentative, and the more complex the problem we are faced with, the messier it gets. Naturally, our massively shared obligations to contribute to distributive, large-scale action differ – phenomenally and morally – from our collective obligations to address those small- to mid-scale collective action problems that the bulk of my discussion focuses on. Ultimately, however, the message of the book is clear, and it is positive: we – together – have obligations to effect change at the large and the small scale even if our individual actions by themselves are (or seem) inconsequential.

Further, the book makes significant headway in tackling a related question: the importance of social cohesion and 'we-framing' for the success of collective endeavours such as the provision of public goods and the overcoming of less entrenched collective action problems. It shows how it is plausible to expand the unit of moral agency beyond individuals much more than we currently do in ethical theory. Suggesting that we shift away from the notion of the discreet, individual moral agent to recognising the social dimensions of our agency and decision-making is less a programmatic manifesto than an acknowledgement of how we actually operate in the world. Our moral categories must expand to accommodate what I believe is and always has been part of our moral practice and intuitive way of thinking: we are essentially social and cooperative creatures.

Glossary

This glossary contains brief definitions of key terms in the book.

Collective action: this is used as an overarching term to describe actions by both → group agents and agents in → unstructured groups.

Collective moral obligations: are obligations held in a collective *mode,* where two or more agents jointly hold an obligation to do x (for instance, where x is only collectively feasible). To jointly hold an obligation is a plural moral predicate – it can only meaningfully apply to two or more agents.

- **Strongly** collective moral obligations exist where collective obligations generate special normative links between group members, require them to take on more wide-ranging contributory duties, including taking some responsibility for the success of the collective action, coordinating the joint activity and generating the required level of group knowledge, as well as obligations towards other group members in that they may be required to pick up the slack left by others or that they have treat other group members fairly in the distribution of burdens.
- **Weakly** collective moral obligations: the collective obligation has primacy over individual contributory obligations in the metaphysical, logical, functional or deliberative sense.

Common knowledge: in order for common knowledge of x to obtain in a group, the individual members of the group need to have knowledge about what the others know with regard to x. Or else, common knowledge is often formulated in terms of beliefs such that common knowledge of x requires that each group member (i) believe x, (ii) believe that each member believe x, (iii) believe that that each group member believe that each other group member believe x, and so on.

Group action: an action performed by a constituted or structured group agent (where group agency is understood in the way described by List and Pettit in their 2011 book *Group Agency*). See also → joint action → group agent

Group agent: a constituted group with a decision-making procedure and other mechanisms in place that ensure it can act as a group. A group agent as described by List and Pettit (2011).

Joint ability: the ability of a plurality of agents to act together in the most minimal sense required for ascribing a joint duty to the agent.

Joint action: an action performed by two or more agents together where these agents together do not form and not act as (part of) a group agent. Minimally, these agents need to share a goal and perform their individual contributory actions with a view to (with the intention to) producing that joint goal (or outcome).

Joint necessity: obtains when in order to achieve a morally desirable outcome or perform a morally desirable action at least two agents need to cooperate. Joint necessity can be

- *analytic*: playing a duet is something that by definition cannot be done by one agent on her own
- *circumstantial*: one person alone cannot tilt the train, as a matter of fact
- *wide* joint necessity obtains where the number of available contributors is greater than the number of minimally necessary contributors, which means it is not strictly necessary that all contribute in order to guarantee the success of the joint effort
- *strict* joint necessity obtains where the number of available contributors equals the number of minimally necessary contributors, which means that all available contributors must contribute in order to guarantee the success of the joint effort.

Massively shared obligations: are usually weakly collective obligations that ordinary citizens have to address large-scale moral problems.

Plurality of agents: set of agents who are not organised or are not forming a structured group agent. May or may not have normative links between them

Public knowledge: A proposition is public knowledge if (a) most people believe that the proposition is true and (b) most people believe that (a) is the case.

Random group: set of agents who are not organised or are not forming a structured group agent. There are no normative links between agents.

Team-reasoning: a type of deliberation that agents do *together*. It is a way of jointly establishing team (or collective) preferences as well as collective and individual strategies for satisfying those preferences.

Unstructured group: same as plurality of agents.

We-framing: the cognitive act of perceiving a joint-necessity scenario as a problem for (or of) the (or a) group. It is something an individual does. I 'we-frame' a problematic situation if I consider it to be a problem *for us*. It is the act of including the collectively available option in one's option set when deliberating.

We-reasoning: a type of deliberation whereby an individual agent independently establishes the course of action she should take with a view to an outcome that is only collectively available. We-reasoning explains why agents choose 'hi' in the hi-lo game or else when they choose to cooperate in a prisoners' dilemma.

References

Aas, Sean. (2015). Distributing Collective Obligation. *Journal of Ethics and Social Philosophy*, 9(3), 1–23.

Albertzart, Maike. (2015). Der Vorrang des Pflichtbegriffs in kollektiven Kontexten. *Zeitschrift für Praktische Philosophie*, 2(2), 87–120.

Ashford, Elizabeth. (2013). Severe Poverty as a Systemic Human Rights Violation. In Gillian Brock (Ed.), *Cosmopolitanism Versus Non-Cosmopolitanism: Critiques, Defenses, Reconceptualizations* (pp. 129–155). Oxford: Oxford University Press.

Bacharach, Michael. (1999). Interactive Team Reasoning: A Contribution to the Theory of Co-operation. *Research in Economics*, 53(2), 117–147.

Bacharach, Michael. (2006). *Beyond Individual Choice: Teams and Frames in Game Theory*. Princeton, NJ: Princeton University Press.

Barry, Christian, and Øverland, Gerhard. (2016). *Responding to Global Poverty: Harm, Responsibility, and Agency*. Cambridge: Cambridge University Press.

Beck, Valentin. (2016). *Eine Theorie der globalen Verantwortung*. Berlin: Suhrkamp.

Bicchieri, Cristina. (2017). *Norms in the Wild: How to Diagnose, Measure, and Change Social Norms*. New York: Oxford University Press.

Björnsson, Gunnar. (2014). Essentially Shared Obligations. *Midwest Studies in Philosophy*, 38(1), 103–120.

Björnsson, Gunnar. (forthcoming). On Individual and Shared Obligations. In Mark Budolfson, Tristram McPherson, and David Plunkett (Eds.), *Philosophy and Climate Change*. New York: Oxford University Press.

Blok, Kornelis, Hohne, Niklas, van der Leun, Kees, and Harrison, Nicholas. (2012). Bridging the Greenhouse-Gas Emissions Gap. *Nature Climate Change*, 2(7), 471–474.

Blomberg, Olle. (2016). Common Knowledge and Reductionism about Shared Agency. *Australasian Journal of Philosophy*, 94(2), 315–326.

Bratman, Michael E. (2014). *Shared Agency: A Planning Theory of Acting Together*. New York: Oxford University Press.

Buchanan, Allen. (1996). Perfecting Imperfect Duties: Collective Action to Create Moral Obligations. *Business Ethics Quarterly*, 6(1), 27–42.

Butler, David J. (2012). A Choice for 'Me' Or For 'Us'? Using We-reasoning to Predict Cooperation and Coordination in Games. *Theory and Decision*, 73(1), 53–76.

Butler, David J., Burbank, Victoria K., and Chisholm, James S. (2011). The Frames Behind the Games: Player's Perceptions of Prisoners Dilemma, Chicken, Dictator, and Ultimatum Games. *The Journal of Socio-Economics*, 40(2), 103–114.

Cohen, Jonathan L. (1981). Who Is Starving Whom? *Theoria*, 47(2), 65–81.

Collins, Stephanie. (2013). Collectives' Duties and Collectivisation Duties. *Australasian Journal of Philosophy*, 91(2), 231–248.

Collins, Stephanie. (2019). *Group Duties*. Oxford: Oxford University Press.

Cripps, Elizabeth. (2013). *Climate Change and the Moral Agent: Individual Duties in an Interdependent World*. Oxford: Oxford University Press.

Cullity, Garrett. (2004). *The Moral Demands of Affluence*. Oxford: Clarendon Press.

Dietz, Thomas, Gardner, Gerald T., Gilligan, Jonathan, Stern, Paul C., and Vandenbergh, Michael P. (2009). Household Actions Can Provide a Behavioral Wedge to Rapidly Reduce US Carbon Emissions. *Proceedings of the National Academy of Sciences*, 106(44), 18452–18456.

Duijf, Hein. (forthcoming). Cooperation, Fairness, and Team Reasoning. *Economics and Philosophy*.

Erskine, Toni. (2001). Assigning Responsibilities to Institutional Moral Agents: The Case of States and Quasi-States. *Ethics and International Affairs*, 15(2), 67–85.

Erskine, Toni. (2003). Assigning Responsibility to Institutional Moral Agents: The Case of States and 'Quasi States'. In Toni Erskine (Ed.), *Can Institutions Have Responsibilities?: Collective Moral Agency and International Relations* (pp. 19–40). Houndmills, Basingstoke, Hampshire; New York: Palgrave Macmillan.

Erskine, Toni. (2014). Coalitions of the Willing and Responsibilities to Protect: Informal Associations, Enhanced Capacities, and Shared Moral Burdens. *Ethics and International Affairs*, 28(1), 115–145.

Estlund, David. (2017). Prime Justice. In Kevin Vallier and Michael Weber (Eds.), *Political Utopias* (pp. 35–55). Oxford: Oxford University Press.

Fara, Michael. (2008). Masked Abilities and Compatibilism. *Mind*, 117(468), 843–865.

Faulmueller, Nadira, Kerschreiter, Rudolf, Mojzisch, Andreas, and Schulz-Hardt, Stefan. (2010). Beyond Group-level Explanations for the Failure of Groups to Solve Hidden Profiles: The Individual Preference Effect Revisited. *Group Processes & Intergroup Relations*, 13(5), 653–671.

Fiebich, Anika, and Gallagher, Shaun. (2013). Joint Attention in Joint Action. *Philosophical Psychology*, 26(4), 571–587.

Fischer, P., Krueger, J. I., Greitemeyer, T., Vogrincic, C., Kastenmüller, A., Frey, D., . . . Kainbacher, M. (2011). The Bystander-effect: A Meta-Analytic Review on Bystander Intervention in Dangerous and Non-dangerous Emergencies. *Psychological Bulletin*, 137(4), 517–537.

French, Peter A. (1984). *Collective and Corporate Responsibility*. New York: Columbia University Press.

Fukuyama, Francis. (1989). The End of History? *The National Interest* (16), 3–18.

Gilbert, Margaret. (2006). *A Theory of Political Obligation: Membership, Commitment, and the Bonds of Society*. Oxford: Oxford University Press.

Giubilini, Alberto, Birkl, Patrick, Douglas, Thomas, Savulescu, Julian, and Maslen, Hannah. (2017). Taxing Meat: Taking Responsibility for One's Contribution to Antibiotic Resistance. *Journal of Agricultural and Environmental Ethics*, 30(2), 179–198.

Gold, Natalie, and Sugden, Robert. (2007a). Collective Intentions and Team Agency. *Journal of Philosophy*, 104(3), 109–137.

Gold, Natalie, and Sugden, Robert. (2007b). Theories of Team Agency. In Fabienne Peter and Hans Bernhard Schmid (Eds.), *Rationality and Commitment* (pp. 280–312). Oxford: Oxford University Press.

Goodin, Robert E. (2012). Excused by the Unwillingness of Others? *Analysis*, 72(1), 18–24.

Goodin, Robert E. (2016). Duties of Charity, Duties of Justice. *Political Studies*, 65(2).

Guala, Francesco. (2016). *Understanding Institutions: The Science and Philosophy of Living Together*. Princeton, NJ: Princeton University Press.

Hakli, Raul, Miller, Kaarlo, and Tuomela, Raimo. (2010). Two Kinds of We-reasoning. *Economics and Philosophy*, 26(3), 291–320.

Harbin, Ami. (2014). The Disorientations of Acting against Injustice. *Journal of Social Philosophy*, 45(2), 162–181.

Hart, H. L. A. (1955). Are There Any Natural Rights? *Philosophical Review*, 64(2), 175–191.

Held, Virginia. (1970). Can a Random Collection of Individuals Be Morally Responsible? *Journal of Philosophy*, 67(14), 471–481.

Himmelreich, Johannes. (2017). The Paraphrase Argument Against Collective Actions. *Australasian Journal of Philosophy*, 95(1), 81–95.

Isaacs, Tracy Lynn. (2011). *Moral Responsibility in Collective Contexts*. Oxford: Oxford University Press.

Jackson, Frank. (1991). Decision-Theoretic Consequentialism and the Nearest and Dearest Objection. *Ethics*, 101, 461–482.

Jackson, Frank, and Pargetter, Robert. (1986). Oughts, Options, and Actualism. *The Philosophical Review*, 95(2), 233–255.

Karnein, Anja. (2014). Putting Fairness in Its Place: Why There Is a Duty to Take Up the Slack. *Journal of Philosophy*, 111(11), 593–607.

Killoren, David, and Williams, Bekka. (2013). Group Agency and Overdetermination. *Ethical Theory and Moral Practice*, 16(2), 295–307.

King, Alex. (2017). 'Ought Implies Can': Not So Pragmatic After All. *Philosophy and Phenomenological Research*, 95(3), 637–661.

Latané, Bibb, and Darley, John M. (1970). *The Unresponsive Bystander: Why Doesn't He Help?* New York: Appleton-Century Crofts.

Lawford-Smith, Holly. (2012). The Feasibility of Collectives' Actions. *Australasian Journal of Philosophy*, 90(3), 453–467.

Lawford-Smith, Holly. (2015). What 'We'? *Journal of Social Ontology*, 1(2), 225–249.

Le Morvan, Pierre. (2011). On Ignorance: A Reply to Peels. *Philosophia*, 39(2), 335–344.

Levy, Neil. (2018). Socializing Responsibility. In Katrina Hutchison, Catriona MacKenzie, and Marina Oshana (Eds.), *Social Dimensions of Moral Responsibility* (pp. 185–205). New York: Oxford University Press.

List, Christian, and Pettit, Philip. (2011). *Group Agency: The Possibility, Design, and Status of Corporate Agents*. Oxford; New York: Oxford University Press.

List, Christian, and Spiekermann, K. A. I. (2013). Methodological Individualism and Holism in Political Science: A Reconciliation. *The American Political Science Review*, 107(4), 629–643.

Louis, Winnifred R., Taylor, Donald M., and Neil, Tyson. (2004). Cost-Benefit Analyses for Your Group and Yourself: The Rationality of Decision-Making in Conflict. *International Journal of Conflict Management*, 15(2), 110–143.

Ludwig, Kirk. (2016). *From Individual to Plural Agency: Collective Action I*. Oxford: Oxford University Press.

Maier, John. (2014). Abilities. In E. N. Zalta (Ed.), *Stanford Encyclopedia of Philosophy*. plato.stanford.edu/archives/spr2014/entries/abilities.

May, Larry. (1987). *The Morality of Groups*. Notre Dame, IN: University of Notre Dame Press.

May, Larry. (1989). Mobs and Collective Responsibility. *Social Philosophy Today*, 2, 300–311.

May, Larry. (1992). *Sharing Responsibility*. Chicago: University of Chicago Press.

May, Larry, and Hoffman, Stacey. (1991). *Collective Responsibility: Five Decades of Debate in Theoretical and Applied Ethics*. Savage, MD: Rowman & Littlefield.

McGarty, Craig. (2009). Collective Action as the Material Expression of Opinion-based Group Membership. *Journal of Social Issues*, 65(4), 839–857.

Miller, Daniel J. (2017). Reasonable Foreseeability and Blameless Ignorance. *Philosophical Studies*, 174(6), 1561–1581.

Miller, David. (2011). Taking Up the Slack? Responsibility and Justice in Situations of Partial Compliance. In Carl Knight and Zofia Stemplowska (Eds.), *Responsibility and Distributive Justice* (pp. 230–245). Oxford: Oxford University Press.

Miller, Seumas. (1992). Joint Action. *Philosophical Papers*, 21(3), 275–297.

Miller, Seumas. (2010). *The Moral Foundations of Social Institutions: A Philosophical Study*. New York: Cambridge University Press.

Morton, Adam. (2005). *The Importance of Being Understood: Folk Psychology as Ethics*. New York: Taylor and Francis.

Murphy, Liam B. (2000). *Moral Demands in Nonideal Theory*. New York: Oxford University Press.

Nussbaum, Martha Craven. (2006). *Frontiers of Justice: Disability, Nationality, Species Membership*. Cambridge, MA: Belknap Press of Harvard University Press.

O'Neill, Onora. (2013). *Acting on Principle: An Essay on Kantian Ethics*. New York: Cambridge University Press.

Øverland, Gerhard. (2009). Forced Assistance. *Law and Philosophy*, 28(2), 203–232.

Pacherie, Elisabeth. (2018). Solution Thinking and Team Reasoning: How Different Are They? *Philosophy of the Social Sciences*, 48(6), 585–593.

Parfit, Derek. (1984). *Reasons and Persons*. Oxford: Clarendon Press.

Peels, Rik. (2010). What Is Ignorance? *Philosophia*, 38(1), 57–67.

Peels, Rik. (2016). *Perspectives on Ignorance From Moral and Social Philosophy*. New York; London: Routledge.

Pettit, Philip. (2007). Responsibility Incorporated. *Ethics*, 117(2), 171–201.

Pettit, Philip, and Schweikard, David. (2006). Joint Actions and Group Agents. *Philosophy of the Social Sciences*, 36(1), 18–39.

Pinkert, Felix. (2014). What We Together Can (Be Required to) Do. *Midwest Studies in Philosophy*, *38*(1), 187–202.

Pinkert, Felix. (2015). What If I Cannot Make a Difference (and Know It). *Ethics*, *125*(4), 971–998.

Pogge, Thomas. (2005). World Poverty and Human Rights. *Ethics & International Affairs*, *19*(01), 1–7.

Pummer, Theron, and MacAskill, William. (forthcoming). Effective Altruism. In Hugh LaFollette (Ed.), *International Encyclopedia of Ethics*. New York: Wiley Blackwell.

Rainbolt, George. (2000). Perfect and Imperfect Obligations. *Philosophical Studies*, *98*(3), 233–256.

Regan, Donald. (1980). *Utilitarianism and Co-Operation* (Vol. 33). Oxford: Oxford University Press.

Rosen, Gideon. (2003). IV – Culpability and Ignorance. *Proceedings of the Aristotelian Society (Hardback)*, *103*(1), 61–84.

Roy, Olivier, and Schwenkenbecher, Anne. (2019). Shared Intentions, Loose Groups, and Pooled Knowledge. *Synthese*, online first.

Schlothfeldt, Stephan (2009). *Individuelle oder gemeinsame Verpflichtung?: das Problem der Zuständigkeit bei der Behebung gravierender Übel*. Paderborn: Mentis.

Schmid, Hans Bernhard. (2016). On Knowing What We're Doing Together: Groundless Group Self-Knowledge and Plural Self-Blindness. In Michael S. Brady and Miranda Fricker (Eds.), *The Epistemic Life of Groups: Essays in the Epistemology of Collectives* (pp. 51–72). Oxford: Oxford University Press.

Schroeder, Andrew. (2014). Imperfect Duties, Group Obligations, and Beneficence. *Journal of Moral Philosophy*, *11*(5), 557–584.

Schweikard, David. (2008). Limiting Reductionism in the Theory of Collective Action. In Hans Bernhard Schmid, Katinka Schulte-Ostermann, and Nikos Psarros (Eds.), *Concepts of Sharedness: Essays on Collective Intentionality*. Frankfurt: Ontos.

Schwenkenbecher, Anne. (2011). Punishing Collective Agents. Non-Compliance with Moral Duties by States (Response to Toni Erskine). *Ethics & International Affairs*, online exclusive.

Schwenkenbecher, Anne. (2013a). Bridging the Emissions Gap: A Plea for Taking Up the Slack. *Philosophy and Public Issues*, *3*(1), 273–301.

Schwenkenbecher, Anne. (2013b). Joint Duties and Global Moral Obligations. *Ratio*, *26*(3), 310–328.

Schwenkenbecher, Anne. (2014a). Is There an Obligation to Reduce One's Individual Carbon Footprint? *Critical Review of International Social and Political Philosophy*, *17*(2), 168–188.

Schwenkenbecher, Anne. (2014b). Joint Moral Duties. *Midwest Studies in Philosophy*, *38*(1), 58–74.

Schwenkenbecher, Anne. (2017). Gemeinsame Hilfspflichten, Weltarmut und kumulative Handlungen. *Zeitschrift für Praktische Philosophie*, *4*(1), 123–150.

Schwenkenbecher, Anne. (2018). Making Sense of Collective Moral Obligations: A Comparison of Current Approaches. In Tracy Isaacs, Kendy Hess, and Violetta Igneski (Eds.), *Collectivity: Ontology, Ethics and Social Justice* (pp. 109–132). London: Rowman & Littlefield.

Schwenkenbecher, Anne. (2019). Collective Moral Obligations: 'We-reasoning' and the Perspective of the Deliberating Agent. *The Monist*, *102*(2), 151–171.

Schwenkenbecher, Anne. (2020). Structural Injustice and Massively Shared Obligations. *Journal of Applied Philosophy*, first view.

Seemann, Axel. (2007). Joint Attention, Collective Knowledge, and the "We" Perspective. *Social Epistemology*, 21(3), 217–230.

Seemann, Axel. (2016). Reminiscing Together: Joint Experiences, Epistemic Groups, and Sense of Self. *Synthese*, 196, 4813–4828.

Shapiro, Scott. (2014). Massively Shared Agency. In Manuel Vargas and Gideon Yaffe (Eds.), *Rational and Social Agency: Essays on the Philosophy of Michael Bratman* (pp. 257–293). Oxford: Oxford University Press.

Singer, Peter. (1972). Famine, Affluence, and Morality. *Philosophy and Public Affairs*, 1(3), 229–243.

Singer, Peter. (2009). *The Life You Can Save: Acting Now to End World Poverty*. Melbourne, Vic: Text Publishing.

Sinnott-Armstrong, Walter. (1984). 'Ought' Conversationally Implies 'Can'. *Philosophical Review*, 93(2), 249–261.

Sinnott-Armstrong, Walter. (2005). It's Not My Fault: Global Warming and Individual Moral Obligations. In Walter Sinnott-Armstrong and Richard Howarth (Eds.), *Perspectives on Climate Change* (pp. 221–253). Bingley: Emerald Publishing Limited.

Slovic, Paul. (2010). If I Look at the Mass I Will Never Act: Psychic Numbing and Genocide. In Sabine Roeser (Ed.), *Emotions and Risky Technologies* (pp. 37–59). Dordrecht: Springer Netherlands.

Stemplowska, Zofia. (2016). Feasibility: Individual and Collective. *Social Philosophy and Policy*, 33(1–2), 273–291.

Sugden, Robert. (2015). Team Reasoning and Intentional Cooperation for Mutual Benefit. *Journal of Social Ontology*, 1(1), 143–166.

Talja, Jari. (1985). On the Logic of Omissions. *Synthese*, 65(2), 235–248.

Tamminga, Allard, and Duijf, Hein. (2017). Collective Obligations, Group Plans and Individual Actions. *Economics and Philosophy*, 33(2), 1–28.

Tamminga, Allard, and Hindriks, Frank. (2020). The Irreducibility of Collective Obligations. *Philosophical Studies*, 177(4), 1085–1109.

Thomas, Emma F. (2009a). The Role of Efficacy and Moral Outrage Norms in Creating the Potential for International Development Activism through Group-based Interaction. *British Journal of Social Psychology*, 48(1), 115–134.

Thomas, Emma F. (2009b). Transforming "Apathy into Movement": The Role of Prosocial Emotions in Motivating Action for Social Change. *Personality and Social Psychology Review*, 13(4), 310–333.

Thomas, Emma F. (2010). Social Psychology of Making Poverty History: Motivating Anti-poverty Action in Australia. *Australian Psychologist*, 45(1), 4–15.

Thomas, Emma F. (2013). Doing Democracy: The Social Psychological Mobilization and Consequences of Collective Action Doing Democracy. *Social Issues and Policy Review*, 7(1), 173–200.

Thomas, Emma F., and Louis, Winnifred R. (2013). Doing Democracy: The Social Psychological Mobilization and Consequences of Collective Action. *Social Issues and Policy Review*, 7(1), 173–200.

Thomas, Emma F., McGarty, Craig, and Mavor, Kenneth I. (2009). Aligning Identities, Emotions, and Beliefs to Create Commitment to Sustainable Social and Political Action. *Personality and Social Psychology Review*, 13(3), 194–218.

Thompson, Janna. (2006). Collective Responsibility for Historic Injustices. *Midwest Studies in Philosophy*, 30(1), 154–167.

Tollefsen, Deborah. (2015). *Groups as Agents*. Cambridge: Polity Press.

Tomalty, Jesse. (2014). The Force of the Claimability Objection to the Human Right to Subsistence. *Canadian Journal of Philosophy*, 44(1), 1–17.

Tomasello, Michael. (2014). *A Natural History of Human Thinking*. Cambridge, MA; London: Harvard University Press.

Tomasello, Michael. (2016). *A Natural History of Human Morality*. Cambridge, MA; London: Harvard University Press.

Tuomela, Raimo. (2013). *Social Ontology: Collective Intentionality and Group Agents*. New York: Oxford University Press.

UNEP. (2017). *The Emissions Gap Report 2017. A UN Environment Synthesis Report*. Retrieved from https://wedocs.unep.org/bitstream/handle/20.500. 11822/22070/EGR_2017.pdf?isAllo. . . .

van Zomeren, Martijn. (2013). Four Core Social-Psychological Motivations to Undertake Collective Action. *Social and Personality Psychology Compass*, 7(6), 378–388.

Vranas, Peter B. M. (2007). I Ought, Therefore I Can. *Philosophical Studies*, 136(2), 167–216.

Woodard, Christopher. (2003). Group-based Reasons for Action. *Ethical Theory and Moral Practice*, 6(2), 215–229.

Woodard, Christopher. (2011). Rationality and the Unit of Action. *Review of Philosophy and Psychology*, 2(2), 261–277.

Woodard, Christopher. (2017). Three Conceptions of Group-Based Reasons. *Journal of Social Ontology*, 3, 107–127.

Wringe, Bill. (2005). Needs, Rights, and Collective Obligations. *Royal Institute of Philosophy Supplement*, 80(57), 187–207.

Wringe, Bill. (2010). Global Obligations and the Agency Objection. *Ratio*, 23(2), 217–231.

Wringe, Bill. (2016). Collective Obligations: Their Existence, Their Explanatory Power, and Their Supervenience on the Obligations of Individuals. *European Journal of Philosophy*, 24(2), 472–497.

Wynes, Seth, and Nicholas, Kimberly A. (2017). The Climate Mitigation Gap: Education and Government Recommendations Miss the Most Effective Individual Actions. *Environmental Research Letters*, 12(7), 074024.

Young, Iris Marion. (2004). Responsibility and Global Labor Justice. *Journal of Political Philosophy*, 12(4), 365–388.

Young, Iris Marion. (2006). Responsibility and Global Justice: A Social Connection Model. *Social Philosophy and Policy*, 23(1), 102–130.

Young, Iris Marion. (2011). *Responsibility for Justice*. New York: Oxford University Press.

Zimmerman, Michael J. (1996). *The Concept of Moral Obligation*. Cambridge: Cambridge University Press.

Zimmerman, Michael J. (2014). *Ignorance and Moral Obligation*. Oxford: Oxford University Press.

Zimmerman, Michael J. (2016). Ignorance as a Moral Excuse. In Rik Peels (Ed.), *Perspectives on Ignorance From Moral and Social Philosophy* (pp. 77–94). New York; London: Routledge.

Index

Aas, Sean 36n2, 38, 116, **125–127**
action-guidance 22, 85, 129, 130, **157–158**
agency principle: compliance with 114–115, 120, 123, 124; critique thereof 33–36; introducing the principle 32–33

Bacharach, Michael 22n1, 24n21, 78–79, 80, 82, 95n15
Björnsson, Gunnar 35n5, 108, 117, **128–129**
blameworthiness *see* joint blameworthiness
Bratman, Michael 40–45, 62n7

capacity principle 31–34, **37–38**, 60, 115, 117–118
claimability objection 152–155, 160n23
collective action 38, 43, 56–57, 62n10, 62n11, 85; cooperative collective action 93, **143–147**, 160n15; distributive collective action 137, **143–149**; large-scale collective action 46, 110–113, 137–139, **143–144**, 152, 159n3; *see also* joint action; joint intentional activity; massively shared agency
collectively available options 11–14, 23n11, **64–66**, 74, 78, 114, 142
collective moral obligations: conditions for 19, **93, 129–130**; epistemic conditions 90–91; failure to comply 106–108; introduction to 6–7, 11, 25–28; second-order **94**, 130–131, 141; strongly collective obligations 25, 105, **151–152**; and substantive moral theories

69; weakly collective obligations 105–106, 151–152, 156; *see also* contributory obligations; duty collectivism; massively shared obligations
Collins, Stephanie 9, 39, 116, **117–118**, 133n2
common knowledge 24n17, 40–41, **44–46, 90–92**, 137, 144–145, 148–149; *see also* public knowledge; shared knowledge
contributory obligations 21–22, **99–106**, 126, 133; failure to comply 106–108; *see also* joint blameworthiness
Cullity, Garrett 127, 135–137, 146–147, 160n15

duty collectivism 32; *see also* collective moral obligations

enforceability objection 155–156
epistemic simplicity 19–20, **92**, 137
Erskine, Toni 116–117, **121–122**, 125; on Virginia Held 120–121

global obligations *see* massively shared obligations
Goodin, Robert 24n26, 30–31, 119, 155
group action 38–39, 58, 148; group agency 39, 96n17, 118; group agent 9–10, 35, 58–59, 96n19, 116, 117–118, 120–121, 127, 158
group-based reasoning *see* team-reasoning
group knowledge *see* common knowledge; public knowledge; shared knowledge

Held, Virginia 28, **120–121**, 133n5
hi-lo game 14, **78–82**

ignorance: blameless 24n19; factive
16; propositional 15–16; *see also*
group knowledge
I-mode reasoning 13, 65, 78, **79–81**,
83–87; *see also* we-reasoning
individual duties *see* contributory
obligations
individual impotence objection 22,
115
Isaacs, Tracy 26, 68, **123–125**, 160n20

joint ability 14–17, 27, 32, **37–38**,
47–48, 54–55, 57–58, 60, 62n10,
62n11; basic conditions 15; as
combined ability 48–51; definition
of 54; *see also* Stemplowska, Zofia
joint action 38–43; basic account 40;
cooperative 144; distributive 144;
extended basic account 42–43;
large-scale 137
joint blameworthiness **108–109**, 155
joint intentional activity 38, 43–48,
60, 148
joint necessity 8–9, 99–104; analytic
8; circumstantial 8; strict 8,
100–101, 107, 112; wide 8, 85,
100, 107, 112
joint rescue analogy 136, 146

Lawford-Smith, Holly 9, 29, 36n1,
57–58, 133n4, 157–158

massively shared agency 44, 46–48,
148–149, 160n21
massively shared obligations 135,
137–139, **150–152**
May, Larry 122–123

noncompliance *see* collective
moral obligations; contributory
obligations

objective view of moral obligations
17, 71–72, 75, 76, 154, 157

Parfit, Derek 9, 97n30, 110–112
Pinkert, Felix 48–50, 62n10, 62n11,
66, 124, 127–129, 147–148
plurality of agents 58–60
prisoners' dilemma 78, 96n16
prospective view of moral obligations
17–18, 70–77, 157
public knowledge 90–91, 138, **145**, 149

reasons: group-based (or pattern-
based) 24n24, 79, 87, 151
reductionism about collective
obligations 119, 131–132

Shapiro, Scott 43–48, 148–150;
see also joint intentional activity
shared agency 41–47, 148–149;
see also Bratman, Michael;
massively shared agency
shared knowledge 90–91, 145
Stemplowska, Zofia 23n14, 56–57

team-reasoning 65–66, 77, **88–89**,
95n12, 96n17, 97n29, 97n31, 109
Tomalty, Jesse 153–154

unstructured group *see* plurality of
agents

we-framing 13, 19, **65–66**, 78, 110,
137–139, 159n3
we-reasoning 12, 24n21, **65–66**,
77–90, 95n2, 96n16
Woodard, Christopher 22, 76–77,
79–80, 87–88
Wringe, Bill 21–22, 33–35, 124–125,
135–137, 146, 160n23

Zimmerman, Michael 17–18, 24n20,
37, 43, 51, 55–56, 63–64, 71–77,
95n6, 98